The Hearing Impaired Child
In a Regular Classroom

The Hearing Impaired Child
In a Regular Classroom

Preschool, Elementary, and Secondary Years

A Guide for the Classroom Teacher and Administrator

Winifred H. Northcott, Ph.D., Editor

 The Alexander Graham Bell Association for the Deaf, Inc. Washington, D.C.

Contents

Part V.   The Elementary Years

Part VI.   The Secondary Years

Part VII. Parent-Teacher Interaction

Preface

It is a distinct privilege for the Alexander Graham Bell Association to present *The Hearing Impaired Child in a Regular Classroom: Preschool, Elementary, and Secondary Years* to an audience interested in the exceptional child. Many months of concentrated effort on the part of more than 45 talented individuals in special education and allied disciplines have resulted in its publication.

Dr. Winifred Northcott is to be complimented on her conceptualization of the structural framework of this comprehensive book and on her sustained direction as its professional editor. Her choice of authors who relate directly to hearing impaired children in a wide variety of educational settings, including the home, assures the reader of practical information and lively illustrations.

Dr. Bell envisioned this educational setting for the hearing impaired child many years ago and wrote eloquently in support of his belief. Today, the demonstrated competencies of hearing impaired children and youth around the world are helping his dream to become a reality.

—Addison Neal Smith
Acting Executive Director
Alexander Graham Bell
Association for the Deaf
September 1972 — July 1973

GRANT B. BITTER

Foreword

The Hearing Impaired Child in a Regular Classroom: Preschool, Elementary, and Secondary Years is important reading for all who are concerned with the development of potential abilities of hearing impaired children. Its comprehensive treatment of integration offers intelligent and timely insight into the educational processes essential to academic and cultural emancipation of children with auditory defects. The book is also evidence that integration is becoming a reality for increasing numbers of children and youth, with the assurance of greater opportunity for their educational and social development and heightened appreciation of individual differences among all children.

The content is a concise and systematic arrangement of pertinent articles describing the philosophy of an integration program; strategies and skills for identifying and alleviating potential sources of academic and social dysfunction; adaptations which can be made to enhance the quality of the hearing impaired pupil's interpersonal relationships; and guidelines for regular classroom teachers and support specialists in implementing successful integration at the preschool through secondary levels. A selected bibliography suggests valuable references from which the reader may obtain additional information over a broad spectrum concerning the content and supervision of partial or full-time integrated programs.

The book focuses on the basic concern that America should have for all hearing impaired children: the guarantee of an educational program which utilizes all available resources to enhance a student's dignity and productivity. It reflects a steady, progressive movement within the educational hierarchy to consider the rights of these children — regardless of degree of hearing loss — to be fully-participating citizens in our culture according to their capabilities. It

---

Dr. Bitter is Assistant Professor in the Department of Special Education of the University of Utah, Salt Lake City.

emphasizes the need for both excellence and accountability on the part of each member of the multidisciplinary team who is involved with the hearing impaired child in a regular school setting.

These important developments in contemporary educational practices are due largely to the cooperative efforts of regular and special educators, parents of hearing impaired children, legislators (national, state, and local), and specialists in the medical, social, and community services. Each group senses the urgency to unite and organize their skills in a combined effort to dispel the labeling of children by audiogram, the stereotyping of performance expectations, and the perpetuation of isolating conditions which may too frequently characterize the educational environment for hearing impaired children and youth. Their efforts reflect a recognition that educational placement of hearing impaired children in regular classes should be based on a diagnostic profile of each child — considering multiple physiological and environmental factors — and that any judgments must thus be reversible, tentative, and subject to continual monitoring.

The Authors

The contributors to this publication include enthusiastic, highly competent specialists in the fields of education, communication disorders, audiology, psychology, and sociology, as well as parents and deaf individuals who have personally been involved in integration programs. Their diverse experience is interfaced with one common goal: promoting the welfare of each child through the maintenance of a variety of educational options. The emphasis is on ability rather than disability, capacity rather than incapacity, normality rather than abnormality, high-level expectations rather than mediocre standards. Indeed, these authors are an articulate and positive team who demonstrate through their writing a special personal and professional commitment and who share their knowledge and observations in a most stimulating manner.

Educational Issues

A paramount concern is the establishment of the environmental parameters which determine to a great extent whether or not the hearing impaired child will ultimately enjoy the personal, educational, and vocational freedom of complete involvement in society. Each of the primary institutions of our culture — the family, the school, the church, and the larger community — contributes significantly to the self-fulfillment and productivity of the individual. There is no adequate substitute for the genuine involvement in the mainstream culture, and our expertise should be focused toward strengthening this natural environment for hearing impaired children.

The central challenge in the educational setting is to provide the regular classroom teacher with realistic support — in information and in personnel (academic tutors, hearing clinicians, integration specialists). A comprehensive system of inservice training must be provided for volunteers, educators, administrators, and hearing peers. In addition, continuing programs of family education are vital to effective integration.

Questions and Answers

Integration of hearing impaired children into regular classes is a fact. The focus of this book is on the improvement in delivery systems. The content furnishes substantive answers to the questions that are most frequently asked: What are the significant characteristics of hearing impaired children who are making a successful adjustment in regular classes? At what age and to what degree should educational integration be encouraged? Are there guidelines and diagnostic tools which may be used in initiating and maintaining the integration process? What evaluation procedures can help in determining entry points? Is it possible to develop objective measurements which can be used as accurate predictors of success? What special support personnel are required, and what are their functions? Are there effective orientation procedures for families, hearing peers, and educators? How should the audiological and environmental factors be assessed and utilized? What modifications in curriculum are required? How can hearing impaired students in a residential school participate in an integrated program? What are the educational and psychological effects on hearing impaired children of prolonged placement in regular classes? What are the most effective ways to assure widespread dissemination of procedures and practices pertaining to successful integration?

Conclusion

The book is a useful tool in the hands of a professional educator or concerned parent striving for the best in educational opportunity for the hearing impaired individual. Although it offers no panacea that will automatically assure successful integration for every child, it provides a remarkable opportunity for regular classroom teachers, administrators, parents, and support personnel to examine the objectives, current activities, and evaluation procedures related to this educational concept. It is designed to be stimulating and provocative and forms the basis for thoughtful discussion at meetings, conferences, and workshops which may contribute in the future to expanded publications on the hearing impaired child in a regular classroom.

Children learn for the same
reason that birds fly.
The question, then, should be
Why do some children *not* learn?
— *Edward Zigler*

WINIFRED H. NORTHCOTT, EDITOR

Introduction

Increased numbers of children who bear the medical label "deaf" or "hard of hearing" are being integrated today into regular classes with their hearing peers in preschool, elementary, and secondary schools of the United States. This fact is, in part, a reflection of the current political, social, and educational climate, which is increasingly responsive to the idea of accommodation to individual differences among exceptional children within their neighborhood schools.*

At the present time, the "state of the art" of integration of hearing handicapped children is not advanced. There are gaps in existing technology and knowledge — as well as a paucity of written information — concerning a systems approach to the admission and maintenance of hearing impaired children in regular classrooms on a partial or full-time basis. Models of pupil assessment, supplementary support services, inservice training, parent involvement, and evaluation subsystems are still in the process of definition.

However, the prognosis for a hearing impaired child's successful assimilation in an ordinary class must not be left to chance. *The Hearing Impaired Child in a Regular Classroom* is offered as a single step, among many, to counteract this possibility. The emphasis is on *clarity* of role definition of members of the regular and special education team; *diversity* of educational models to support the hearing impaired child and the regular classroom teacher; and *flexibility* in the application of information gleaned from these pages according to the unique educational environment in which the reader functions.

---

*Instructional Alternatives for Exceptional Children, E. N. Deno, Editor. Arlington, Virginia: Council for Exceptional Children, 1973

Dr. Northcott is Consultant, Early Childhood Education Program for Hearing Impaired Children, 0-6, Minnesota State Department of Education, St. Paul.

1

From the outset there has been a unified sense of excitement among the authors over the potential of reaching a *new* audience — the classroom teacher, administrator, and resource specialist in regular or "mainstream" education. This audience will bring to the reading an invaluable background knowledge in child development and the behavioral and instructional techniques that contribute to an optimum learning environment in an ordinary classroom; however, it is assumed that the reader has minimal knowledge of the accommodations which can and should be made to ensure maximum comprehension and active participation by a *hearing impaired* child in all facets of regular classroom and school activities. Careful attention is given to the description of current procedures and practices as well as organizational and administrative patterns designed to ensure that the integrated hearing impaired child is not supported in isolation by a single classroom teacher.

In this practical yet serious and personal book, there has been little attempt to modify the unevenness of literary style from one chapter to another since the cumulative effect is hoped to be one of rich diversity in useful information contributed by 45 authors. In the aggregate, their classifications reflect the full spectrum of responsibilities and activities required to initiate or improve supplementary services and educational programs for children with hearing losses. Each contributor writes from a particular vantage point — as a hearing impaired individual, a family member, a classroom teacher, or a person in frequent contact with them in the role of special educator or administrator; resource specialist (academic tutor, speech and hearing clinician); or participant in the diagnosis, educational programming, or evaluation of hearing impaired children in regular classes.

The Population

"A hearing impaired (deaf or hard of hearing) individual is a person who requires specialized education because of a hearing impairment."* The generic term *hearing impaired* is used deliberately throughout this book because it is relatively neutral in emotional content; it does not arouse automatic prediction of the level of personal, academic, or social performance that will be achieved by any students whose hearing loss may range from mild to profound by audiological assessment and audiogram.

The Bureau of Education for the Handicapped, U.S. Office of Education, cites the figure .075 (3 in 4,000 persons) as the incidence of children of school age (5-19 years) in the United States who are *deaf* (91 dB ISO hearing loss or greater in the better ear) and .5 (1 in 200 persons) who are *hard of hearing*. One would predict on the basis of this information (i.e., the small percentage of *deaf* children) that a correspondingly small number of the total population of hearing impaired children would be receiving their education in self-contained classes. However, this is not the case.

Standards for the Certification of Teachers of the Hearing Impaired, Developed by the Committee on Professional Preparation and Certification. Adopted by the Council on Education of the Deaf, January, 1972. P. 1.

The most recent demographic studies of characteristics of hearing impaired students by hearing status* (published in March 1973) reveal some significant information relating to the 41,109 hearing impaired (deaf and hard of hearing) students in the United States:

1. Audiological data was available for only 32,054 (78%) of the 41,109 students examined.

2. 49.5% could be classified as hard of hearing *by unaided audiogram* even though the dividing line for classifying students as "deaf" was lowered to 85 dB ISO (loss in the better ear).

3. Only 10.6% of the 41,109 hearing impaired students were integrated with hearing students either in itinerant programs (6.5%) or part-time special educational services (4.1%). The majority were located in residential schools for the deaf (45.5%), day schools for the deaf (7.2%), or self-contained classes for the hearing impaired (30.8%).

The conclusion can be drawn that too many hearing impaired children in the United States are receiving their education today in self-contained classes in either day or residential schools. The implied mandate to local school boards, public school administrators, and ombudsmen for hearing impaired children is to initiate and expand educational alternatives to traditional programs of self-containment.

Characteristics of Integrated Hearing Impaired Children

The Hearing Impaired Child in a Regular Classroom focuses on a total systems analysis of 1) hearing impaired children who are candidates for admission to or continuation in regular classes, and 2) the educational environment which may support or restrict their academic progress and social interaction with hearing classmates. Although the unaided audiogram may indicate a hearing loss ranging from moderate to profound, these children have certain characteristics in common:

1. Active utilization of residual hearing and full-time hearing aid usage, if prescribed.

2. Demonstrated social, academic, cognitive, and communicative (auditory and oral) skills *within the normal range of behaviors* of hearing classmates at a particular grade level.

3. Intelligible speech and the ability to comprehend and exchange ideas with others through spoken, written, and read language.

4. Increased confidence and independence in giving self-direction to the tasks at hand.

Current Trends in Education of the Hearing Impaired

The literature and topical conferences relating to present educational models for the handicapped, across disabilities, reveal a number of significant trends

Annual Survey of Hearing Impaired Children and Youth, United States: 1970-1971. Washington, D.C.: Office of Demographic Studies, Gallaudet College, March 1973.

which mandate the individualization of educational services and programs for the hearing impaired child in the regular classroom:

1. *The rights of the child to an educational program as soon as the diagnosis of a handicapping condition is established and without cost to the family.* In response, the U.S. Office of Education, Bureau of Education for the Handicapped, has given highest priority to support for early education programs.

Educational practices in the management of infant and preschool hearing impaired children can be summarized by these descriptors: (a) parent guidance, counseling, and education; (b) aural (listening) and oral procedures; (c) experiential, inductive approaches to learning; (d) early amplification and systematic training of residual hearing; and (e) group educational experiences with hearing children. As a result of early identification, parent training, and emphasis on what the child can *hear* and what he can *do* during the preprimary years, burgeoning numbers of hearing impaired children are ready for placement in regular classes during the elementary school grades.

These candidates for integration are effective full-time hearing aid users and, for the most part, are well-disciplined and trusting. They expect adults to be useful to them in their play and verbal conversations. Having been placed routinely in regular nursery schools, they have confidence in group interaction and high motivation to use their aural (listening) and oral communication skills, despite imprecise articulation. The principal of an elementary school in Sweden spoke to me of the parents of integrated hearing impaired children who were "graduates" of infant and preschool special education programs: "My parents are so ambitious for their children, and so helpful to them."

Parents around the world expect to participate in decisions relating to their hearing impaired child's educational setting and social experiences once he reaches formal school age. The parents of primary school-age children who are entering regular classes expect assurance that the individually prescriptive program designed for each family during the early years, as described in this book, will be continued. They also expect that special education support will be forthcoming for the general educator, as it had been for the regular nursery school staff. This holds implications for the examination of parental roles and responsibilities as an integral part of the redesign of a total special education system.

2. *Identification of the public school as the logical and accountable fiscal agency to coordinate a program for hearing impaired children.* The public school would contract with other agencies in the community or region, as appropriate, to provide a full range of educational services. This is particularly pertinent during the preprimary years; integration in regular nursery schools and day care centers is a critical factor in a child's learning to listen and to utilize his aided residual hearing in acquiring normal inflectional contours of speech (rate, rhythm, inflection) prior to the use of functional language for verbal self-expression.

3. *Adherence to the principle of normalization throughout the educational years, as far as reasonable.* The home and community educational program is considered preferable to education in a residential facility. Integration of the hearing impaired child into a more verbal, nonhandicapped group is the desired goal, whenever possible.

4. *A shift of emphasis from a medical to an educational model of intervention by the schools.* There is ample evidence in current literature and research that the terms *deaf* and *hard of hearing* are diagnostically and psychologically unsound as a basis for judging how well a hearing impaired child will perform in the classroom. The focus today is on labeling not the child but the supplementary services and resource personnel (e.g., specialists in developmental reading, language arts, and behavior management; the itinerant teacher; the academic tutor; and the speech clinician) required to assist the child and his family.

5. *A systematic program of sequential auditory training activities offered throughout the school years, based on individually prescriptive behavioral objectives.* They should relate to the child's developmental level and to concepts being presented in academic subjects in order to assure the incorporation of the dynamic use of residual hearing into the child's daily interpersonal experiences.

6. *The development of a new classification of specialist in the neighborhood public school — the Consultant, Services for the Hearing Impaired —* with a different set of competencies from those of the special or regular classroom teacher, administrator, or itinerant teacher. This individual can serve as a catalyst to initiate and coordinate the support services subsystem required by hearing impaired children who are integrated. In addition, this individual has major responsibility for developing an inservice training program, based on a formal needs assessment, to determine the professional experiences required by the educational personnel who will provide instruction or services to hearing impaired children assigned to regular classes.

A Continuum of Educational Services

The cascade system of special education services was adopted by the delegate assembly of the Council for Exceptional Children at its national convention in Dallas, Texas, in April 1973 as a major policy statement on the organization and administration of special education. It outlines the concept of a continuum of educational services and program alternatives for exceptional children, regardless of etiology. The assumption is that a handicapped child may begin his formal educational program at any level in the cascade, according to his entry level skills and performance. The expectation is that periodical reassessment and observation of the effects of educational intervention will result in gradual movement of an individual child to a less intensive level of special education services as an adjunct to increased participation in regular classes, as demonstrated progress justifies. Local school boards, pressured by mandates from the courts and

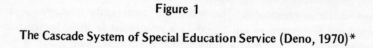

Figure 1

The Cascade System of Special Education Service (Deno, 1970)*

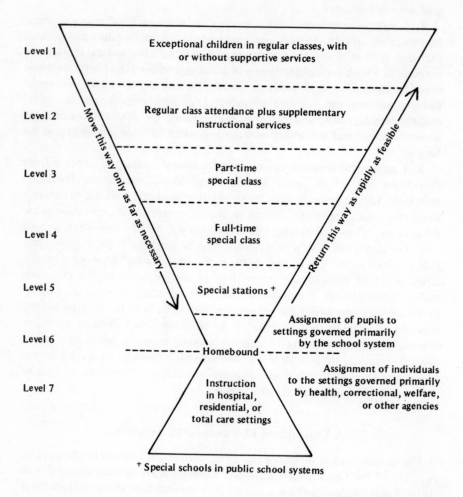

† Special schools in public school systems

creative school personnel to realign specialists and subsystems within their jurisdiction, are moving steadily toward modification of the total educational system of public school services for exceptional children, including increased interaction with the general education program.

In the case of the hearing impaired, partial or full-time integration in regular classes is not a realistic goal for *every* child; nor is a policy of automatic self-

---

*Reprinted by permission of the Council for Exceptional Children from "Bulletin," *Exceptional Children,* March 1973, Vol. 39, p. 495.

containment from kindergarten through grade 12 — which has been the general practice of residential schools for the deaf in the United States. Readers should consider the position responsibilities and activities of the state-supported residential school and the desirability of requesting legislative study of the feasibility of placing the educational program of the state school under the direction and supervision of the state department of education, special education division. Such action would permit implementation of a written state plan affecting educational programming for *all* hearing impaired children, 0-21 years of age, within a state. It would encourage the development of guidelines for a unified monitoring and assessment system to be used in reassigning hearing impaired children to their home districts or to a more intensive level of service in self-contained classes in a regional day or residential school. One considered modification in state laws would require the local school district of residence to assume the full cost of tuition, room, and board for a hearing impaired child placed in any residential school program; this would accelerate regionalization of public school services.

A promising first step would be the establishment of an Admissions and Discharge Committee of the state residential school, with membership including the hearing consultant in the state department of education and regional public school administrators. The committee would develop written policies concerning admission and demission of pupils and act as catalyst to initiate support services for children recommended for placement in their home school district.

Parent Involvement in Educational Change

The personal chronicles by hearing impaired youth and their parents might suggest that they have not always been consumers of educational services for exceptional children — but have indeed been victims of deficits in educational programming. (A reader may note, however, that the parents' tireless knocking on educational doors, on behalf of a son or daughter being integrated, has been answered with increased hospitality in more recent years by the educators responsible for decision-making.) When parents are forced to assume the role of resource specialist to the regular classroom teacher on the subject of classroom seating, modifications of teaching style, and peer group orientation, the natural relationship between parent and teacher is jeopardized. Even more significantly, the art of parenting may be neglected.

In their role as ombudsmen and child advocates, regardless of their concern for a particular handicapping condition, parents must work through councils for exceptional children, as partners of the schools, for initiation and expansion of nonspecial class alternatives. It is hoped that the practices and procedures described in this book will accelerate the efforts in communities across the United States to develop an instructional and behavioral support system based on the distinctive, identified needs of the exceptional child and of the regular classroom teacher. The total spectrum of educational services should be tailored to assign high priority to a program of continuing parent guidance and education throughout the hearing handicapped child's formal school years.

Implications for the Future

Local school districts.

The identification and retraining of specialists within a school system to remediate educational deficits of integrated hearing impaired children (Levels I, II, III in the cascade) is a major trend today. Thus, national attention must now be focused on: 1) identification and expansion of the skills, behaviors, and attitudes of regular classroom teachers and supplementary personnel to ensure efficient individual operation as well as routine and continuing discussion between regular and special educators; and 2) written descriptions of the processes of (a) identification, (b) diagnosis, (c) assessment, (d) program design, and (e) alternative procedures for the implementation of individualized services for integrated children. Each subsystem should be designed for easy modification in response to changing population requirements and new instruction and service alternatives which may be developed in the future.

The prediction of how well hearing impaired children will perform in a regular classroom — once they are determined to be eligible candidates for admission — depends largely on whether certain actions are initiated, *beyond* the local school district, by state education agencies, teacher training institutions, and legislative bodies.

State education agencies.

In every state, the major responsibility for developing a unified management system of educational services for exceptional children (including the hearing impaired) in the public schools resides with the state department of education. If this role is accepted, it will require the appointment of broadly based task forces to examine and modify state guidelines and regulations for program implementation. Updating of teacher certification standards will also be necessary. In many states today, hearing impaired children are denied publicly supported supplemental instruction (academic tutoring, speech and language therapy, auditory training) during the school day — which may be essential to their assimilation in regular classes.

Legislative action.

Existing state laws must be examined and statutes amended, as required, to permit the downward extension of state aid patterns to support infant and preschool educational programs and to encourage the employment of itinerant teachers who would provide academic tutoring on a one-to-one basis to integrated pupils in the public schools. There should be no minimum age requirements for state aid, and the support should be based on current rather than reimbursable formulas, including excess transportation costs.

Teacher training institutions.

The professional preparation of a new specialist in services for the hearing impaired in general education — to serve as consultant to regular classroom teachers and supportive personnel — highlights the relevance of performance-based teacher education programs. The *Standards for the Certification of Teachers of the Hearing Impaired,* published in 1972 by the Council on Education of the Deaf, delineate the general competencies required to provide appropriate educational services in one or more areas of specialization. As educational agencies identify the skills and techniques required to support hearing impaired children in regular classes, teacher training institutions will be challenged to permit each student and his adviser to enter into an individualized compact to determine the student's "curriculum" — both in readings and in professional growth experiences. His progress would be dependent on demonstrated competence. Experienced school personnel should be actively utilized in the management of field-based university programs of observation and demonstration teaching as supplements to interdepartmental seminars and conferences.

Research.

To date, nearly all research studies conducted in the United States by educators of the deaf have examined characteristics (personal, social, academic) of hearing impaired students by utilizing samples drawn from the population in self-contained classes in day and residential schools. In too many instances, a quantum leap has then been made from findings on this population to *non sequitur* generalizations and assumptions about limited capabilities of the entire school-age hearing impaired population, regardless of educational setting. The most auditory and oral hearing impaired children are no longer to be found in self-contained classes. Research specialists in psychology, child development, and family life are invited to look to the hearing impaired population *in regular or mainstream programs at the preschool, elementary, and secondary levels* for their research subjects. Comparative studies should be made of matched groups of children in integrated and self-contained classes for identification of critical variables in child management, speech intelligibility, approaches to cognitive tasks, and academic and social performance.

Concluding Remarks

The chilling concept of *one* educational setting for all hearing impaired children who have been labeled *deaf* by audiogram — prior to the fitting and daily full-time use of an individual hearing aid(s) — is outmoded and no longer defensible. Every hearing impaired child and youth is entitled to an individualized program of instruction and services at whatever age (0-21) and in whatever educational setting is likely to decrease his isolation from society and encourage the development of a reasonably optimistic, competitive, and productive individual.

Educators today are fully aware that this is a decade of accountability — to legislators, to the taxpaying public (including parents), to professional personnel, and to the courts — that guaranteed assurance of the rights of exceptional children will be an integral component of every total educational system in the public school districts of our country.

The Hearing Impaired Child in a Regular Classroom is offered as a set of working papers to encourage the future development of educational alternatives to self-contained classes through the concerted action of state, regional, and local agencies. It is expected that a description of innovative service models designed for the integrated hearing impaired child will be shared through subsequent publications, to which this book is a modest prelude.

*   *   *

Special acknowledgment is given here of the critical role assumed by Mrs. Robin Wittusen, Assistant Editor of *The Volta Review*, as Technical Editor of this book. Her personal serenity and professional acumen made her an invaluable colleague.

Appreciation is also extended to Mrs. Bettie Loux Donley, Director of Publications, Miss Esther L. Hiney, Editorial Assistant, and Miss Suez Kehl, Production Assistant, for their advice and assistance throughout the production of this book.

Part I
Preparation for Integration:
Issues and Objectives

MARK ROSS
DONALD R. CALVERT

The Semantics of Deafness

The dynamics of the "self-fulfilling prophecy" occurring with the hearing impaired child are described in this paper. The authors believe that either by labeling a person as "deaf" or by responding to people with different degrees of loss as if they were "deaf," the outcome is behavior in the predicted direction. That is, the presence of differing amounts of residual hearing is ignored in fact. If ignored, it cannot be effectively utilized, and the child's behavior and achievement become consistent with the original label. This affects the hearing impaired child in four general areas: (1) diagnosis, (2) parent-child interaction, (3) determination of educational placement and treatment, and (4) expected standards of achievement.

One well-recognized phenomenon in the field of education is that placing a label on a child can shape his teacher's response to him and, ultimately, strongly influence his behavior. For example, if a child is labeled "bright," his teacher may expect him to act intelligently and he will frequently respond by acting as the teacher expects. On the other hand, if the teacher reads on a child's record that he is a "discipline problem," she may be particularly alert to misbehavior, and the child, sensing what is expected of him, may begin to disrupt the class. The teacher, unaware of her effect on the child's behavior, may resign herself to an attitude of "I told you so," or "Just as I thought"; the prophecy she had made about the child's behavior has been fulfilled. Similarly, the self-fulfilling prophecy can also result either from labeling a child as "deaf" or from treating

Dr. Ross is Director of the Willie Ross School for the Deaf, Longmeadow, Massachusetts. Dr. Calvert is Director of the Central Institute for the Deaf, St. Louis, Missouri.

children with different degrees and types of hearing losses as if they were "deaf."

How do parents, relatives, and teachers react to a child who is considered "deaf"? Because he has been placed in this category, those around him assume that he has certain characteristics, and they treat him accordingly. Since he is "deaf," they reason, he cannot hear; and since he cannot hear —

- There is little point in speaking to him.
- He will need a special means of communication.
- He will need to be educated in a special school environment with special means of instruction.
- He cannot be expected to use a hearing aid to good effect.
- He will not be expected to succeed or excel at intellectual, social, or vocational endeavors.

Faced with such reactions, a child with a *moderate* hearing loss who is labeled "deaf" can become "deaf" by fulfilling the expectations of those around him.

The root of the problem lies in the very human tendency to polarize concepts and to stereotype; for example, one is either conservative or liberal, guilty or innocent. Degrees between these poles which do not lend themselves to familiar vocabulary are often ignored or dismissed as fuzzy thinking. It is not surprising, then, that lay people often assume that a person is "deaf" or is not. What *is* surprising is the frequency with which professional personnel continue to make the same faulty generalization—despite repeated experiences and studies showing that people with hearing losses have important quantitative differences in their ability to hear, to understand and develop speech, to use hearing aids, and to succeed intellectually, socially, and vocationally, if differential treatment is given.

There are several areas in which the hearing impaired child is adversely affected by the self-fulfilling prophecy embodied in the label "deafness": diagnosis, parent-child interaction, educational placement and treatment, and expected standards of achievement.

Diagnosis

The diagnosis of any disorder is based upon our understanding of the symptoms associated with it. If we understand "deafness" to include inability to respond to sound, then it follows that any individual who responds to sound cannot be "deaf." Because of this misunderstanding of the nature of hearing loss, we have frequently seen, for example, children with high-frequency hearing losses misdiagnosed as aphasic, emotionally disturbed, or mentally retarded. We have also seen the corollary of these misdiagnoses; that is, mentally retarded, aphasic, or emotionally disturbed children may be diagnosed as "deaf" if they fail to respond to auditory stimuli. In both cases, the child's behavior is forced into one of the discrete diagnostic categories created by the examiner's use or understanding of descriptive labels.

An individual examiner may have a good understanding of the phenomenon of hearing loss, but may nevertheless create a situation leading to the self-fulfilling prophecy by using the terms "deaf" and "deafness" loosely. There are several reasons why even a good understanding of the phenomenon of hearing loss does not preclude the use of simplified labels to describe it.

First, it is convenient to label with one word, the lowest common denominator that will carry meaning, have familiar connotations, and elicit predictable emotional reactions.

Second, diagnostic thinking is limited when only classes for "deaf" children and classes for normal children are available for educational placement. How different our diagnostic terminology might be if we always had many classes for children with hearing losses, with placement based at least partially on the degree of hearing loss!

A third factor is the tradition of medical diagnosis, which is generally based on labeling a disease syndrome, with the appropriate treatment ensuing when the cause is established. However, the children we deal with have varying degrees and types of auditory problems and varying degrees and types of many secondary problems, all of which have diverse therapeutic significance. By incorrectly adhering to medical tradition, educators frequently obscure individual differences by using and responding to single-term diagnostic labels and consequently searching for a single treatment for the condition.

The lay public and many professionals demand and are satisfied with a single word or figure to summarize the hearing loss. This urge toward simplicity in diagnostic terminology perpetuates the simplistic view of hearing loss. The audiologist, in turn, may tend to administer only those tests necessary for his report without exploring dimensions of hearing necessary for better understanding of the problem.

Parent-Child Interaction

Once a child has been diagnosed as "deaf," very often the parents' first reaction is to stop talking to him and to stop exposing him to auditory experiences. The parent may substitute gestures for vocalizations or deliver speech in monosyllables with whispered voice. Auditory training procedures may have been instituted in a clinic, and a hearing aid may have been fitted; but if the parents are reacting to the child as if he were completely "deaf," the child's residual hearing will not be used effectively. Therefore, counseling should begin when the loss is first determined and continue until the parents or dormitory personnel fully understand the nature of the problem and demonstrate that they are treating the child appropriately with respect to his hearing ability. Such counseling is the initial responsibility of the audiologist and the continuing responsibility of the child's teacher. A good understanding of the dimensions of hearing and the quantitative nature of hearing loss and sound will assist parents or dormitory personnel in setting realistic goals as well as help them structure their behavior for the child's benefit.

Educational Placement and Treatment

The placement of a hearing impaired child in a school for "the deaf" is often determined not by an analysis of the dimensional and quantitative nature of his hearing loss, but by the general tendency to polarize the concept and terminology of hearing loss: children who are "deaf" are to be educated in schools or classes for "the deaf." Although the administrative convenience of placing children in a limited number of comprehensive categories cannot be denied, this type of placement has plagued our progress in developing effective special education programs for children with significant hearing losses.

Educational placement has been the prime factor in determining educational treatment. Facilities for children with significant hearing handicaps have typically offered a method or approach that is applied to all children enrolled therein. Differences in a child's age and learning ability are recognized as grounds for differential educational treatment; when it comes to the state of his hearing, however, he is considered just like the other children. He uses *the* classroom amplifier and is taught by *the* classroom approach, despite significant variations in hearing ability which call for significantly different educational treatment. We believe that, in addition to grouping children by age, intelligence, and other factors, they must also be grouped in accordance with their ability to hear so that differential educational treatment may be established and residual hearing may be utilized to the fullest possible extent.

Expected Standards of Achievement

For every person, standards of achievement in social, educational, and vocational endeavors are set by parents, schools, and society. These expectations become part of our motivation to achieve. The label of "deafness," however, frequently results in greatly lowered standards, reduced motivation, and, consequently, limited achievement. As parents become aware of the limitations imposed by a hearing loss and as they broaden their experience with other hearing handicapped children, they tend to underestimate their child's potential. Schools disregard formal achievement standards and either aim for a norm based on previous experience or seek to get "whatever they can" from the child. Our society seems willing to adopt a paternal attitude toward "the deaf." The low standards set for "deaf" people reduce their external motivation, which we all need to achieve potential; they reduce competition with people who hear, whether or not the task is associated with reduced hearing, e.g., the "Deaf Olympics." Low standards can be and have been used to explain all failures and shortcomings of hearing impaired persons, and they can reduce the opportunities a hearing handicapped person has to achieve by making certain vocations taboo. The result is that a person labeled "deaf" achieves less than his real potential. Norms are established on such reduced achievement, and these norms become the target for future generations of "deaf" people. Those who predict the low achievement of "deaf" people see their prophecy fulfilled.

Discussion

In the preceding sections we have alluded to the "dimensions" of hearing and the "quantitative" nature of hearing loss. What are some of these dimensions? Certainly, the degree of hearing loss is basic; by using a single figure for this dimension, however, we obscure the variations in hearing loss across frequency. The individual who shows a progressively increasing hearing loss with increasing frequency may receive the same average figure as the individual with a flat hearing loss across all sound frequencies. Are we to assume from this that the degree of their impairment is similar?

Also important is the ability to integrate and make consistent configurations out of complex auditory signals, particularly speech. Hearing impaired children vary in the extent of damage they have sustained in the auditory pathways to the brain and consequently vary in their ability to integrate speech sounds into meaningful and consistent patterns.

Other dimensions of hearing include variations in: tolerance for loud sounds, growth of loudness of an auditory signal once threshold is exceeded, ability to detect small differences of intensity and frequency, growth of aural harmonics in the inner ear, extent of threshold decay of a sustained pure tone signal, ability to resolve time differences, auditory memory span, ability to localize sound sources, and ability to function auditorily in a noisy environment. Are all these dimensions relevant to the use a child makes of his residual hearing? Without a doubt, some are. For the rest, we do not presently know. Fortunately, we can now measure some important dimensions, one of which is the threshold configuration of an individual's hearing loss, or the audiogram. Given the widespread availability of audiograms for hearing impaired children, it is distressing that the information they portray is so frequently ignored.

Certainly, the authors realize that there are many diagnosticians and educators who are not easy prey to the generalizations implied by the categorical grouping of hearing loss and the self-fulfilling prophecy. Even for these, however, the inertia of tradition is difficult to overcome. Diagnostic terminology in the area of hearing impairment is embedded in our medical textbooks, our statutes, and in time-honored educational approaches. Recent developments in the measurement of hearing loss, in acoustical amplifiers, and in the skilled use of these amplifiers have not yet sufficiently influenced traditional practices. It should not be surprising that in educational programs for "deaf" children, the product is a "deaf" child. In spite of an apparent understanding by many professionals of recent developments, a cultural lag persists which continues to generate the self-fulfilling prophecy. It is time to generate a new hypothesis, one which has as its basis the dimensional and quantitative nature of hearing loss. We firmly believe that it is only after this step that hearing impaired children can begin to realize their maximum potential for growth.

2

E. W. JOHNSON

Let's Look at the Child, Not the Audiogram

There is potential harm in labeling a child "deaf" or "hard of hearing" solely on the basis of an audiogram. It is how the hearing impaired child functions, not the degree of his hearing loss, which should determine the type of educational system to which he is assigned. In the three cases described, although the pupils had severe hearing losses, they were entirely capable of adjusting to a school program designed for the hard of hearing and were functioning well. After two were transferred to programs for the deaf, they retrogressed and developed other problems.

As professional clinicians, trained in the evaluation of children, we have been admonished not to place a label on a child. When evaluating an individual child whose primary deficiency is in the development of speech and normal communication processes, we would not think of calling him brain-damaged, mentally retarded, or aphasic until we are reasonably certain of the diagnosis.

Why is it, then, that a child is labeled a deaf child as soon as we have recorded his responses to audiometric testing? It is just as improper to call the child with an audiogram of 70, 80, or 90 dB a deaf child without investigating his use of residual hearing as it is to label him brain-damaged or retarded without careful evaluation.

We must be deeply concerned at the tendency of some school administrators or school placement officers to assign a child to a school for the deaf solely on the basis of his audiogram. It is entirely possible that a child who is called

Dr. Johnson is Director of Clinical Audiology, Otologic Medical Group, Inc., and Consultant in Audiology, University of Southern California School of Medicine.

profoundly deaf on the basis of a threshold pure tone audiogram functions with hearing aids as a hard of hearing child. It is also entirely possible that the so-called hard of hearing child with adequate use of residual hearing can function as an essentially normal youngster.

Three cases handled in our Otologic Medical Group provided the impetus for writing this article.

Case Report #1

The first instance is Jeff, a 9-year-old who was first seen for evaluation at age 5. Audiologic studies revealed a flat sensorineural impairment of approximately 85 dB on the right ear and hearing only through 1000 Hz on the left ear (Fig. 1). Otologic diagnosis established a sensorineural congenital hearing loss. The history revealed that the mother had had rubella during the third month of pregnancy. There was some history of variation of hearing level with colds. Jeff had started using a hearing aid at a little over 2 years of age.

Jeff returned to the office the following year at age 6. At this time speech reception thresholds were obtained at 80 dB on the right ear and 90 dB on the left ear. He was using binaural hearing aids at this time and seemed to function very well with the two instruments.

Figure 1

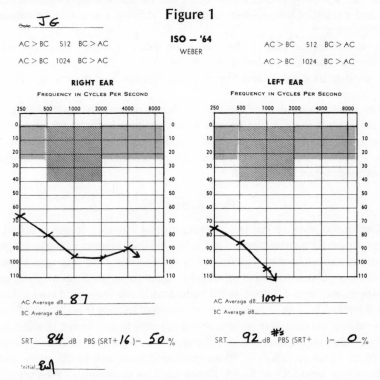

(Note: All references to dB in this book may be understood to be ISO calibration unless otherwise noted.)

He was enrolled in a school for hard of hearing children rather than deaf children and remained in this school environment one and one-half years. His attendance in a hard of hearing program appeared to be satisfactory in terms of educational progress. He was passed at the normal intervals and received grades of A's, B's, and a scattering of C's.

In December of his second year, he was told that on the basis of his hearing level he had been classified as a deaf child and that he must attend the school for the deaf. He was subsequently transferred to the school for the deaf and, in the re-evaluation at the school, was classified as an aphasic child. The following semester Jeff seemed to lose all interest and motivation in the educational process. His mother reported that behavior problems that had not previously existed began to occur. She further reported that his language and speech seemed to deteriorate and that his interest in reading and in school subjects was almost nil. At the end of that semester, Jeff returned to the office for another evaluation. The same hearing levels were established as for previous tests. Speech testing established a threshold for speech on the right ear of 84 dB and (at plus 16 dB) a speech discrimination (PB) score of 50%. We were unable to establish a threshold for spondee* words on the left side although he could repeat a number series that was presented at a level of 92 dB. He was still using binaural hearing aids and a retest of his responses to speech established a sound field threshold of 45 dB.

It would appear that by his audiogram this is a child who might well be classified as having a profound hearing loss. Yet his use of his residual hearing with good hearing aids places him into a category of hard of hearing rather than deaf.

The parents were determined that he should not return to a deaf program in the fall even if it would be necessary to provide private tutoring or to make other arrangements for his education outside of the public school system. They were convinced that it was to his educational advantage that he be transferred out of the program for the deaf.

Case Report #2

The second instance involves a young man of 16 years. Ronny was first seen at age 10, and a bilateral sensorineural hearing impairment, probably congenital in origin, was established. Ronny had used a monaural aid since age 3 and had attended a school for hard of hearing children in an Eastern state before moving to this area. Looking at the audiogram alone, we would tend to classify him as hard of hearing or perhaps severely hard of hearing (Fig. 2).

A hearing aid consultation was carried out with Ronny at age 10 and binaural hearing aids were recommended. At that time we were able to establish a speech reception threshold (SRT) of 50 dB on the right ear and 52 dB on the left ear with a sound field SRT of 53 dB. Ronny was able to establish a PB score of 64%

---

*Spondee words — words containing two stressed syllables.

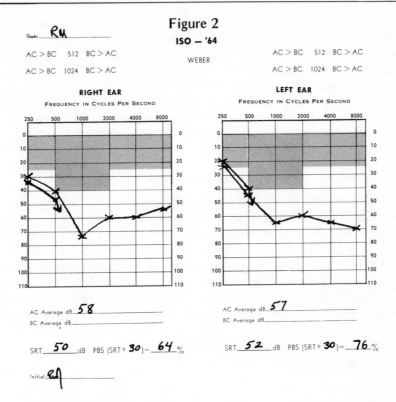

Figure 2

Date _RM_

ISO — '64

AC > BC   512   BC > AC   WEBER   AC > BC   512   BC > AC

AC > BC   1024   BC > AC   AC > BC   1024   BC > AC

RIGHT EAR   LEFT EAR

FREQUENCY IN CYCLES PER SECOND   FREQUENCY IN CYCLES PER SECOND

AC Average dB _58_   AC Average dB _57_

BC Average dB   BC Average dB

SRT _50_ dB   PBS (SRT+ _30_) = _64_ %   SRT _52_ dB   PBS (SRT+ _30_) = _76_ %

Initial _RN_

on the right ear and 76% on the left side. Working with binaural hearing aids it was possible to shift his hearing level from 53 dB sound field to 25 dB sound field with a 74% discrimination test score.

Ronny was enrolled in a program for the hard of hearing in an integrated school system where a substantial part of his work each day was carried out in classes with normally hearing children. Ronny responded well to this program and progressed from grade to grade with average or slightly better than average grades.

In September of the year that Ronny was 15 years old, his parents were told that he was a deaf child and must be sent to a school for the deaf. The parents were informed that the hearing tests clearly indicated that he did not belong in the hard of hearing program. He was subsequently assigned for that school year to a deaf program. The school was located a long way from his home and it was necessary for Ronny to get up at 5:30 each morning for a one and one-half hour bus ride. His mother reported that he regressed in his school work and completely lacked motivation during that school term. She reported further that his grades fell off, that his reading level declined, and that his speech seemed to be more impaired.

At the end of the year, his mother insisted on returning Ronny to the integrated school program for the hard of hearing. The results were: improved

grades, significant improvement in motivation, and better all-around performance. In the seventh grade he came up with 2 A's, one B, 2 C's, and one D.
Ronny came back for a new audiologic evaluation in June and once again speech
tests established a threshold of 50 dB on the right ear, 52 dB on the left ear,
with discrimination scores of 64% on the right and 72% on the left. Using
binaural hearing aids we were able to establish a threshold of 26 dB with 84%
discrimination. Here is a boy classified as severely hard of hearing who is
functioning as essentially normal with the use of his hearing aids. Certainly he
does not belong in a school for the deaf.

Case Report #3

A third example is a child who would normally be classified as profoundly
deaf (Fig. 3) and who is now functioning in a high school with normally hearing
children and passing all of her classes. Donna's hearing loss was established
before age 2 and a hearing aid was given to her immediately. She had a twin
brother to help to stimulate a constant flow of communication. She also was
blessed with parents who began working with her with auditory training and
speechreading before age 3. Donna has been periodically re-evaluated and the
hearing results are essentially the same with each re-check.

Figure 3

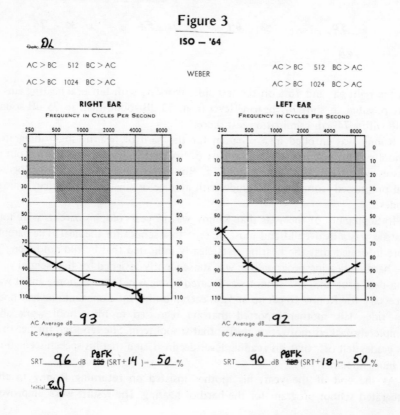

She was 9 years old when the second aid was added for true binaural hearing, and she has continued to use two aids to the present time. Initially it was possible to establish speech thresholds only through recognition of picture spondee words, but later tests established PB scores with the PBFK* list. Speech testing at age 9 established an SRT of 96 dB and approximately 50% on the PBFK words. Donna was seen again in the next year and had essentially the same audiogram; new binaural hearing aids were recommended. With this equipment she was getting an unusually good threshold shift sound field to 43 dB. Three years later she was re-evaluated with no change in her responses to pure tones or speech through the audiometer head phones. Testing the use of her hearing aids, her threshold for warble tone and speech in the sound field was shifted to approximately 40 dB.

Donna could well have been a child classified as profoundly deaf and could have remained in a program geared to the profoundly deaf for the rest of her educational life. The fact remains that she does not function as a profoundly deaf youngster because of her excellent use of every bit of residual hearing. She did remain in a deaf education program until the junior high level. She then functioned in a hard of hearing program until the high school level, and she graduated as the only hearing impaired child in a normal hearing high school with a senior class of over 300.

These three examples may help stir us to look at the child and the way he functions with hearing aids through utilizing whatever residual hearing he has rather than to look at the audiogram and to decide that *this* youngster is profoundly deaf and *that* youngster is severely hard of hearing. It behooves us as parents, as audiologists, as clinicians, and as teachers of the deaf, to look at the youngster and to determine how he functions as a person and not as a particular category of deafness.

Conclusions

Different children respond differently to hearing aids. If aids are placed on the child early in life, and if he lives in an enriched environment with constant auditory and verbal stimulation, much can be achieved. It is grossly unfair to label a child "deaf" or "hard of hearing" solely on the basis of an audiogram. Some children will utilize every scrap of residual hearing to *function* as hard of hearing in spite of a "deaf-type" audiogram. Other children may *function* as essentially normal hearing youngsters in spite of a "hard of hearing" type audiogram.

Let us adopt, as our guiding principles for educational placement and for therapy, the basic idea that we will always look at the child and the way the child functions and responds to environmental sound, rather than merely at the type of audiogram he may present.

---

*Discrimination of kindergarten-level words.

3

RAYMOND A. STASSEN

"I Have One in My Class Who's Wearing Hearing Aids!"

Hearing aid technology has permitted pupils with severe to profound hearing impairments to function in the classroom as though they were only mildly to moderately hearing impaired. The pupil and his amplifying system are only two of the elements that contribute to this increased educational potential. Teachers, if they become aware of the hearing and listening needs of the pupil who wears hearing aids, can become the third important element.

No teacher should have to experience the surprise of discovering a hearing aid user among the pupils in his classroom. Pupil placement personnel, special education staff members, the classroom teacher who worked with the pupil the previous year, the audiologist responsible for monitoring the child's hearing status, the parents, the pupil — somebody should have prepared the teacher before the first class meeting. However, institutional communication systems sometimes fail, parents may be unable to resolve their conflicting feelings about their "imperfect" child, and the pupil may hesitate to advertise the fact that he is different. Consequently, every year there are teachers who are alarmed to discover, "I have one in my class who's wearing hearing aids!"

Contemporary American culture conditions us to prize the attractive physique and the intact nervous system. We may respond to hearing aids in the same way we respond to leg braces, extraordinarily thick eyeglasses, or a wheelchair. The appliances obviously are beneficial to the users, but they are unattractive. We are eager to help the handicapped person, but we also wish to avoid any embarrassment that might come from speaking about the appliance

Mr. Stassen is Supervisor of Clinical Audiology, Speech and Hearing Center, Teachers College, Columbia University, New York.

the person must use. When a school child with both hands holding crutches stands before a heavy door he cannot manage, we immediately open the door for him. Our role in the solution of this child's immediate problem is obvious. But what is our role when we talk to a student who wears hearing aids? All we know about hearing aids is what we read in newspaper advertisements.

The initial surprise and alarm of discovering hearing aids worn by a pupil in the classroom may be followed by the wishful and unrealistic assumption that the amplifying appliances themselves will do the work of overcoming the hearing problem and that the teacher and pupil can proceed as usual with the business of teaching and learning. Not true. The hearing aid user does more work than the hearing aids in understanding a spoken message. His energetic and persistent efforts are crucial to adequate comprehension of the aided sound. By developing some basic understanding of the operation and limitations of hearing aids, a teacher can become the student's ally in this effort.

Hearing Aids

Few teachers have ever touched a hearing aid, much less listened to one. Inexperience allows persons with normal hearing to attribute a level of complexity to the hearing aid that it does not possess. Manufacturers of hearing aids, if they expect the public to purchase their products, must make the aids manageable by elderly persons with arthritic fingers and by 6-year-olds who do not always have parental supervision. Operation of a hearing aid is essentially uncomplicated. Although the procedure for battery replacement and the location of on/off switches, volume controls, and telephone amplifying circuits may vary from one brand of hearing aid to another, the teacher can be assured through practical demonstration that manipulation of the hearing aid is straightforward and simple.

There are hundreds of different types and models of hearing aids. *Low-frequency emphasis* aids, *transposer* aids, *CROS* and *BiCROS* aids, *directional microphone* aids: all these are terms symbolizing recent innovations in hearing aid technology. There is no reason to doubt that the next decade will require new jargon because of further modifications in hearing aid engineering and design. Nevertheless, all hearing aids are, and will continue to be, instruments that are sensitive to air-borne sound, amplify its energy, and deliver the increased sound level to the user's ear by means of a loudspeaker or earphone.

The hearing aid amplifying system begins with a pick-up microphone, much smaller than those for tape recorders or public address systems. But, like all microphones, it responds with sympathetic physical movement to the sound, or acoustic energy, that strikes it. The movement is changed into minute electrical variations that correspond to the intensity (loudness) and frequency (pitch) of the original sound. The electrical variations are increased, or amplified, by a series of transistors powered by a small battery housed within the hearing aid case. Their function is to change these minute electrical variations produced by the microphone into larger electrical variations, feeding them to the loudspeaker component.

A loudspeaker is something of a microphone in reverse. The microphone is physically moved by sound waves, but the loudspeaker *generates* sound waves. The electrical changes amplified by the hearing aid transistors are translated by the loudspeaker components into physical movements. Whether in a radio, a public address system, or a hearing aid, the physical movements of the loudspeaker components are greater in degree than are the movements of the microphone components at the beginning of a sound amplifying system. Usually, the amplified sound energy from the loudspeaker is carried to the listener by a custom-fitted mold worn in his ear. In some cases involving conductive hearing loss (external or middle ear problems), the sound energy may be delivered by a small plastic-encased vibrator held in contact with the bone behind the ear by a spring steel headband.

Specific hearing aids differ in their power and in the pitches, or frequencies, that they amplify. Some hearing aids may be housed in eyeglass bows, be perched behind the ear in flesh-colored cases, or be contained in larger cases worn on the chest. But, despite these differences, all hearing aids include a signal pick-up system, an amplifying system, a volume control device, and a loudspeaker system. There is, consequently, a similarity between hearing aids and the commonplace transistor radios that are equipped with earphone attachments. (A significant difference, of course, is that transistor radios pick up inaudible radio waves while hearing aids pick up sound in the near environment.) With only a little exposure, educators and therapists will find a child's hearing aid no more intimidating than the familiar transistor radio. Comfortable acceptance of the hearing aid by persons responsible for the training and education of a hearing impaired pupil will work to the advantage of the pupil.

Realistic Expectations for Hearing Aids

A hearing aid cannot completely eliminate the problems associated with hearing loss. Rather, it may reduce the dimensions of the problems so that they can be managed through the persistent efforts of the hearing aid user with support and understanding of persons who communicate with him.

One factor that may limit the benefits to be expected from hearing aids is the nature of the individual's hearing impairment. Most hearing aid users, whether children or adults, rely on amplification for hearing problems that cannot be treated by medical or surgical procedures. When the sensorineural system, or nerve structures, of the inner ear have been damaged, environmental and speech sounds are perceived with less than normal loudness, and the sounds are usually less clear as well. The person with this type of loss must listen with a low fidelity system. To compensate, he can use an amplifying system to increase the loudness level of conversational speech. However, adequate loudness of speech sounds cannot be equated with adequate clarity of the sound. Damage to the nerve receptor portion of the inner ear may make it difficult or impossible for a person to detect the acoustic energy in some speech sounds, no matter how loudly and clearly the spoken message is produced at its source. Even if the sounds can be amplified to a level at which some elements of speech can be detected, the built-in distortion of the ear can obscure the differences among the elements. With adequate hearing aids in place, for instance, the child with a sensorineural hearing loss may not hear the differences among words like *mass, gnat, math, nap, mat,* and *map.*

The effectiveness of a hearing aid may also be limited by the size of the amplifying equipment. Adult male speech includes a constantly varying array of pitches and overtones ranging over six octaves, with the lowest pitch in the region of one octave below middle C. The range of women's and children's speech sounds includes middle C and five octaves above. If one considers the size and weight of high fidelity radio receivers and record playback systems designed to respond faithfully to the full array of pitches in speech, it becomes obvious that similar fidelity cannot be expected from a package of components small enough to be worn conveniently during all waking hours by a school-age child. Hearing aids worn on the head are rarely more than two inches long and half an inch wide.

There are larger box-like hearing aids that are worn on the chest in a pouch secured by a harness. These body-worn instruments have a separate loudspeaker (earphone, or receiver) attached to the user's earmold, and the loudspeaker is connected to the hearing aid box by an electrical cord. The larger size of the body-worn instrument allows the engineer more opportunity to improve fidelity. Although the person with a severe loss of hearing usually wears a larger hearing aid, his lower fidelity hearing mechanism may counter-balance whatever improvement in fidelity has been built into the body-worn hearing aid.

The hearing impaired pupil and his teacher thus cannot look to the hearing aid as the *complete* solution for the learning and teaching problems that are predictable consequences of a hearing handicap. Yet, for a large proportion of the hearing impaired population, the benefits of hearing aid usage far outweigh the limitations. Since conveniently wearable amplifiers have become available, thousands of hearing impaired persons have been offered the potential for speaking to others and for understanding speech. Use of a hearing aid offering appropriate amplification for the peculiar needs of the wearer can lead to primary reliance on residual hearing, with speechreading as a supplement, for maximum comprehension of spoken language.

The Ideal Communication Environment

There are steps teachers can take to capitalize on the benefits offered by hearing aids. One of the most important is to maintain a good communication environment in the classroom. The ideal communication environment for the hearing aid user includes neither mystery nor surprise. Briefly it is one where the talker is close at hand, where there are a number of nonauditory cues to support and emphasize the spoken content of the message, and where there is little or no extraneous sound competing with the speech signal that is to be understood. Such an environment enhances understanding of spoken language for all hearing impaired persons. Yet, while these characteristics are easy to specify, they may sometimes be overlooked or forgotten by a teacher who has two good ears, who has had little or no contact with a hearing impaired child, and who has not felt the compelling need to recognize ways of controlling environment to the best advantage of those who do not hear normally.

The work of understanding speech is made easier for a pupil with hearing aids when his teacher is nearby while speaking. The intensity of an acoustic signal decreases markedly as the distance from the source of the signal increases. If a talker moves from a position four feet from a listener to a position eight feet away, the intensity of the talker's speech decreases fourfold. If the talker then moves twelve feet away, intensity decreases ninefold. The implications of this acoustic phenomenon should be considered when a teacher plans seating arrangements. An important factor in determining the best place for the hearing impaired student to sit is the position in the classroom his teacher customarily takes when talking to the class. If the pupil wears only one hearing aid, he should be seated with the aided ear directed toward his teacher. If two aids are worn, but one ear is better than the other, the better ear should be directed toward the teacher. Expect best understanding to occur when speech is offered face-to-face to the hearing aid user. Expect poorer understanding when the hearing impaired pupil is in the auditorium, is seated far back in the study hall, or is struggling to comprehend the speech of a classmate reciting from a distant corner of the classroom.

Controlling Extraneous Sounds

A crucial consideration in maintaining a good communication environment is the control of sounds extraneous to the spoken message. Noise is the archenemy of hearing aid users. Unfortunately, while the hearing aid is designed to amplify and deliver pitches perceived in spoken messages, it will also amplify those same pitches when they are part of background conversation, rustling papers, air conditioning noise, babble on the playground, the custodian's lawn mower outside the window, or the footsteps of students moving from class to class. The degrading effect of even moderate levels of noise upon the hearing aid user's understanding of speech is difficult for those of us with normal hearing to understand because we relegate extraneous noise to the background with almost reflexive efficiency. But the dynamics of sensorineural hearing loss and hearing aid amplification make selective listening much more difficult for the hearing aid user. If the source of noise is closer to the pupil than is his teacher, the pupil will be more aware of the noise than of the teacher's speech. Therefore, noise sources must be considered when planning seating arrangements.

Another source of unessential sound that is a predictable part of many school settings—and that sabotages the hearing aid user's attempts at understanding speech—is what we call echo, or reverberation. This phenomenon is most conspicuous in large, enclosed areas with few sound-absorbing surfaces. The school gymnasium is a prime example of a reverberant environment that renders a hearing aid virtually useless. Similarly, the hearing aid user cannot trust his hearing perception in hard-surfaced corridors or lunchrooms. Even some large classrooms without carpeting, draperies, or acoustical tile force the hearing impaired student to deal with unfavorable reverberation much of the time.

Consideration of the limitations of hearing aid amplifiers and of competing sounds in the environment underscores the importance of providing nonauditory cues to meaning along with sounds of speech. Seating the child so that he has face-to-face visibility of the teacher's speech movements, employing appropriate and natural hand gestures, glancing in the direction of an object being discussed, using supplementary pictures and diagrams, and writing key words on the blackboard (but don't talk while facing the board) are all uncomplicated nonauditory techniques that will fill in the gaps left by an imperfect listening system.

There are particular problems of hearing aid usage that are peculiar to the age and grade level of the pupil. These problems are outlined below.

Nursery School Through Kindergarten

Because hearing loss is diagnosed and hearing aids are fitted at progressively earlier ages as time goes by, the youngster who is just beginning his half-day school exposure may already have tallied an impressive number of practice hours with amplification. Yet, even though a child may be using a hearing aid full-time before the age of 3 years, he may not have the manual dexterity to manipulate the instrument. To complicate matters, the very young child may not have mastered the clarity of speech or the expressive language to alert his teacher to the fact that his aids are not working and are consequently acting as plugs in his impaired ears. Therefore, teachers of a very young hearing impaired child should develop some expertise in manipulating the controls of the particular model of hearing aid worn by that child, learn the technique of inserting the earmold, and master the soap and hot water approach to removing ear wax from the opening of the earmold. They must also know how to replace a spent hearing aid battery and should have spare batteries available as needed. Parents of the hearing impaired youngster can supply the extra batteries and can usually offer the simple instructions and demonstrations that will take care of hearing aid needs during school time. If the mother and father are unable to provide help, one may consult the dealer who sold the hearing aid or the audiologist who monitors the child's hearing status. A conference should then be arranged so that the parents can become acquainted with the hearing aids.

Typically, very young children easily accept the presence of hearing aids on one of their peers. If curiosity is stirred and questions do come from the hearing children, their teacher can make a comparison between the function of eyeglasses and the function of hearing aids. The analogy, while not quite accurate, allows young children to associate unfamiliar hearing aids with familiar glasses, and it encourages an understanding of the need to protect the instruments.

The Elementary Grades

By the first or second grade, the child who began hearing aid usage prior to the age of 3 should have developed a high level of independence in the utilization and care of his hearing aids. If the recommended hearing aids are appropriate to the pupil's hearing needs, his acceptance of them will be relaxed and certain. When asked to draw portraits of themselves, hearing aid users at this age level usually include their hearing aids in the picture. Teachers should encourage this easy acceptance of hearing aids, and please don't suggest that the child remove his hearing aids when class photographs are taken!

Hearing children aged 6, 7, or 8 may begin to show an active curiosity about the hearing aids worn by one of their classmates. Don't squelch this natural curiosity because unsupervised and potentially damaging explorations of the instruments may result. A child's hearing aids are entirely suitable subjects for his turn at show-and-tell. Satisfy the classroom's predictable curiosity about the amplifying devices; once familiar with them classmates will hardly think them worthy of mention.

Teachers who work with a hearing aid user during the elementary school years would do well to borrow from the experience and insight developed by the child's previous teachers. Arrange a conference to discuss last year's successes and failures. A word of caution, however: if you find last year's teacher dwelling exclusively on observations of the hearing impaired pupil's inability to pay attention, or on the suspicion that the pupil's inconsistent understanding points to brain damage, or on the accusation that the child can hear when he wants to hear, you have found a person who has confused inconsistent behavior due to fluctuating acoustic conditions with misbehavior due to the secondary social and emotional stress which can accompany central nervous system pathology. Seek advice elsewhere.

Since the development of reading skills is important in the elementary grades, the impact of hearing impairment and hearing aid usage on this area of academic training should be recognized. For instance, phonic approaches to reading instruction are directed to the least reliable sensory system of the hearing impaired pupil. It might be wise to request the services of the remedial reading teacher even before the hearing impaired first-grader shows a need for remediation. Reading coaching sessions will be all the more effective if they take place in a quiet, one-to-one communication environment.

The advancement from nursery school and kindergarten to elementary school usually means a change from half-day to full-day attendance. For the hearing impaired pupil, the act of listening is demanding and fatiguing; so expect better performance early in the day. If flexibility in scheduling is possible, allow the hearing aid user to grapple with verbally dependent subjects in the morning and reserve art and physical education for the afternoon.

Junior and Senior High School

Aided hearing that seemed adequate at the elementary school level may suddenly seem less than adequate when the pupil enters either junior or senior high school. Instead of becoming familiar with the communication habits of only one teacher, the hearing aid user must adapt to several teachers each day. Classroom lights are forever being turned off so that film strips and slides can be shown in a darkened environment in which the teacher's face and gestures are difficult to see. Or motion pictures are shown, narrated by an off-screen voice that meets noisy competition from the sound of the movie projector. Notetaking plays an increasingly important part in classroom activities, and with his eyes on the notebook page, the hearing aid user is denied many of the nonauditory cues to meaning that may be offered by the lecturer. Panel discussions, questions and responses from students in all parts of the classroom, committee meetings, and assembly programs all become part of a complex communication environment much more taxing than the "ideal" environment described earlier. Ears and hearing aids may be functioning as well as they always have, but communication demands have become dramatically more stringent. In some schools, the practice of recruiting "listening buddies" has been an effective way of meeting the greater listening demands of the secondary level. The buddy's ears and carbon copies of his class notes and assignments can be used to fill the gaps in the hearing aid user's understanding.

In Conclusion . . .

Of all handicapped pupils, those with amplifiable hearing losses are among the most potentially teachable. Yet, this group historically has been among the most undereducated. Too often the poor academic standing of the hearing impaired pupil begins with the stultifying alarm that fills the teacher when hearing aids in the classroom are discovered. Yet there is a more productive response to the sight of hearing aids than alarm. View them as a clear signal that some uncomplicated but consistent modifications of good teaching techniques are in order to help the pupil with hearing aids approach his true potential in the classroom. The pupil and his hearing aids will do most of the work, but they need your help.

4

DORIS J. LECKIE

Creating a Receptive Climate
In the Mainstream Program

To facilitate integration of hearing impaired children into regular public school programs, administrators in the special schools for the hearing impaired must initiate a selling effort to convince mainstream educators of the importance of accepting hearing impaired students and of providing adequate programming for them. The process of preparing a receptive climate for integration can parallel that of developing a market for a product in the business world; it involves the consideration of market conditions, sales method, product quality, advertising, price, and warranty.

The placement of hearing impaired children into mainstream programs necessitates a two-fold willingness on the part of mainstream educators. They must first accept such children into regular schools and, second, make adequate provision for their education. To create and sustain a receptive climate requires a selling effort on the part of schools for the hearing impaired, which have not been traditionally sales-minded. For too long we in the schools have tended to isolate ourselves, doing our own thing, rather than exploring the world of hearing education all around us.

This attitude must change if we are to be successful in our commitment to the philosophy of oral education which, in its logical extension, requires:
a) an end to the initial segregation of deaf children who do not really need the special services of a school for the hearing impaired, and
b) integration into mainstream programs as quickly and extensively as possible for those who have been initially segregated.

Mrs. Leckie is principal of the Montreal Oral School for the Deaf in Montreal, Quebec, Canada.

It has thus become the responsibility of a school for the hearing impaired to conduct a highly persuasive "selling campaign" directed specifically toward educators of normal children with a supporting spillover throughout the community at large.

Over 10 years of integration experience in Montreal suggest the following guidelines for the development of an optimum "marketing strategy" based on analogies to the business world: market conditions, sales method, product quality, advertising, price, and warranty.

Market Conditions

At no time in the history of education has our task been easier. Many mainstream educators are realizing that they must accept the concept that education is an individual matter. Programs are now being tailored to the individual child, and mainstream educators are at least willing to talk with interested groups of special educators about handling all types of handicapped children in the regular classroom. But there still remain many formidable obstacles to successful integration. Educators may have a general appreciation of its desirability, but they often feel that they are not equipped to undertake the particular task. Specifically, when integrating deaf children, we have encountered the following typical objections:

1) The regular teachers are not trained to teach children with hearing problems.
2) The teachers are already overworked.
3) It will be too costly.
4) Deaf children cannot keep up.
5) It will disrupt a class to have a deaf child.
6) Parents of hearing children will object.
7) It will lower the level of class achievement.

We must strive to overcome these objections as we continue in the development of the suggested "strategy."

Sales Method

Essential to the program are the continuing services of an integration officer from the school for hearing impaired children and the provision of amplification equipment for the regular classroom. The integration officer, in a supportive role, facilitates the operation and fills in gaps for the regular teacher. There are a variety of ways in which he may be useful—e.g., he may provide interesting materials to share with the hearing children or have two or three hearing children join in tutorial sessions with the deaf child.

Such a liaison is easier at the elementary level where there are only one or two regular teachers involved. In high school, however, the integration officer works best through the guidance department, for close contact with each individual teacher is not always possible. A written progress report on the hearing impaired child, obtained through a counselor from each teacher, focuses attention on the child and usually brings to light any problems that are being ignored. One principal felt that the very fact that an outsider was going to ask questions about a particular child created a greater interest in that child.

Occasionally regular teachers ask about training courses. It would seem desirable that every teacher have as part of his preparation some minimal training in dealing with all types of handicapped children. However, in keeping with the philosophy of individualizing programs, the best approach is surely regular consultation with the integration officer. The teacher of the hearing class then learns to deal with each problem as it arises.

For each integrated child the best and most easily operated amplification equipment should be installed. If possible, a cordless mike is advisable to give the teacher freedom of movement, and the liaison officer should make sure that the regular teacher is completely comfortable and confident in the use of the equipment.

Product Quality

Efforts to create a receptive climate in the mainstream will hardly succeed without a good product from the school for the hearing impaired—an emotionally balanced, socially mature child whose academic and communication skills have been developed to a stage adequate for his introduction into a mainstream classroom.

Naturally, the progress and achievement of hearing impaired children will vary greatly, as do those of hearing children. The integration officer must know and understand the child's capabilities and the range of mainstream programs offered in most school systems and then carefully seek the most suitable program for the child's individual needs. Ingenuity or creativity may be necessary to show how existing programs may be further adapted to special needs. For example, a boy in his final year of high school was having trouble with English literature. Since he had a block of free time during oral French, the liaison officer persuaded the school to enter the boy into a second English course, and the double dose eliminated the troubles. Most schools are receptive to such ideas but do not have the time to work them out themselves.

Advertising the Product

It is a well-known fact that you can't sell if you don't advertise. The public in general is curiously ignorant about hearing impaired people, and a good publicity campaign is a must. If you plan an integration program, every opportunity must be utilized to stimulate interest in deafness and overcome any fears or objections that may arise.

All levels of government must be made aware of the possibility of educating hearing impaired children in the mainstream. This can be done through pressure groups, lobbying, writing to members of the legislature, sending letters to newspapers, etc.

At the school board level it is usually easiest to work through the special education department—often a very receptive climate waiting to be cultivated. Through the department you can make contact with principals of regular schools, guidance counselors, and teachers.

Within the community are numerous avenues to explore. Lecture to service clubs, medical students, teachers-in-training, nurses-in-training, etc. Invite principals and teachers of regular schools to visit hearing impaired classes. Invite members of influential groups such as Junior League and Jewish Junior Welfare League to serve as volunteers and teaching aides in the school. Persuade radio and TV commentators to talk about the integration work. The very best form of advertising is the graduates themselves. As soon as you can show results, your work becomes much easier.

Integration is probably easier for a program which has always operated in a regular school. This year our school decentralized and established classes in five regular schools so that we could cut down on the ratio of hearing impaired to hearing. Even in this type of setup, it is easy to become a separate entity; it is necessary subtly but consciously to promote goodwill in the school with a view toward using the classrooms for integration. Teachers of the deaf who become personal friends of regular school teachers might plan interesting activities to which the hearing children would be invited, e.g., theater groups or special movies. They can offer to share equipment and programs; for instance, the Montreal Oral School offers an exciting art program and an Orff music program to which hearing children are invited. On the playground teachers of the deaf can organize games which hearing children will ask to join. The possibilities are endless; but unless you really work at it, you will end up with two separate schools in the same building.

To Sell—Be Competitive and Cost-Wise

In Canada many school boards are suffering budget cuts, increased teacher-pupil ratios, and stricter government controls. Taxpayers are complaining bitterly while at the same time demanding innovative programs, new and expensive equipment, and more individual attention for their children.

Therefore, one of the most influential points when trying to persuade a government or a school board to favor a mainstream program is the fact that integrating hearing impaired children into regular schools brings about a reduction in costs. Using Montreal figures as an illustration only, we estimate that we save several hundred dollars per child when we place him in regular school. These calculations include the basic cost of educating a normal child, to which we add a percentage of the integration officer's salary and the cost of the amplification equipment which we provide.

Warranty for Success

One thing you cannot do when selling an integration program is to give a guarantee—success is too unpredictable and the outcome undefinable. However, if it is a new program, be highly selective in the initial students that are integrated so that success is quite probable. Flexibility must be built into a program to enable adjustments if a child is having difficulty. On two or three occasions we have had some very pleasant surprises—students on whom we "gambled" rose to the challenge and did very well. During our 10-year program we have returned only two students from total integration to a partial program—one for social reasons, the other for academic difficulties.

In summary, let me outline the creed that did the most to create a warm, friendly atmosphere in our regular schools.

1) I am here to sell an idea.
2) If they buy, it will help a deaf child.
3) I am here to facilitate—not to demand.
4) When success comes, I will let the others have the glory.
5) When problems arise, I will shoulder the responsibility and find the solutions.
6) I will find tactful ways of pointing out errors and making suggestions.

When you are frustrated and discouraged because of indifference and lack of understanding, you may find this creed too idealistic, but it was effective for us.

Have You Thought Of . . .

. . . planning some integrated experiences for teachers of the hearing impaired in order to facilitate the successful integration of students? We at Tucker-Maxon Oral School feel that teachers of the deaf can more skillfully prepare deaf students for integration if they have some actual teaching experience with hearing children on the same age level. Next year two of our junior high teachers will assume part-time positions in a nearby parochial school and will have one or two deaf students in each class. This placement will provide the faculty with an opportunity to observe the deaf child from the point of view of the regular classroom teacher and will hopefully result in suggestions for improving the curriculum in our elementary grades. — *Wallace Bruce, Portland, Oregon.*

5

PHYLLIS GILDSTON

The Hearing Impaired Child in the Classroom

A Guide for the Classroom Teacher

The number of hearing impaired children placed in regular classrooms is increasing. Teachers who understand the difficulties such children encounter will be able to help them more effectively. This set of guidelines summarizes the major problem areas involved and suggests procedures for avoiding or ameliorating them.

General Considerations

DO try to accept the hearing impaired child positively — no matter how inadequate his speech, his comprehension, or his vocabulary (unless, of course, there are other reasons for not doing so). Since you often set the example for the class, your reactions are likely to trigger similar response patterns in the other children.

DON'T *pamper or overprotect the hearing impaired child, however. Don't treat him any differently from another child of his age, intelligence, etc. With only the limitations of his handicap to modify the goals you set for him, he will feel that he belongs.*

DO remember that even two children with *almost identical* hearing losses may function very differently and hence cannot be effectively lumped into one generalized category — the hearing impaired — for teaching purposes. They must be motivated, taught, and challenged according to their ability to function as total individuals.

DON'T *forget that intelligence, social maturity, family background, etc., of these children vary considerably. Any one or a combination of the above factors may be even more significant than the child's hearing loss in determining his ability to function or to learn — e.g., don't expect a dull child with a mild hearing loss to do nearly as well as a brilliant child with a profound loss.*

Dr. Gildston is Associate Professor, Communication Disorders, Brooklyn College, Brooklyn, New York.

DO discover and encourage the child's special capabilities and interests just as you would with any normally hearing child who is not top-notch in everything. It is, of course, of great psychological benefit to the youngster to know that he can excel in something.

DON'T *assume that the child can't be gifted in science or art or poetry simply because he has a significant hearing loss.*

DO try to discuss his problem objectively with the class. Children can be much less cruel when they are helped to understand another's problem. The content of the motivational material may be as simple as the book, *Tim and His Hearing Aid,** or as complex as a discussion of sound propagation in the secondary school science lab.

DON'T *miss any opportunity to turn the hearing handicap into an asset. Units in physiology, mechanics, physics, communication problems, etc., may provide the fulcrum for swinging the attitudes of his classmates in the right direction. The "dross into gold" approach can be adapted at all levels.*

DO make certain that the hearing impaired child is *attending* (not just "listening") when you begin new work, when you ask him a question, or when you give him a job.

DON'T, *however, expect continuous attention on his part. Some inattention must be tolerated if you are not to wear the child out. (Remember how tired you were when you returned from that lecture given by a foreign authority and could only get a seat at the rear of the auditorium?)*

DO consider instituting the buddy system. A buddy is a child who can help the hearing impaired child with directions he has missed without wasting the teacher's time. The buddy may also "cue him in" should he miss out on some of the class discussions or need notes to copy over at home.

DON'T *expect the hearing impaired child to understand at all times no matter how bright he is or how diligently he tries! The child must make an extra effort much of the time and fatigue alone could cause him to miss out on what is going on. Furthermore, some of the many obstacles he must hurdle daily are bound to trip him up every so often.*

DO try to use many visual aids (you probably do, anyway) to increase the number of sensory associations the hearing impaired child can store in order to facilitate his learning.

DON'T *rely solely on auditory cues in teaching the hearing impaired child.*

DO be aware that some hearing impaired children have special vocabulary limits. Many words which normally hearing children use in the course of everyday conversation may be new words to the child with a hearing impairment.

DON'T *assume he starts off with the same vocabulary as the normal hearing child. The hearing child has heard multiple repetitions of many, many words without attending particularly to their meaning or to the speaker who uses them. He "absorbs" the meaning. The hearing impaired child must learn by attending directly to the speaker and concentrating on the communication with all his resources.*

---

*Available from the Alexander Graham Bell Association for the Deaf, Washington, D.C.

DO use some of the slang that is popular with the child's peers (within bounds, of course). You may be the link that connects him to the group.

DON'T *be a "fuddy-duddy" in your speech or language.*

To Help the Child Understand More Adequately Via Speechreading

DO write on the board without speaking. Then turn back to the class and speak.

DON'T *speak with your back to the class at any time.*

DO try to articulate clearly and with moderate speed.

DON'T *mumble and gallop in speaking. On the other hand, don't exaggerate your speaking pattern in a gallant attempt to make the hearing impaired child understand. He has to live with normally speaking people and has acquired speechreading skills for comprehension of normally articulated words.*

DO try to speak to the class from a position in the room which allows for adequate light to fall upon your face.

DON'T *stand with your back to the window in an unlighted room, for it puts your face in shadow. Similarly, don't talk to a hearing impaired child when he must assume a position which forces him to try to speech-read in an intense glare.*

DO be flexible in your standards for notetaking for the hearing impaired child. Remember that he must watch your face in addition to writing.

DON'T *expect the hearing impaired child always to be able to take decent lecture notes. He can't write and listen as most of us can, but must keep his eyes peeled to the speaker's lips in order to get the gist of what is being said. Don't expect him to be able to take notes in a darkened room.*

DO keep your book down when you read orally. (It's a good example for your students, anyway). Good eye contact is important.

DON'T *read with your eyes glued to the page.*

DO try to stand fairly still when talking. This may be difficult for you at first but give it a try.

DON'T *perambulate while talking -- particularly if you're giving an oral test.*

DO try to seat the child so that he may have a clear view not only of your face, but of every other student's face as well.

DON'T *seat a child in a class that has a great deal of group and class discussion with thoughts of his understanding only your conversation.*

DO allow the child to move his seat or to exchange seats with one or two others when he feels this move to be advantageous for comprehension.

DON'T *make the child feel he must be confined to only one location in the room.*

DO rephrase a question or message if the child does not appear to understand it in its original form. You may be employing words that look and/or sound alike to him but are in reality quite different.

DON'T *repeat the same question over and over again in its original form when the child appears not to understand. Raising your voice will not necessarily help either.*

DO write new vocabulary words for any subject on the board and say them for the class to give the hearing impaired child a chance to see how these words look on the lips — or — give him a list of the new vocabulary words to take home so that a member of his family may read them for him prior to the class discussion. He will thus become familiar with their visual properties and recognize them more easily in class.

DON'T *expect every hearing impaired child to understand new vocabulary words if he is given aural clues and explanations only. (Some may, but many will depend on speechreading as a supplement.)*

DO give the child and, if necessary, the child's parents, a preview of topics to be discussed the next day or week so that he (and his parents — if the child is young) may prepare at home for the coming units.

DON'T *spring a topic "cold" on the hearing impaired child.*

DO make a blackboard outline of any complicated topic being discussed to orient the student after tangential discussions along the way.

DON'T *shift topics without "tuning in" the child with verbal and visual connectives and transitions. ("Now we're going to discuss last night's homework." "Now let's move on to our science project.")*

DO remember that not all children speak clearly. Hence some are very difficult to speechread. Should something of importance be said or reported by another such child, it would be most helpful to repeat the highlights.

DON'T *hesitate to repeat for the hear-impaired child what another child says even though this is sometimes considered to be a poor teaching technique.*

DO remember to put all spelling words into a sentence as so many words look alike to the hearing impaired child.

DON'T *be content to give a spelling test in which a list of words is presented without an accompanying meaningful carrier sentence.*

DO try to keep the child within reasonable visual range so that he may listen and speechread without straining.

DON'T *expect him to speechread as well from a distance.*

To Help the Child Understand More Adequately Via Hearing

DO try to learn something about the extent and nature of the child's hearing loss in order to understand his communication handicap. Although many hearing impaired children face similar problems, each child's particular hearing disability makes his comprehension problem different.

DON'T *assume that all hearing impaired children hear in the same way. Don't hesitate to consult with the school doctor, nurse, speech and hearing clinician, etc., to get this specialized information. They will be happy to save you the trouble of having to dig it up yourself.*

DO try to learn something about hearing aids and the extent to which the child's hearing aid can help *him* to understand better; e.g., 1) children with moderate losses may benefit much more from a hearing aid than children with either very mild or very severe losses; 2) not all children who have hearing losses can be fitted with a hearing aid without compounding their comprehension problem.

DON'T *assume that hearing aids are like prescription eyeglasses — that wearing a hearing aid can "correct" the child's hearing problem. No hearing aid is completely free of distortion. No hearing aid will permit a child with even a moderate loss to hear exactly as he would hear if he had normal hearing.*

DO learn how to patch up minor breakdowns in hearing aids for the youngest children. It's a cinch to change a battery or cord.

DON'T *imagine you have to be a mechanic to do simple repair work on hearing aids. It may mean the difference between a useful or a wasted day for the child if you can make these simple repairs.*

DO seat the child so that if he wears a hearing aid in only one ear he is able to get the best reception not only from the teacher but from most of the children. Remember that, with or without a hearing aid, distance from the speaker is a significant factor in the child's ability to understand.

DON'T *assume that just because the child is wearing a hearing aid he can be seated anywhere in the room and hear as well. The further he is from the source, the more difficult it is to receive the message.*

DO reduce the noise level in the classroom at various times throughout the day to give the child with a hearing aid some respite from listening. The hearing aid is not selective and even a highly skilled listener may experience undue tension after a long session of listening in intense ambient noise.

DON'T *assume the hearing impaired child can focus upon important sounds in the environment and ignore background noises as successfully with his hearing aid as the normally hearing child does with his ears.*

DO speak in a natural tone of voice. Only with certain types of losses will raising the voice have any effect.

DON'T *shout. Shouting at someone who wears an aid will either "blast" him out of his seat or distort the sound considerably.*

DO remember that assignments which require a very long auditory memory span may not be best suited to the hearing impaired child.

DON'T *expect every hearing impaired child to remember a long list of items aurally presented. He is never sure whether he has caught all of the items correctly since they are in list form rather than part of a meaningful context. This task is hard enough for the child with normal hearing.*

DO encourage him to be unashamed if he does not understand and to state his confusion or apprehension immediately.

DON'T *become impatient with the child who so often comes up to your desk "just to make sure" he understands. (But do encourage longer intervals between visits if you are certain he is leaning on you unnecessarily.)*

DO remember that the hearing impaired child may not hear as well after he has had a cold or sore throat or earache. A temporary hearing loss may, after such an illness, be ADDED to the child's permanent hearing loss, thus further complicating his hearing problem for days or weeks after the respiratory infection has subsided. Weather conditions may also contribute to fluctuations in hearing level. Should you suspect a change of this nature, ask the nurse to run another hearing test on the child; if the hearing level has dropped considerably, the nurse will want to keep the child under close surveillance.

DON'T *assume that a child's inattentiveness or inability to follow class work after an absence is necessarily due to "laziness" or to his having missed certain lessons. The child may be functioning with a temporarily greater loss than usual. Not all parents of hearing impaired children are aware that an additional loss may follow an ear, nose, or throat infection. Such a temporary loss may become permanent if it persists and is not treated by an ear specialist.*

DO remember that children who have been tested at the beginning of the year and who have been found to have *normal* hearing may also develop temporary hearing losses after respiratory infections. You may be the first to notice the loss. You should refer the child to the nurse for another hearing test. Such an awareness on your part may save the child from sustaining a permanent loss due to ignorance or neglect.

DON'T *assume that the child reported to have* normal *hearing cannot develop a hearing loss during the year. If the child's behavior, in terms of comprehension and the ability to follow directions, appears to be significantly impaired after an illness, the possibility of such a loss should always be investigated.*

DO remember that a child with specific allergies may have normal hearing most of the time. On certain days, however, his hearing may be impaired. The season, certain foods, and environmental stress may all contribute to temporary hearing difficulties.

DON'T *feel that all children who complain of not hearing well on one day or who don't seem to be attending as they ordinarily do are necessarily delinquent or falsely exonerating themselves.*

To Help the Hearing Impaired Child Communicate More Adequately Via Speech

DO remember that most hearing impaired children do not hear many of the sounds we hear (particularly sounds like s, f, th). Furthermore, many of the sounds they *do* hear come through in distorted manner. Hence many of them will have a speech impediment. Although the speech clinician will probably help the child to acquire and correct omitted or defective sounds, you can help by following through in the classroom. Occasionally, remind the child to use the sounds he is working on in his special speech classes when he is with you.

DON'T *be discouraged if years and years of outside speech help bring only slow improvement. The hearing impaired child has to learn consciously to feel and remember many of the correct articulatory patterns which normally hearing individuals acquire unconsciously through the medium of sound. Of course, you won't wish to interrupt his communication with constant corrections. Wait until he has finished what he has to say and then, if you find it opportune, you can inform him of his errors.*

DO compliment him when he does manage to use correctly the sounds he is working on.

DON'T *think success is its own reward in this case — unless the success is called to his attention. Often, after all his hard work, he cannot hear his own improvements but must depend upon the listener to let him know when he's right.*

DO remember that although some hearing impaired children shout, many will speak with inadequate projection and flow of tone. Reminders to speak up and to reach out to the back of the room when he talks will help the child to project more adequately.

DON'T *accept either shouting or inaudibility from the child. He* can *be taught, with your help, to modulate his voice and project efficiently.*

DO give him as much opportunity to speak — if at all possible — as any other child in the class.

DON'T *make him feel inferior by "protecting" him from speaking assignments.*

Have You Thought Of . . .

. . . teaching the normal-hearing classmates of the hearing impaired student about hearing, hearing loss, and amplification devices? Mini-inservices can be developed in which the hearing consultant and the user of a hearing aid and/or loop system talk to classmates about the equipment. Units on the ear and hearing can also be presented to a class with participation by the hearing impaired child to the extent he wishes, as determined by prior consultation with him. — *Anne Seltz, Minneapolis, Minnesota.*

. . . writing lesson plans in pencil, and at the end of the day writing over them in red ink, indicating what was actually accomplished or how the plan had to be changed? — *Dorothy Hedgecock, Rochester, Minnesota.*

Part II

The Multidisciplinary Team

6

LEE F. AUBLE

The Integrated Superintendent: Normalization Can Be a Reality

A public school superintendent describes the role of parents and educators in developing and implementing an integrated program for hearing impaired children within the public school system. Among the challenges to be met are locating the children to be served, securing qualified and committed staff members, obtaining and utilizing effective equipment, developing a unifying and workable philosophy, and involving the parents for support and interaction. In the Berrien Springs Program the goal is complete "normalization" of each hearing impaired child.

Parents have the right to an education for their children. However, having a right and securing the effects you want from that right may be two different things. If you're driving down the road, you have the right to half of it—we say. I had the personal experience a few years ago of assuming this to be automatic. It was in early winter—we'd experienced a heavy snowfall and there were snowbanks on each side of the road. I was driving along at slow speed, came to a sharp turn in the road, and met a truck right on the turn. When we met, our vehicles overlapped by about two feet. Both of us had the right to half of the road, and we got it; but the road wasn't wide enough for two cars. We had assumed too much.

Education for hearing impaired children is somewhat the same. You can't, with safety, assume too much. You have to be involved, as a parent, on a personal basis.

Mr. Auble is Superintendent of Schools in Berrien Springs, Michigan.

Perhaps there is no one claiming the same road you want—perhaps there is. If it's just a vacant road, and your car won't run—if it's just no program, and you need to get one going—that's one problem. If it's a conflict as to what *type* of program is going to run, that's another.

Initiating a Program for the Hearing Impaired

Let's address ourselves to the no program situation. Certainly there are areas where this is the case. It was true in the southwest corner of Michigan just a few years ago. I believe it was in about 1959 that a mother came to me and said, "I have a daughter who will be of school age next fall and who is profoundly deaf. While she does quite well at home, I don't suppose she could get along in a regular classroom." Knowing what I did (really, knowing no more than I did) at the time, I said, "You are certainly right. She needs special help. Why don't you take her to Flint to the State School and ask their advice, or take her to Kalamazoo to the Upjohn School and talk with them?"

What happened after that is a long story—about 14 years long—and I won't give you all of the details and travail this family has gone through. But they illustrate, as do many others, that it is possible for people who can't hear a thing to live in our society as regular contributing members. (Sometimes it is to their own advantage: imagine yourself as a totally deaf parent of a teen-ager afflicted with the loud music bug! Handicapped? Not altogether.)

The establishment of our program at Berrien Springs was cued by the enactment of state legislation setting up Intermediate School District Special Education programs. These are pretty general in Michigan now. I don't know how easy or difficult it is if you live in another state. Certainly the situation varies. But let me tell you how our program grew to reality in Berrien Springs. If you have a program, you could parallel or contrast our situation.

Our school district is located in the center of the county, and a survey indicated that it seemingly made sense for us to be a program sponsor—although to our knowledge we had only one deaf child in our district. Five children were known in the general area, though, whose parents were anxious—to put it lightly—that something get going. We had employed a County Director of Special Education, Walt Wend, who is a "doer"; we found a teacher, through the staff at the Kalamazoo program, who was disenchanted with work in the big city of Chicago; and we started off in 1961 with five pupils. These rapidly grew to eight by mid-year, and to a dozen by the next fall.

I well remember our remedy for the problem of having such a large number of pupils for the one teacher. Although we couldn't find another teacher, state law allows us to employ aides. We had annexed a one-room rural school to our district, and a teacher employed there was no longer considered qualified, according to state certification standards, for the job. She had only had two years of college. We thought better, though, and employed her as an aide in our program. We gave her half of the pupils, under supervision of the certified teacher.

This worked fine the first few days, but then I got a call from the Principal one morning. He said, "Our aide in the deaf ed program didn't make it yesterday; said she didn't feel well. She called again this morning, crying, and said she just can't come." I thought, of course, it was some problem at home—teachers do have them now and then, you know. I said, "We'll give her a little time, but tell her we really need her and maybe it'll work out. In the meantime, let the kids come on alternate days or something so you won't lose *both* teachers." He said, "No it isn't the home that causes the problem, it's the school. She says she feels so sorry for these kids that every time she gets ready to start for school, she breaks down crying and can't bring herself to come."

I didn't know enough to recognize it then, but that was, and is, one of the big problems in education of the hearing impaired. These children tend to be treated with special care and special concern from birth. The man who came to us in 1964, Andy Gantenbein, had the philosophy that this is wrong—that these children need special help, yes, but that if they are to succeed in this world they must recognize their handicap and not expect any unusual recognition from society because, except on special occasions, they won't get any. We employed Andy in 1964. (By the way, the aide did overcome her handicap, and is still with us as head office girl and general manager. We really don't have a title for her, I don't think, but we'd be in trouble without her.)

Our first teacher's health gave out from trying to deal with the vast differences in the dozen pupils on an almost individual basis, and neither she nor I saw soon enough that our problem was that we needed more help. She forced it on us by leaving, and we combined our program with one Andy had going at Benton Harbor, 15 miles away. This gave us 25 pupils, enough so that we could specialize by having one teacher for small kids, another for medium-sized kids, and another for big kids. But getting the teachers was the biggest problem. Andy had been around and had connections, but we had to go all over the eastern half of the United States to find people—and even then we had to resort to growing our own.

At that point in time, speech clinicians were our best potential. We let the county office recruit speech therapists, and then we talked them into taking a course or two to get special certification for our program.

We began a summer school and offered jobs as aides to college juniors in the deaf education departments at Kent State, Michigan State, and others, with the intent of bringing them back a year later as graduated, certified teachers. It worked; we filled our staff. And we found pupils who needed the program in numbers we hadn't dreamed of. We now have 110 enrolled, all living within "reasonable" bus transportation distance of Berrien Springs.

Progressing Toward a Goal

If you do have a program in operation, then you may feel as we at Berrien Springs do, that you are achieving. However, I know that you aren't satisfied, any more than our staff is. We don't think we have it made, and you don't think so either. If you've caught the developments of the last few years, you've learned of new things which can be tried, new things which seemingly should have been evident long ago.

As a non-participant, an innocent bystander, so to speak, I've watched the development of this educational process we call normalization. I've seen the demands made on students to get them the place in society which is rightfully theirs. And I've felt the thrill a boy experienced last summer when he got his first driver's license, something he doubted he would ever accomplish—not because he couldn't, but because he didn't have the picture of himself as the driver of an automobile. He imagined himself as even more disadvantaged, to use a modern term, than any of the rest of us did.

This year, the girl whose mother introduced me to the problem of education of the hearing impaired back in 1959 will graduate from our high school. She's been a full-time attendant in regular classes all through high school, has been on the honor roll, has been a co-op student holding a half-time secretarial job, has been admitted to Eastern Michigan University at Ypsilanti for next fall, and wants to become a special education director, not teacher, mind you. She wants to see programs develop and operate.

And she isn't an isolated example. Of our 110 students, 40 will be fully integrated into regular classrooms this next year. We aim for and expect to achieve 90% integration.

Really, there isn't anything about our program that can't be duplicated. There certainly are people who think it shouldn't be duplicated, but we can't see that they are people we should be paying attention to. If they say that we shouldn't do it—that normalization isn't possible—but we know we can accomplish it, why waste time arguing with those who protest? We should be getting about the business we've set out to do.

Believing in What You're Doing

Of course, this involves many factors, many necessities, many things that make the job possible. One of these is staff. You have to have people who believe in what you're doing. These are not just typical teachers. They're a different breed. They're dedicated to the task, and they'll go to all lengths to achieve it. It isn't that they have great ability, necessarily; but rather that they believe in what they're doing and work at it full-time.

Second, you have to have a parent program. Normal, typical education sort of goes along without the parents. They send the children to school every morning and welcome them back every night; but they're not really involved themselves, as they could be. The parent of a hearing impaired child *must* be involved. These children need special training as soon as the difficulty is recognized. This is before school bus age—before the child is ready for a full day's dose of "education." So the parent brings the child to school and waits until it's time for him to go home. The parent thus becomes well-acquainted at school—becomes, in most cases, a real part of the school program. If not the actual parent, for one reason or another, then a substitute must be found: either a brother or sister, a friend, or someone who will play that role, because it will be a very unusual child who can accomplish normalization by self-discipline alone. We think in terms of 100% participation—100% of parents and 100% of teachers. Think of the potential for the typical school program with this kind of togetherness.

Importance of Working Together

The third essential for normalization, it seems to me, is a cooperative, interested, and sympathetic total staff—including the teachers of the typical classrooms, the office girls, the custodians, and the administration. A few years ago, as we moved toward what we call integration—placing hearing impaired children in regular classrooms—we found real problems here.

Even though our special classrooms were in a building with regular classrooms, we found that many teachers didn't want to cooperate. Some were sure they couldn't do the job of giving an education to a child who couldn't hear what they were saying. Some didn't want to try, and some still don't. We have avoided forcing anyone, and we have avoided artificial means such as extra pay incentives. We *have* lightened the class load of those who have accepted hearing-loss children. We have provided them extra help, by having one of the special education staff serve as a helping teacher in an area such as science or math where they would most appreciate it. And we have achieved a cooperative atmosphere for learning.

Another necessity is equipment. Michigan law has made it possible for us to purchase a considerable amount of materials and equipment. We've tried just about everything we have heard of. In many cases it hasn't been sensationally effective, but just the trying has had a salutary effect.

Living Oralism

We've gone to great lengths to make sure that the youngsters converse in oral language, not only at school, but also on the bus; we put an aide on the bus to remind them that oralism goes home with them. We've set up a tape recorder program which the teachers use with students at school, and which parents use with the student at home. The tape goes back and forth daily and is "homework" in a real sense, with everyone involved. Also, it carries daily messages back and forth between home and school.

Certainly we don't claim to be any miracle workers—that's the point. We believe we are demonstrating that, at least to our own satisfaction, we can do things we didn't at one time think possible. I believe the results are worth the effort, and I know that the parents who live in our area think so, too. And I don't think it's beyond you either.

7

SUSAN BILEK

The Integrated Teacher

In advising on techniques and methodology for a teacher of integrated hearing impaired children, it is extremely difficult to set down firm guidelines; for each integrated child is in a highly individualized situation. While there are numerous practical suggestions which can and should be provided for the teacher, these "do's and don'ts" must not override the basic fact that the teacher's first responsibility is to the child as an individual, discovering and learning among other individuals — not as a "deaf person." A teacher in a public school where hearing impaired children are integrated herein responds to the reactions and questions of her co-teachers on the subject of integration by describing her approach to teaching — an approach which considers the child first, the hearing impairment second.

Reactions to the subject of integration from my co-teachers in a public elementary school are widely varied. Many of the concerns reflect an unfamiliarity with a hearing impaired child and with the fact that his needs are essentially those of *any* child. Perhaps an approach toward educating each child as an individual might be more helpful to the "newly integrated teacher" than specific answers to specific questions, which would vary with each case. Right and wrong solutions are sometimes less productive in the classroom than the confidence to teach, experience, and learn *with* the hearing impaired child.

Preparing to write this, my attention was first drawn to the great diversity of the comments, and it occurred to me that the usual way of ordering ideas will

Mrs. Bilek is a classroom teacher at Iona Avenue School in Montreal, Quebec, Canada.

not work very well here; i.e., arranging thoughts in a logical order and attempting to present a premise and arguments. This is not my intention, for I don't feel I am trying to win an argument, nor that I am in one. I am trying to see some aspects of integration in a different way and would like to share some of the thoughts that have come to me when hearing the questions and comments of other classroom teachers.

The Teacher's Role

"How can I help a hearing impaired child without special training?"
"We're not specially trained — we need to know more."
"I don't have time for another 'special' child."
"If hearing is their problem, how can I help?"

While considering these comments, my own perceptions were being side-tracked by a question John Holt, educational philosopher, had often posed at meetings of educators: "If I were to ask you what was the best way out of town, [wouldn't you] ask me where I wanted to go?" The obvious yet essential point here is that only if we know where we want to go can we decide. Thinking about my own class and about the responses of the other teachers, it seems to me that more often than not our destination has not been clear or well planned.

As teachers we must decide — long range — what we hope to accomplish with the children as people — not just the facts which need to be covered. We must set a goal as teachers to accept each child's uniqueness and encourage his contribution to the group. Our job is not necessarily to teach him to "hear," nor to make him less "special." So these two characteristics should not dominate our teaching.

The Subject Matter

"If hearing impaired children are to fit into a regular world,
shouldn't they be prepared academically?"
"What about the written projects or subjects
requiring research and extensive reading?"
"What of the discussions and subject matter
hearing impaired children miss?"

Perhaps we can accomplish more if we remember not to try to *make* the children learn, but to let them learn, setting increasingly realistic standards for participation and performance as we come to appreciate each child's capabilities. As teachers we often believe we can take something developed in our minds out of long experience and familiarity and, by modeling it into a string of words, transplant it whole into the minds of children. Perhaps once in a thousand times this works — but most of the time repeated explaining does not increase understanding, and may even lessen it.

Classrooms are full of children who have become so distrustful of words and their ability to get meaning from words that they will not do anything until they are shown something they can copy. Also, too many schools are too far removed from the real world, or real things and real people. The crazy idea persists that to educate children one takes them out of the world they live in and shuts them up in brick boxes.

For many children the conventional curriculum is inappropriate and undesirable. Rather than giving children extra time to work at what they like and are good at, schools seem to insist on what children do worst and most dislike. True education, it would seem, requires faith that children want to make sense out of life and will work at it, and courage to let them do it without continually poking, prying, prodding, and meddling.

In the Classroom

"Should I talk louder in class?"
"What if the 'thing' falls out of the ear?"
"I can't handle another 'difficult' child in my class."
"Maybe in a 'special education' class you can give individual attention,
but you ought to try it in my class of 36!"

No one should underestimate the importance of small classes in permitting individualized instruction; however, it is important to state that even in a large class one cannot afford *not* to diversify children's work — or rather not to allow children to diversify, as they inadvertently will, if given the choice.

James Herndon has pointed out in *The Way It Spozed To Be* that people who work with children in new ways need to be helped to find the meaning of much that is happening in their classes. Often they are anxious about whether they are doing the right thing, or indeed doing anything at all! Consider his statement:*

> In school certain things are spozed to happen, the kids are spozed to sit still, be quiet, read the texts, do the workbooks, and pass the exams. If none of these things happens, if the kids learn nothing, meet in the halls, drop out, — that's O.K. as long as you tried to make happen what is spozed to happen. But if you tried to make something else happen, even if your kind of order worked and your kids found things worth doing and actually did them, you are a threat.

Is this the kind of teaching we really believe in?

**In *The Lives of Children*, George Dennison writes that "the proper concern of a primary school is not education in a narrow sense, and still less preparation for later life, but the present lives of children." This, I feel, is the critical issue. In the classroom there will be unexpected incidents, problems, surprises — for us and the children. But this is so in all areas of life. What better place for each

---

The Way It Spozed To Be, James Herndon. New York: Simon & Schuster, 1968.
**The Lives of Children,* George Dennison. New York: Random House, 1969.

child to learn to cope with these than in our classrooms? Can we look past the unfamiliar speech patterns of the hearing impaired child — and the unevenness of his predicted responses — to appreciate the freshness of his ideas and the courage he shows in wanting to express them day after day?

The Hearing Impaired Child Among Hearing Peers

"What kind of special attention will the child require?"
"How much extra tutoring will he get with his subjects?"
"How will other children react to the hearing impaired child?"
"What about the social situation?"
*"Should the hearing impaired child have to meet
the same requirements as the others in the class?"*

Let us not concern ourselves always with his special handicap and how this affects our classroom — but with our role as teachers to respond to him as an individual member of a "normal" class. If I appear to be more concerned here with schools and classes than with the hearing impaired integrated child, that is so; for they are inextricably intermeshed. The hearing impaired child should not be subjected to an additional burden of an irrelevant, bureaucratic machinery. To speak only of the "integrated hearing impaired child" seems to beg the issue, to avoid the realities of the situation and to place the full burden for success on the child. It is as if once having stuck the child's finger in the dyke, any further damage to the dyke could be blamed on the child. More important, it really lets everyone else off the hook. Thus, perhaps a more proper subject for discussion is *the integrated teacher.* This teacher's tolerance, patience, and capacity for welcoming all children are critical to her effectiveness.

In another part of his book, Dennison writes:

> Let us imagine Maxine in a regular classroom. (And let me say here that every child is plagued by apparently special problems and unmet needs.) She is quite capable of concentrating for short periods of time. She learns rapidly and well. But the lesson goes on and on ... She feels herself vanishing in this swarm of children, who are not only constrained to ignore her, but constitute a very regiment of rivals interposed between herself and the teacher, her one source of security. The deep confusions of her life are knocking at her forehead — and who better to turn to than a teacher? She does it indirectly. She runs across the room and hugs her favorite boy, and then punches her favorite boy, and then yells at the teacher who is now yelling at her ... All these are the facts of her life. If we say that they do not belong in a classroom we are saying that Maxine does not belong in a classroom. If we say that she must wait, then we must say how long, for the next classroom will be just like this one, and so will the one after that ...

Thus, it may well be that the teachers who accept hearing impaired children in their classrooms may become more aware of the vital importance of their role in the education process as it affects all children; i.e., they will be, in fact, "integrated teachers."

Conclusion

Too often we are all too likely to see, and only to see, what we look for, or what we expect to see. Every child should have a chance everyday to make a fresh start, as should every teacher. Going to class with every step and every detail thoroughly planned and ready often produces anxiety and dullness in children. On the other hand, faint beginnings or ideas, a tentative first step, sometimes not even that — allow one to see what the children might offer and to work from that. For all of us know much more than we can say, and many times we cannot really put it into words at all.

Have You Thought Of . . .

. . . sending a brief letter with a checklist of helpful items to teachers who will be having a hearing impaired child in their classrooms for the first time? These letters should arrive approximately a day or two before school begins, be very brief, and include the names and the phone numbers of people whom the teachers may call if they have questions about the hearing impaired child during the first few days of school before a regular helping professional can be there. — *Verna Yater, St. Louis, Missouri.*

. . . attending — and encouraging other parents, teachers, and supervisors in general education to attend — meetings or discussions where qualified, experienced, and well-motivated people describe the very best methods and practices of integrating hearing impaired children in regular classes? — *Bruce Shepherd, Sydney, Australia.*

ANDREW GANTENBEIN
LYNNITA MATTOCK

8

Report from a Team Teacher
In an Integrated Program

The Head Teacher of a day school for hearing impaired children describes the integration program in which the hearing impaired students attend classes with normally hearing students at an adjoining public elementary school. An important feature is the provision of trained teachers of the deaf to team-teach with the regular classroom teachers for part of the school day. Excerpts from a fifth-grade teacher's annual report indicate how the public school students and teachers respond to this arrangement.

In the Berrien Springs school system, trained teachers of hearing impaired students are assigned to teach for three years in public school classes as "integrated teachers." They team-teach with regular classroom teachers in at least two subjects (science and math) for third-, fourth-, and fifth-grade students. During this three-year transitional period, the hearing impaired children who are integrated in the classes take achievement tests by which their progress can be charted. The administrators feel that the placement of certified teachers of the hearing impaired into the typical classroom setting is justified because 1) there are so many children fully integrating that the need for trained teachers of hearing impaired children permeates the entire school system, and 2) all teachers in Michigan are certified in general as well as special education.

Once the class of hearing impaired children moves into a typical classroom, all of the children are regrouped. One group then stays in the regular classroom setting, and the other (consisting of normal-hearing children as well as children

---

Mr. Gantenbein is Head Teacher at the Berrien County Day Program for Hearing Impaired Children, Berrien Springs, Michigan. Miss Mattock was a fifth-grade teacher in Berrien Springs Elementary School when she wrote this account.

with defective hearing) goes to the room previously used by the teacher of the hearing impaired. All of the reasons why *"children can't"* melt away when both team teachers are committed to solving the same problems and accomplishing the same goals. Some excerpts from the year-end report (1971-72) of Miss Lynnita Mattock, a fifth-grade "integrated teacher," illustrate how this system works.

Report from a Team Teacher

The goals of the integrated fifth-grade classroom this year were: 1) to help hearing impaired students adjust to a regular public school class full-time; 2) to introduce an intermediate III class of hearing impaired students to regular classroom procedures and aspects in two subjects (science and math); 3) to gain an understanding of the problems faced by regularly certified teachers who take hearing impaired children into their classrooms without having had any previous experience with children with hearing handicaps; 4) to establish better relationships and understanding between both staffs involved; and 5) to promote mutual understanding and empathy among hearing and hearing impaired people in general.

This fifth-grade class consisted of 13 to 16 hearing children and three to four hearing impaired children (depending on the subject studied). The hearing children were selected by the principal according to a principle of heterogeneous grouping: among every three children there was one low performer, one average performer, and one above average performer. In the group of four hearing impaired children, one (who had a severe-profound loss) had previously been fully integrated in a regular classroom. The others had been in a partially integrated class; two had profound losses and one had a mild loss. The objective for *all* students was to participate fully in a regular fifth-grade academic setting, to work toward the same goals as the other fifth-graders, and to take part in all available activities with children of other fifth-grade rooms. There were five other fifth-grade classes staffed by teachers certified in regular education. Three of these had one hearing impaired student each.

At first the integrated room was regarded as a dumpyard for low performers, but an alert and understanding principal soon straightened this out. The other fifth-grade teachers were very helpful in supplying material, information, and advice.

The team teacher's responsibilities were: 1) to teach all students in the class on a fifth-grade academic level; 2) to carry out the normal functions of any regular fifth-grade teacher; 3) to assume the more specialized functions of a teacher of the hearing impaired; and 4) to preserve a normal educational environment by meeting the needs of *all* children within the classroom — hearing as well as hearing impaired.

Social Considerations

Within the class itself, social integration was achieved in most aspects. Hearing impaired students were picked first on spelling teams because it was known that they studied. There was hesitancy in choosing hearing impaired students who had poor speech as partners in discussion groups, probably because interaction had to be slowed down to make sure that everyone understood. But it was also apparent that hearing impaired students were chosen before those students who were known to be lazy workers.

We had to stress the fact that hearing children must talk and not just mouth (speak without voice) words to their hearing impaired classmates. In turn, hearing impaired children, when talking with each other, were cautioned not to mouth but to talk audibly. (We felt that, in general, it was better for the children to speak out loud when they were not expected to than to whisper or mouth their words.)

A talk by a teacher of the hearing impaired on the subject of hearing testing and the problems connected with hearing loss sharply altered the attitudes of two children who formerly had an edge of mockery toward the hearing impaired students. After the discussion, they began to support the integrated students.

The main problem socially was caused by students in other classes. Hearing impaired students were teased not because they wore hearing aids but because of their sometimes faulty speech. One girl had a bombastic voice that easily drew attention. She got along very well with people who knew her — both hearing and hearing impaired — but the first reactions of students who were unfamiliar with her were, "She's funny," or "What's wrong with her?" The only people this hurt, however, were her friends. She didn't hear most of the teasing. Her friends were quick to correct the other students in their judgment and remarks.

One occasion in the cafeteria is worth noting: a hearing girl from another class was using gesture language in talking to two hearing impaired students. A hearing boy from my class went up to her and calmly explained to her that those kids could understand her without that.

One time, however, protection for a hearing impaired student was overdone. A boy from another class made the mistake of teasing a boy who had cerebral palsy and a hearing loss. His entire class rose in defense, and we had to disperse the group and explain the situation to the offender. I introduced the boys to each other and, finally, they shook hands without my prompting.

Team Teaching for Academic Subjects

The team teacher and five or six hearing impaired students came into my class for science and math. This teacher's responsibilities were oriented toward helping hearing impaired students prepare for full-time integration into a regular classroom. At the beginning of the year we each took a subject and concentrated on teaching it. We soon discovered, however, that there were too many diverse abilities among our students and decided to divide the children into two groups: high performers and average performers. Hearing ability had nothing directly to do with this placement — performance in the subject itself was the key factor. One of us took the front half of the room for the lesson and the other took the back. It worked well except for the noise level; there were times when both groups had discussions at the same time and the students had trouble concentrating. We then decided to use the team teacher's room as well, and she took her math group there while I stayed in my regular room. This way each of us was able to deal with an even smaller group of students and provide each with the attention required.

At the first of the year it took time for a few students to give up, willingly and understandingly, their first-row desks in order for a hearing impaired student to sit at the front of the class. This sacrifice caused a little resentment — more toward the teacher than toward the students. The majority of the hearing children immediately got up and moved without question.

Problems arose during softball season when we observed what could be called reverse segregation. Instead of hearing children discriminating against the hearing impaired, hearing impaired boys excluded hearing children from their game. But after reasoning with them, we finally had integration once again on the baseball diamond.

These problems arose more from the selfishness of individual students (both hearing and hearing impaired) than from any other cause. Students who were unable to stop thinking "I" and "Me" were the culprits — but they were in the minority. Those who naturally understood that there were other people around them whose needs were as important as their own were able to adjust very well.

The staff members in the regular elementary school contributed significantly toward making integration work. It is this type of attitude — cooperation and flexibility — that will accomplish the goal of banning a "self-containment" policy in a public school. True integration cannot be achieved by convincing students alone; general and special education staff members must share the common goal of educating all children. It will not do to have regular teachers who are qualified to teach only the typical children and teachers of the hearing impaired who are prepared to educate only the hearing impaired. Not only must regular teachers educate hearing impaired children — but teachers of the hearing impaired must be able to educate *hearing* children, too. Only when *all* teachers are equally committed to understanding and solving the problems of *all* children will integration have a firm foundation.

Have You Thought Of . . .

. . . having the hearing impaired class host a "Getting to Know Us" party for hearing children (who come in shifts)? Set it up like a fair, with hearing aids, school work, art projects, scrapbooks, etc., on display. After the visitors view the exhibits, play a game and serve Kool-aid. It's a good way to learn about the "special" class. — *Lois Germain, Lexington, Kentucky.*

9

WINIFRED H. NORTHCOTT

The Academic Tutor
And the Hearing Impaired Child

The academic tutor functions as a support specialist to 1) the hearing impaired child with identified characteristics of academic, personal, and social need; 2) the regular classroom teacher; 3) the child's parents; and 4) other members of the multidisciplinary team who participate in an annual evaluation of the child's progress. The competencies required by the tutor are described as well as the objectives and major activities related to the individualized tutoring sessions with the child.

The tutor who provides supplementary instruction to a hearing impaired child is faced with a challenging task requiring not only a full understanding of the needs and competencies of the individual child, but also an awareness of the procedures utilized in the child's regular classroom and a working relationship with the classroom teacher. The following guidelines, originally prepared for use in the Minnesota Public Schools, are directed to the tutor of the elementary-age hearing impaired child who attends classes in an integrated setting.

Eligibility for Tutoring Services

It is not the degree of hearing loss, as indicated on an audiogram, which determines the amount and type of supplemental instruction required by a deaf or hard of hearing pupil in order to compete successfully in a classroom with his hearing peers. Instead, the characteristics of need include: defective speech with substitutions and distortions of individual elements (remediation provided by a

Dr. Northcott is Consultant, Early Childhood Education Program for Hearing Impaired Children, 0-6, Minnesota State Department of Education, St. Paul.

speech clinician); reading problems; immature language patterns and lowered level of abstractions; inadequate performance in one or more content areas; and social inadequacy arising from frustrations.

Teacher Talent

The daily period of individual tutoring in academic subjects is part of the regular school day and may be provided by a teacher holding valid state certification at the appropriate grade level. It is not necessary to hold certification as a teacher of the hearing impaired, although this would sometimes be more desirable.

After trying to compete successfully in the classroom, which can be a frustrating and fatiguing experience, a deaf or hard of hearing pupil looks forward to the "oasis" you, as his tutor, provide. Patience, tolerance, and active enjoyment of your student will motivate him to utilize his residual hearing and intellectual potential to the fullest during the remainder of the school day.

When a hearing impaired child realizes that you have confidence in him, are proud of his accomplishments, and expect him to be increasingly independent in his thinking, progress is inevitable. If you care more about the substance of his conversation and his response to your questions than the preciseness of his articulation, he will be motivated to listen, to learn, and to think reflectively.

If you are imaginative and able to relate well to children on an individual basis in the face of challenging circumstances, the hearing impaired child's self-confidence, as well as his academic skills, will increase noticeably.

It is critical that you work directly with the classroom teacher who will provide you with a set of textbooks and weekly assignment pages for review or preview of content and concepts to be covered. During the period of tutoring you might clear up the student's questions about his daily work, discuss the meanings of spelling words presented in appropriate context, review assigned reading pages for clarification of concepts, or sing the new song presented in class, while at the same time building some wholesome attitudes toward work and independent thinking.

Goals

Although the specific purpose of supplemental instruction is academic tutoring in the subject-matter areas requiring supportive assistance, the education of the whole child emphasizes these objectives: development of reading skills, confidence in approaching new tasks, pride in written work, expansion of vocabulary, a better understanding of abstract concepts, and, above all, development of a sense of humor and the ability to laugh spontaneously.

The need to communicate is basic to life itself, and the hearing impaired child requires your assistance to reach and satisfy this fundamental desire. Take time to listen to him and to respond to his questions. In turn, ask him questions which stimulate independent thinking and judgment. If you're conscious of helping to shape his personality as well as of enriching his understanding of the syntax and semantics of our language, you will motivate your pupil to become a more competent individual, socially, linguistically, and academically.

Language Input

The language presented to the child should be useful; it should be selected and arranged in sequence appropriate to his age, background, and interests. The material presented should concern concepts covered by the classroom teacher in certain subject areas, following the textbook pages assigned for that week. Although the child's linguistic level may be immature, he should be challenged with material appropriate for his chronological age and interest level.

Accept your student's imperfect attempts to express his thoughts, and restate them in correct form. Challenge his intellect as well as his knowledge of syntax so that he feels free to ask, "Why?" or "Please repeat." Answering these questions will be part of your responsibility, too.

A skillful use of the dictionary is critical to the stimulation of cognitive development; and this encourages the student to learn as early as possible to select appropriate meanings of words in different situations.

The hearing impaired child frequently has had limited experience with auditory and verbal stimuli. Often, a late introduction into the world of speech (if he was fitted with a hearing aid at age 3) has deprived him of many growth experiences and reinforcements which are critical to language development.

Language is most meaningful to any elementary school child when it is linked with child-centered activities, the child's feelings, and his reactions to situations as they occur. The experience of the moment gives added meaning to the accompanying language, thus aiding conceptual development.

When a pupil attempts to express his thoughts in a sentence, however imperfectly, you should improve and expand the preciseness of his expression. The child who says, "The doctor gave me a piece of paper for the man in the drug store," should be introduced to the concepts "prescription" and "druggist."

A sentence which is not understood should be rephrased for added meaning; the original expression may contain many words that look alike on the lips or have low visibility. It is not desirable to change the subject of conversation abruptly without calling attention to the change, for this can cause misunderstanding.

The aim of the supplemental instruction is to help the child develop correct speech *attitudes* which motivate him to use with confidence the language he has. This leads ultimately to development of an extensive oral and speechreading vocabulary and a more normal voice quality. Service by a speech clinician will ensure that attention is given to the child's rate, rhythm, and quality of speech production. The speech should be evaluated in a language setting which incorporates vocabulary drawn from textbooks currently being utilized in the classroom.

Your concern as an academic tutor is a pupil's expressive and written language. You should ask questions which will stimulate his cognition. This is equally as important as supportive or remedial action in academic subjects.

Improving Conditions for Hearing and Learning

In the noisy environment of the average classroom, a teacher's instructions and conversation are difficult to hear. In addition, the room may have poor acoustic treatment. The hearing impaired child finds this setting overwhelming at times. He can understand familiar words, yet he may fail to understand new vocabulary during class recitation.

He may function effectively when he is in good physical condition, but may not hear well when suffering from a cold or other illness. He may hear with amplification, but be unable to hear without it. Most important, the hearing impaired child may supplement his imperfect hearing by speechreading so that he appears to hear more than he really does. Hearing problems will most frequently occur when the child is some distance from the speaker and cannot see his face. Fatigue from the strain of listening and watching may reduce his efficiency during the afternoon hours.

During the period of individual instruction, the pupil should face you and should be within a comfortable speechreading distance (three feet or less). Ideal listening conditions are obtained at a distance of 18 inches from the speaker. The light should be on your face, and you should speak in a normal tone of voice. A glance of the eye rather than a hand gesture will convey added meaning. Before beginning to speak, it may be desirable to wait until the student looks up. The ideal combination for the child is speechreading ability plus amplified hearing achieved through the daily wearing of a prescribed hearing aid.

Hearing children learn from each other. "What are four sevens?" the teacher asks the class. If a hearing impaired pupil cannot hear his classmates' response, his own thought is not confirmed or corrected. Speechreading will supplement his hearing but will not be a perfect channel of communication between him and his classmates. Your tutoring is valuable.

Comprehensive Evaluation

It is essential that you participate in the annual comprehensive evaluation of a hearing impaired child's progress. This evaluation should consider social maturity, academic achievement, intellectual potential, hearing aid usage, and personality, and will be valuable in determining appropriate placement for the following year.

10

JOHN NUERNBERGER

The Role of the Psychologist: Evaluating Potential for Integration

The role of the psychologist as a member of a multidisciplinary team involves accurately assessing the hearing impaired child's levels of cognitive, social, and maturational development. He reviews the child's cumulative folder, which includes previous tests and an overview of his academic achievement; observes the child in the classroom and with peers; and evaluates the child's personal interaction with him. The child's receptive and expressive communication skills are assessed in terms of how they affect his behavior, achievement, and educational planning. The psychologist administers various psychometric tests to ascertain the child's levels of cognitive development and psycho-social adjustment. He then relates his findings to the multidisciplinary team so that the total child may be considered for most beneficial educational planning.

The psychologist's role in evaluating the potential of hearing impaired children in regular schools is complex and multifaceted. It is essential that he be acutely aware of the levels of performance expected of normally hearing children in the classroom, for this is the educational environment to which the hearing impaired child will have to adjust. There may be wide variations in the performance of normally hearing children on standardized tests, for instance, and unless the psychologist is experienced in acknowledging and interpreting these variations, he will not be able to weigh and evaluate effectively and realistically

Mr. Nuernberger is a Psychological Examiner for the Special School District of St. Louis County, Missouri.

the scores of the *hearing impaired* children. Also, the psychologist must be aware of changes in performance due to age and/or grade level progression. A young child may adapt satisfactorily in the lower primary grades but, as the levels of communication and educational strivings become more advanced, he may require additional or alternate educational plans. It is in this continual, ongoing process of evaluation that the psychologist is very often involved.

Sometimes parents and teachers seem to look to the psychologist as the kind of person who, because of his title, can say a magic word and make wondrous results appear; their questions and desires will be fully answered or realized through his help. But this simply isn't so. The best evaluation that a hearing impaired child can receive in a regular classroom results from a multidisciplinary approach: each practitioner of a particular discipline provides detailed information, of a nature for which he is specifically trained, while simultaneously evaluating the *total* child in every dimension feasible. The psychologist, audiologist, hearing clinician, regular teacher, and others, as the case may be, can provide − as a team − an infinitely more detailed evaluation of the hearing impaired child in the regular classroom than any one specialist could provide independently.

Review and Observation of the Child in School

For the psychologist who functions on a multidisciplinary team, there are specific procedures that should be considered. 1) A complete review of the child's cumulative folder is essential. If the hearing impaired child is in the upper primary or secondary grades, the cumulative folder should indicate results of all known previous tests and provide a reasonably detailed overview of the child's educational achievement and performance. 2) Observation of the child in a classroom is an invaluable aid and an integral part of the evaluation. In many instances, clinical judgments play an important role here. The psychologist can convey valuable impressions to the team regarding the hearing impaired child's ability to use and/or demonstrate many group-related behaviors and interactions. Observation of peer interaction is particularly important because empirically this may provide very real clues to the hearing impaired child's level of social adjustment and his degree of accommodation to his handicap. A happy, outgoing hearing impaired child is almost always a child who has adjusted reasonably well to his hearing loss. If possible, the psychologist should render an opinion regarding the hearing impaired child's level of group motivation and competitiveness; without a strong motivational set and positive response to group competition, the child may flounder in a sea of uncertainty and insecurity in the regular classroom.

The psychologist's most valuable role is in determining accurate levels of cognitive development, social development, and general maturational strengths and weaknesses. His evaluations and conclusions should be drawn from judgments based on a one-to-one relationship and personal interaction with the child.

Preparing for Psychological Evaluation

Hearing impaired children are generally judged to be rather concrete in their thinking and, as such, may seem less flexible and insightful than many children who have normal hearing. The psychologist must be acutely aware of how the hearing impaired child reacts immediately to a new person in his presence and how the child responds in a one-to-one situation which he may not completely understand. This is particularly important with young hearing impaired children who may be reluctant to leave the comfort of familiar surroundings such as their classroom or the security of the teacher. The child's initial impression of the psychologist may well be determined by the psychologist's first words or his nonverbal language (e.g., facial expressions); some hearing impaired children rely heavily on facial expression in making initial character judgments. Prior to the formal evaluation, therefore, the psychologist should attempt to gain a strong, positive relationship with the child and should become as familiar as possible with his receptive and expressive communication skills, for these will affect the nature of the evaluation and the conclusions drawn from it.

If a 3-year-old child is asked a question and he responds correctly with a one-word answer, it is apparent that he has some hearing or speechreading skill (or both) and is developing receptive and expressive language. However, if an 11-year-old fifth-grader is asked the same question and gives an identical response, it may suggest that he is educationally misplaced in the fifth-grade class. Receptive and expressive communication is essential to the development of cognitive ability. For some hearing impaired children, gestural language may be necessary; however, these children will rarely be found in a regular classroom of hearing children. Hearing impaired children in a regular classroom must possess receptive and expressive verbal communication skills commensurate with their grade placement or they will not realize appropriate educational growth and development. Ongoing development of the child's communication processes is essential to his continual educational success.

Receptive and Expressive Communication

In an assessment of the child's receptive and expressive communication skills and how these relate to his potential placement, the psychologist may draw upon his background knowledge and experience in working with hearing impaired children and upon the child's performance on various psychometric instruments. Receptive, nonverbal vocabulary tests such as the Ammons Full-Range Vocabulary Test and the Peabody Picture Vocabulary Test might be used to acquire base line data on which an evaluator can begin to build judgments. These instruments do not yield a *complete* receptive language picture (only one stimulus word at a time is presented); however, with this information and with knowledge gained from pretest procedures, it is possible to gather some fairly reliable impressions of the child's receptive communication. The psychologist's objective here is not to test communication skills *per se,* but to attempt to determine how this communication ability affects and interacts with the child's behavior, adjustment, achievement, and test performance — and hence how it might influence educational planning.

By closely observing a child's eyes, an experienced psychologist can often tell whether the child relies primarily on visual or auditory input in receiving language. If the child is able to communicate without observing the examiner's lip movements, it may indicate primary use of residual hearing; however, if the child's eyes are continually fixated on the psychologist's lips — or if the child cannot respond when the examiner's lips are shielded — he may be more dependent on speechreading. In evaluating the child the psychologist must be sensitive to the fact that many hearing impaired children do rely heavily on speechreading and that they may not communicate well during an evaluation if the psychologist has his hands close to his mouth or does not enunciate clearly.

The child's expressive communication ability is reflected partially in his language structure (grammar and syntax) and can be judged by an observant listener. Another indicator is the child's general level of speech intelligibility. If the psychologist notes significant articulatory deficits which affect conversational exchanges with the child or depress test results, he should consider their relationship to possible educational problems and/or to necessary supplementary services if the child is admitted to regular classes. Vocabulary subtests of the Wechsler Tests and the Stanford Binet can further contribute to the psychologist's knowledge of the hearing impaired child's expressive communication skills.

Motivation

In evaluating a hearing impaired child for appropriate placement, the psychologist is particularly concerned with the child's insight and motivation. The child with a hearing impairment may well evidence a high level of abstract thought processes on nonverbal tasks, yet perform on a rather concrete, almost dependent level in verbal tasks. The higher the level of abstract conceptualization in both verbal and nonverbal tasks, the better the chances for academic success in a regular classroom.

Such motivational factors as task cooperation, attentiveness, self-reliance, self-confidence, and task persistence should be noted during the psychological evaluation. When observed carefully they yield important data which are helpful in predicting the degree of educational adjustment of the hearing impaired child.

Psychological Testing

After becoming familiar with the child's development through examination of his cumulative record, observation of the child in class, and personal interaction with him, the psychologist chooses the psychometric instrument best suited to the child's abilities and most likely to provide meaningful information in psychological testing. Major psychometric instruments such as the Wechsler Preschool and Primary Scale of Intelligence, the Wechsler Intelligence Scale for Children, or the Wechsler Adult Intelligence Scale may be used to assess the child's cognitive abilities in both the verbal and nonverbal areas of development. Each instrument provides verbal and nonverbal tasks for the child to complete according to his ability. Teachers seem to prefer the administration of these tests because they are able to grasp readily the implications of the Verbal, Performance, and Full-Scale IQ Scores although they may need assistance in interpreting the individual subtest information gained. At times the psychologist may find it desirable to convert Wechsler IQ scores to mental ages to make the IQ scores more meaningful to the teacher or administrator. The Hiskey-Nebraska Test of Learning Aptitude may be appropriate for some children although it does not yield information on the child's verbal responses, which must be obtained through other instruments. The Stanford-Binet Scale, which combines verbal and nonverbal tasks on separate age levels, may be of some value; it does yield a mental age, which is preferred by some teachers and administrators.

Measured levels of comprehension, visual-motor proficiency, arithmetic reasoning, vocabulary, verbal fluency skills, and judgment and reasoning abilities should be determined, if possible. As a matter of routine, one or several instruments involving eye-hand coordination should also be administered. The Beery Developmental Test of Visual Motor Integration and the Bender-Gestalt and Graham-Kendall Memory for Designs Test are relatively quick to administer and permit the psychologist to determine readily the functional level of eye-hand coordination. The hearing impaired child in a regular classroom will undoubtedly experience some moments of frustration and lack of under-standing, and if he has an undiagnosed impairment in eye-hand coordination and does not receive specific remediation, this may increase his educational frustration.

After completing a psychometric evaluation to determine cognitive levels of development and eye-hand coordination, the psychologist should attempt to relate this information to the multidisciplinary team as explicitly as possible.

Social and Emotional Adjustment

Hearing impaired children — like normal-hearing children — will demonstrate various degrees of social adjustment or maladjustment. In addition to the "normal" problems children encounter as they mature to adulthood, these children must also cope with a hearing loss and the natural frustrations it provokes. Infrequently, a teacher may ask if there are tests available to determine if a child has emotional or social problems. Projective instruments which have easily understandable directions, such as the Sentence Completion tests, are recommended for this purpose. Sometimes, older hearing impaired children may prefer to write out their answers to the questions rather than verbalizing them. For the mildly hearing impaired child, instruments such as the Children's Apperception Test (animal and human forms), Thematic Apperception Test, House-Tree-Person, Draw-A-Person, and Kinetic Family Drawing Tests may well be appropriate. Of course, a psychologist who administers projective tests to hearing impaired children must be well-versed in the psychodynamics of the hearing impaired child.

Summary

Working as a member of a multidisciplinary team, the psychologist can provide important and useful information on the functioning of hearing impaired children in a regular or special educational setting. Among the many areas which the psychologist is trained to evaluate are the child's levels of cognitive development, social adjustment, and eye-hand coordination. However, he must view the *total* child in full awareness that, as the child matures, his ability to adapt to and cope with a regular educational environment may alter. A professionally functioning multidisciplinary team will welcome and respect facts, impressions, judgments, and general information about the child from the other team members — and from other sources including the child's parents. After gathering all available information, the team will then consider appropriate future educational plans for the hearing impaired child, which may or may not involve entrance to or continuation in an integrated classroom.

Have You Thought Of . . .

. . . encouraging classmates to help with speech (pronunciation, etc.) of the hearing impaired child? Sometimes his peers are excellent teachers. — *Linda McArthur, Arcadia, California.*

. . . taking photos of children in the classroom and of teachers so that parents can teach their names and talk about school friends? — *Doreen Pollack, Denver, Colorado.*

. . . fostering friendship between two hearing impaired children of comparable age from different schools by suggesting that they become pen pals? The speech clinician who provides therapy for both children can be encouraged to act as a go-between. — *Brenda Green, Minnetonka, Minnesota.*

GENEVIEVE RUSSELL

11

The Place of the Social Worker
In Integration

The role of the social worker in helping a child experience successful integration is embodied in the essence of social work training — to assist each person to live comfortably and productively according to his individual abilities. Social workers act as liaison between the school, the family, the community, and the child in interpreting the needs and feelings of each and in integrating these concerns into a productive experience. In this way the social workers may help implement an effective integration program.

A social worker is committed to helping individuals function efficiently and comfortably within the framework of their life style. Since hearing impaired children are definitely a part of the larger hearing community, the philosophy of maximum integration according to each child's abilities is clearly in accord with the philosophy of social work. Social service workers, in the two years' postgraduate training required to complete a degree in social work, are carefully indoctrinated with an understanding of human needs, the subtle language of overt behavior, the changing demands of cultural surroundings as they affect individuals, and deviations in human emotional growth. About half of each graduate academic year is spent on the job in various social agencies under close supervision, refining the skills of interviewing, understanding the psychodynamics of interpersonal problems, and learning to evaluate various community resources. According to individual abilities and interests, a graduate social worker then chooses an area of professional involvement such as family counseling, child

Miss Russell is a School Social Worker with the Regional Facility for the Deaf and the public school system in Portland, Oregon.

welfare, group work, psychiatric social work, administration, research, school social work, medical social work, or rehabilitation, as in juvenile court work or penology. A professional social worker can usually be identified by his master's degree in social work, membership in the National Association of Social Workers, and state certification.

School social workers, as members of the school teaching staff, are in a particularly advantageous position to facilitate integration of hearing impaired students. Prior to integration, meaningful consultation must be well established with the hearing school and its staff so that they may prepare to modify teaching methods to meet the specialized needs of the hearing impaired child. Plans must also be made for continued communication between the public school and the facility for the deaf from which the child was referred. The social worker should also consider using all available community resources to ensure that the integrated child can receive maximum benefit from health services, audiological assessment, and opportunities for integration in the community.

The hearing impaired child always faces some degree of personal, social, and emotional adjustment at the time of integration. By helping the child to clarify his thinking about his new school setting and by helping him to gain increased understanding and self-acceptance in his new situation, the social worker hopefully aids in making the transition period a positive, comfortable one. At the same time, parents need help in understanding the public school, its personnel, and their own expectations for the newly integrated deaf child.

Integration in the Portland Public Schools

As a staff member of the Regional Facility for the Deaf in Portland, Oregon, much of my time is devoted to implementing effective integration programs. There are three centers for the deaf within the Regional Facility, each attached to a public grade school. Every one of the 245 children in the program is involved in an integrated experience for some part of the day, even if it is only for physical education and lunch. The preschool nursery program, beginning with 4-year-olds, maintains an equal population of hearing impaired and hearing children. Integration begins in kindergarten where the hearing impaired children are a regular part of the hearing public school class although they are equipped with Phonic Ears and their teacher wears a microphone at all times. Each preschool hearing impaired child is given individual tutoring sessions daily in speech and language development by a certified teacher of the deaf (who is part of the kindergarten staff) and a teaching aide.

By first grade full integration begins whenever possible, although the students still return to one of the centers for a daily tutoring session with the teacher of the deaf. As soon as a child is deemed able to adjust in his neighborhood school, he is integrated and provided with tutorial help for one to five hours a week by an itinerant teacher of the deaf. The social worker continues to give support to this child, appraising the adjustment progress and offering help when needed. At high school age, all hearing impaired students are fully integrated into one of several public high schools with special periods for tutorial help. Teacher aides accompany the students to technical vocational classes for further reinforcement.

Implementing an Effective Program

The success of the program rests to a great extent on very careful planning and understanding on the part of all teachers involved. It is at this point that the social worker can be most effective. The first need in successful integration is the parents' sincere desire for an integrated program and their complete cooperation with the plan. Integration is often a threatening concept to parents whose children in various ways have been sheltered from the hearing world. They are sometimes inclined to believe that the solution to a problem as great as deafness lies in isolating the child from his hearing contemporaries, forgetting that the very reason for the existence of any school is to prepare students for future life outside the classroom in a hearing world. A parent with these feelings must be helped to understand that grades may not be as high as the child might receive in a self-contained classroom of hearing impaired children, but that the child's overall adjustment and comfortable acceptance of his hearing contemporaries during the greater part of his life is the balancing weight on the other side of the scale. Part of the task of the social worker is to maintain constant contact with the parents to interpret what is happening in the hearing classroom and to reflect the parents' questions or concerns back to the teacher. The social worker should always be included at report card conference time to represent the child's interests and to help the parent evaluate the responses to any questions he or she may have after the conference is completed.

Working with the Classroom Teacher

As important as the parents' and child's total acceptance of integration is the acceptance of the child by the hearing school. Each member of the staff — from the principal to the secretaries, cooks, and custodians — will influence the child's adjustment in some way. Because the school social worker is already identified with the school personnel, she can gain a more accurate reading of the true feelings of school staff. These feelings must always be respected. Due to previous unfortunate experiences with handicapped persons, some teachers may believe that problems such as deafness preclude learning, and they may find it difficult to overcome their feelings of frustration with the child's limited success. Teaching is a very oral profession, and we are asking teachers to monitor their area of greatest competency by necessarily simplifying or restating their language as they teach the hearing impaired child. Some feel that this challenge is too great and that they should not be asked to include a deaf child in their class structure. The social worker can help these teachers evaluate their feelings and can support their decision in discussions with the administrative staff.

For those teachers who freely express a desire to have a hearing impaired child in the class, the social worker can be particularly effective in explaining the personality needs and behavioral characteristics of the special student before he enters the class. Behavior patterns — such as a hearing impaired child's frequent nodding in acquiescence whether or not he understands — are often not recognized by a teacher totally unfamiliar with hearing impaired children. Some of the personal questions these children are inclined to ask an adult (his age, for example) are difficult for a teacher to accept until he or she understands that hearing impaired children must learn from their hearing contemporaries what questions or areas of information are acceptable conversation, just as the hearing child learned verbal propriety through trial and error at an earlier age.

The social worker should try to get to know the child's teacher so that the teacher will trust her and will not feel threatened when she observes in the classroom. The social worker should spend considerable time introducing the teacher to the world of the hearing aid: how to place an earmold in the ear, how to test an aid and how to respect one, the need for an immediate and serious search when an aid is lost, and the need for contacting the parent with an explanation if one is broken. The social worker should be informed any time the child comes without an aid so that she can learn from the parents what is happening at home. The average teacher needs to be reminded before she enrolls the child that some hearing impaired children are noisy — noisy breathers, noisy eaters, foot draggers, and sometimes audible mumblers. Plans for fire drill must be arranged so that the hearing impaired child who cannot hear the alarm is always accounted for. Lastly, a social worker can emphasize that body language is a natural supplement to normal conversation.

A Team Approach

A team approach is advantageous to successful integration of the hearing impaired child. The team may include the regular classroom teacher, the tutor, the psychologist, the audiologist, and the social worker. Each team member focuses on a specific area: the psychologist on learning assessment, the teacher on classroom management, the academic tutor on language development, the audiologist on hearing evaluation, and the social worker on an understanding of the home, parental goals for the child, and parental interest in home help. The separate reports of the team members are coordinated in a profile of the hearing impaired child. As an adjunct to the integration program in the Portland Regional Facility, the Center for the Deaf provides two full-time teacher aides to the public school. The teachers who have hearing impaired children in their class use the aides in any way they wish, most often as tutorial help for hearing children with reading problems.*

---

*Sometimes a hearing child with severe learning problems is accepted as a full- or part-time student by a teacher of the deaf at the center, where more attention can be given the hearing child because of the smaller classroom load. This integration in reverse is encouraged in the Facility, and groundwork for this process is laid by the social worker.

The social worker should also be involved in promoting extracurricular group activities at the school. Each year the school social worker in the Regional Facility and the social worker from the adjoining public school have developed a Boys Club and a Girls Club, each consisting of four profoundly deaf children and four hearing children 9 and 10 years old. The membership is selected on the basis of teacher referral. The clubs meet twice weekly during school time, with play as the common focus of communication. The activities include a great deal of team play, service projects, checker tournaments, field trips, and crafts. Hearing students from a nearby high school are enlisted to help teach crafts, wrestling, or athletic skills, or just to roughhouse with the boys. This group experience has been particularly valuable to the deaf children in self-contained classes who would have no other means of interaction with hearing children on an individual basis due to a lack of intelligible speech and speechreading (oral) ability. Concomitant with the student club is the parent group which meets in the evenings to discuss each child's progress.

Social workers attempting to expand integration particularly prize the bene-fits to the child of camping in a hearing situation, such as with organized youth group camps. The social worker can make contact with business groups and educational honorary chapters such as Delta Kappa Gamma throughout the year to secure donations for an extended scholarship program providing camping experiences for deaf children. Interpreting the needs of a hearing impaired child to the camp staff during their training is certainly a part of the school social worker's advocacy program. Year-round membership in youth organizations must also be constantly provided; the social worker can help the child with his initial adjustment so that he will not drop out in discouragement before his interest is firmly established. The Portland school system offers a week's out-door school session to every sixth-grade child and teacher during the school year. The hearing impaired children are included in this experience and have an opportunity to live with children from many different schools during the week-long program. The hearing and hearing impaired children are on a somewhat equal level in class content, having completed an ecology curriculum before the camping experience is begun; consequently the outdoor session always proves to be an outstanding integrative experience for both groups of children.

Coordinating Community Services

Finally, in planning for the integration of the hearing impaired child, the social worker should be aware of the services offered through many community agencies and should serve as liaison between the agency and the family or school. If there are serious marital problems in the home affecting the hearing impaired child's adjustment, the social worker can help the family procure counseling that is best suited to their needs and can work with the agency to help bring the problems connected with the child's hearing loss into the proper perspective. Dental and health agencies can be enlisted to provide maximum care when needed; and the school social worker can usually provide an understanding of the family as a unit at all Crippled Children's Division clinic staffings on a deaf child. The social worker also works closely with the State Division of Vocational Rehabilitation in planning adequate training for the hearing impaired high school student. Again, the social worker has a special place as an ombudsman for the hearing impaired, citing areas of needed reform or research and challenging the school and community to set up integrated programs advantageous to these children. Much work needs to be done in encouraging a curriculum rich in visual materials, providing inservice workshops for teachers, establishing parent-teacher groups to discuss problems of mutual concern, encouraging child psychiatrists to prepare to work with the hearing impaired child, and establishing a roster of attorneys experienced and interested in helping parents. There also remains the great need to emphasize constantly to the medical profession the importance of very early diagnosis of infant deafness.

Interaction with the Family

Effects on the family of raising a hearing impaired child are a primary area of concern to the social worker; some alterations in life style normally result, and these must be worked through. Sibling frustration with a nontalking but extremely demanding deaf child need special attention, for the mother can quickly become worn out as an arbitrator. Parents may inadvertently foster helplessness in the child by their constant concern for his physical needs. Overprotection is a common problem when the child is not allowed to exert normal independence for fear of hazards — cars, getting lost, neighborhood disapproval, etc. How the deafness is explained to neighbors, relatives, or friends is an area in which the social worker's experience and perspective can be helpful. The child who is well adjusted in his home and community will have a better likelihood of adjusting to an integrated school and society.

When integration fails, it is not necessarily the children who fail — but the adults responsible for his progress in school and at home. We may be expecting too much specialized teaching by the classroom teacher, too much time and attention from the parent, or too much improvement too fast from the child. "Failure" is often a result of a disregard for the painful reality that integration is not the goal for *all* hearing impaired children. Any educational program should be suited not only to a child's academic needs, but to his social and emotional needs as well. The social worker — with her knowledge of academic and community services and her skill in interpreting the needs, desires, and abilities of hearing impaired children, parents, teachers, and other professionals — can play a vital role in ensuring successful placement and planning for the hearing impaired child.

12

BARBARA L. JONES

The Audiologist
In the Educational Environment

Although the educational audiologist is a newcomer to the educational environment of hearing impaired children, he is providing audiological services essential to their educational program. By adapting and modifying audiological tests and techniques traditionally used in clinical settings, the educational audiologist can more adequately define and provide for the acoustic needs of the children. The selection, monitoring, and maintenance of amplification instruments are also more effectively achieved through his services. It is only as an integral member of the educational staff, however, that the educational audiologist can maximize audiological services to the children.

As a result of the demand in recent years for increased audiological services in programs for the hearing impaired in the public school system, some audiologists have moved from the clinical environment to an educational one. The National Conference on Audiology and Education of the Deaf recognized this growing need for audiological services by supporting the resolution that an audiologist should be a full-time participating member of the instructional staff of each educational program for deaf children (Ventry, 1965).

Whether located in a residential school for the deaf or in a public school program with integrated or self-contained classes for the hearing impaired, the

Dr. Jones is Assistant Professor of Special Education, University of North Florida, Jacksonville. This chapter is adapted from her prize-winning paper in the Student Literary Competition of the Council for Exceptional Children, Division for Children with Communication Disorders, which appears in DCCD Bulletin, *Summer 1973, Vol. X, No. 3.*

educational audiologist is an important addition to the staff and can directly influence the education of the children in that program. The extent to which his influence is beneficial depends to a great degree on his knowledge and experience with deaf children and his understanding of the educational and language problems caused by deafness (Ventry, 1965).

Services To Be Provided

Recommendations concerning the use of hearing aids and residual hearing and presentations to teachers of the deaf concerning the educational implications of audiological findings are important contributions which the audiologist can make to the hearing impaired child's educational environment (Ventry, 1965). Traditionally, audiological evaluations of children have been conducted in clinical settings totally removed from the educational environment. While for some children this procedure has been adequate, the evaluations of many children have produced audiological tests of questionable validity. Recommendations for amplification have often been based on inadequate and/or inaccurate audiological information. Although ongoing evaluation of the child is critical to accurate diagnosis and appraisal (Ling, 1971), it does not occur in the clinical setting with the majority of young deaf children. Once the initial audiological evaluation has been completed, most children are not seen again in the clinic for several years. The diagnosis of deafness in young children is thus based on an incomplete definition of the child's auditory functioning (Fuller, 1971); therefore, decisions resulting from these initial tests should not be binding on the preschool child during the most important years of his life (Bloom, 1964). Furthermore, the incorporation of audiological testing and hearing aid selection into the educational environment would result in better services to the hearing impaired child.

The educational audiologist is the professional person who can minimize the physical and philosophical distance between the audiology clinic and the classroom. He can continue the audiological assessment of the child who is difficult to test in the clinical setting. By adapting audiological tests and test sessions to the child's ability to cooperate, the educational audiologist may secure a thorough and valid delineation of the child's hearing capabilities and amplification needs. The fact that the educational audiologist is a familiar person in the child's educational environment does much to promote successful audiological testing.

Selection of Hearing Aids

It is not an easy task to select an appropriate hearing aid for a young child. Because the provision of proper amplification is in many respects the "single most important therapeutic measure available for young hearing impaired children" (Ross, 1970), the selection of hearing aids should not depend solely on pure tone data (Ling, 1971). Since continued assessments are essential to the selection process, the educational audiologist can obtain considerable information by observing in the classroom the child's auditory behavior with various trial hearing aids. This procedure is particularly important in assessing auditory behavior with monaural versus binaural instruments (Luterman, 1969). Teachers and parents can be involved in the observational process and should be consulted for their assessment of the child's performance with the trial instruments. The child himself may be able to express a preference for a particular instrument, and this contribution is of considerable value in the audiologist's deliberations.

Liaison between School and Professional Agencies

When a speech and hearing clinic is involved in the audiological assessment and hearing aid selection process, the educational audiologist serves as liaison between clinic and school. It is important for him to maintain good rapport with otologists, clinical audiologists, Crippled Children's Service workers, and hearing aid dealers in order to coordinate effectively the various professional services. The educational audiologist is essential in helping to maintain the flexibility necessary in providing for the acoustic needs of the child; for the way the child uses his hearing will not necessarily remain the same throughout his educational experience (Fuller, 1971).

Monitoring and Electroacoustic Testing of Amplification Equipment

In addition to participating in the audiological assessment and hearing aid selection process, the educational audiologist is responsible for the monitoring of hearing aids and auditory trainers and the evaluation of their electroacoustic response characteristics at regular intervals during the school year. Since it has been demonstrated that a significant number of hearing aids worn by children are functioning inefficiently, one cannot assume that merely because a child is wearing an aid, he is getting optimum or even minimal benefit from it (Zink, 1972). Although the educational audiologist might be unable to check all amplification instruments each day, he can train teachers and teaching assistants to perform this task, to replace batteries and cords, and to refer malfunctioning instruments to him for further examination. The audiologist is generally able to perform minor hearing aid repairs but will contact hearing aid dealers and auditory trainer representatives to deal with the more complicated problems.

Amplification instruments which have undergone "repair" may still have inadequate electroacoustic response characteristics (Zink, 1972).* The educational audiologist who has made regular electroacoustic evaluations of the hearing aids and auditory trainers used in his program is familiar with their response characteristics, can identify improper deviations in response patterns,

---

*In one study (Zink, 1972), 60 "repaired" hearing aids were re-evaluated: 65% were acceptable after repair while 35% were again rejected for failing to meet electroacoustic requirements.

and can check the adequacy of acoustic response after the instruments undergo repair.

Provision of Earmolds

Properly fitting earmolds are a necessity for hearing impaired children. Too often the volume of a hearing aid or auditory trainer must be turned down in order to eliminate the acoustic feedback resulting from poorly fitting earmolds. With the services of the educational audiologist, however, earmolds can be replaced whenever necessary.

Usage of Amplification Instruments in the Classroom

A major responsibility of the educational audiologist is to identify those children in the program who should use auditory trainers in the classroom and those who should continue to use their individual hearing aids. Despite considerable time, effort, professional skill, and money involved in the selection of appropriate hearing aids, these instruments are routinely removed in the classroom and replaced with auditory trainers. In contrast to the selection of hearing aids, classroom amplification equipment is often selected by supervisory personnel and/or classroom teachers of the deaf who have limited knowledge of acoustic or instructional criteria upon which to base their evaluations (Krebs, 1968).

The classroom teacher also decides when the children are to use the auditory trainers, where the various controls on the units are to be set, and whether the instrument is to be worn monaurally or bilaterally. Furthermore, in most programs no formal evaluation is made of a child's performance to determine whether he functions better with the auditory trainer or with his individual hearing aid; yet this evaluation is essential. It is the educational audiologist who can provide this service by conducting the necessary audiological assessments, observing the child's performance with the instruments in the classroom, and communicating information on the child's auditory functioning to his teacher.

Dissemination of Information

In many ways the educational audiologist is an educator. He should be prepared to explain his methods, findings, and recommendations to a myriad of people: parents, teachers of the deaf, classroom teachers, teaching assistants, principals, school psychologists, nurses, program supervisors, school bus drivers, and sometimes even Cub Scout leaders. The educational audiologist should be able to offer suggestions to parents regarding therapeutic or rehabilitative procedures to be used in the home (Eisenstadt, 1972) and to teachers regarding instructional methods in the classroom. Audiological information should be presented in such a way as to aid differential diagnosis and educational placement (Ventry, 1965).

Summary of Services

The services which the audiologist can perform in the educational environment are indeed varied and broad in scope including:
— complete audiological evaluation of children related to their admission to the educational program
— annual assessment of children's hearing, including an interpretation of the results to the teacher
— selection, orientation, and maintenance of hearing aids for children
— application of knowledge concerning speech perception and speech pathology to the speech problems of deaf children
— inservice training to orient teachers to new procedures and information
— counseling of parents
— selection, evaluation, and application of amplifying systems and/or equipment used in the school
— liaison service between the school and the college or university training program and/or community speech and hearing center, and
— research   (Ventry, 1965)

Requirements for Educational Audiologists

Academic Preparation

It is imperative that the educational audiologist have the experience and information to make meaningful rehabilitative and educational recommendations to educators, parents, and deaf individuals (Ventry, 1965). Therefore, he should be a certified audiologist (holding the American Speech and Hearing Association Certificate of Clinical Competence in Audiology), and should also be trained in language development, language disorders caused by deafness, history of education of the hearing impaired, educational philosophy, and psychological and social aspects of deafness (Ventry, 1965). Moreover, he should be flexible enough to apply appropriate audiological standards and procedures to the various situations presented by different schools for the deaf (Siegenthaler & Owsley, 1968) and by various regular school settings into which hearing impaired children are integrated.

Personal Commitment

The educational audiologist is committed to improving the educational environment of hearing impaired children. He adds his talents to those of parents, teachers, and administrators in the effort to provide these children with a well-rounded, high-quality educational program. It is only as an integral member of the educational staff that the educational audiologist can maximize audiological services to hearing impaired children. By helping to shape their educational environment, he can help them to function more effectively in it.

(See next page for references.)

REFERENCES

Bloom, B.S. *Stability and change in human characteristics.* New York: John Wiley & Sons, 1964.

Eisenstadt, A. A. Weakness in clinical procedures — A parental evaluation. *ASHA*, 1972, 14(1), 7-9.

Fuller, C. W. The audiological diagnosis of deafness. In D. Hicks (Ed.), *Proceedings of National Forum IV: Medical Aspects of Deafness.* Washington, D.C.: Council of Organizations Serving the Deaf, 1971. Pp. 63-66.

Krebs, D. F. Educational amplification response study (EARS). *San Diego Speech and Hearing Center,* Monograph No. 1, 1968.

Ling, D. The hearing impaired preschooler: A family responsibility. *Hearing and Speech News,* 1971, 39(5), 8-13.

Luterman, D. M. Binaural hearing aids for pre-school deaf children. *Maico Audiological Library Series,* 1969, 8(3).

Røjskjaer, C. Hearing aid treatment in the young child. *International Audiology — Audiologie Internationale,* 1966, 5(3), 355-361.

Ross, M. Hearing aid selection for young hearing-impaired children: A point of view. *Maico Audiological Library Series,* 1970, 9(1).

Siegenthaler, B. M., & Owsley, P. J. Audiologists in schools for the deaf. *ASHA*, 1968, 10(11), 471-472.

Ventry, I. M. (Ed.) *Audiology and Education of the Deaf.* Washington, D.C.: Joint Committee on Audiology and Education of the Deaf, 1965.

Zink, G. D. Hearing aids children wear: A longitudinal study of performance. *The Volta Review,* 1972, 74(1), 41-51.

Have You Thought Of . . .

. . . acquiring skill in salesmanship to help motivate other teachers in mainstream programs to accept happily the extra work that having a handicapped child in the classroom entails and to increase their knowledge on the subject? This type of salesmanship can and should be part of the basic training of a teacher of the deaf or resource specialist serving hearing impaired children. — *Bruce Shepherd, Sydney, Australia.*

. . . using a wireless microphone to enhance the speech intelligibility of the average hearing impaired child fully integrated in a normal classroom? The proper use of this device will result in an average increase in intelligibility score by 30 to 40 percent. The use, however, depends upon the kind of educational environment the children are in, whether formal, structured, or an "open" type topography. — *Mark Ross, Longmeadow, Massachusetts.*

13

WINIFRED H. NORTHCOTT

A Speech Clinician
As Multidisciplinary Team Member

A speech and hearing clinician assumes a variety of roles to help maintain hearing impaired children in regular classes. These involve: 1) supplemental therapy for the pupil; 2) consultant service to classroom teachers, administrators, and resource specialists; and 3) participation in a multidisciplinary team effort to develop new components of hearing services. In the description of these functions, distinctions are made between speech and language lessons; speechreading and auditory training; and class participation and individual academic tutoring. Supportive activities are suggested for parents, and questions are furnished for the discussion of the child's progress during an annual evaluation.

The primary focus in special education today is on the labeling of children according to their educational deficits. This, in turn, requires the identification of certain support specialists and services whose availability may help these children function realistically in regular classrooms (Deno, 1970; Lilly, 1971). Thus, the role of specialists in speech pathology and audiology is expanding beyond the provision of speech, hearing, and language therapy for hearing impaired children to an increased interest in their educational management (O'Neill, 1971).

The populations of concern to the speech and hearing clinician are those children who manifest cognitive, experiential, and linguistic deficits, whether the

Dr. Northcott is Consultant, Early Childhood Education Program for Hearing Impaired Children, 0-6, Minnesota State Department of Education, St. Paul.

etiology is environmental or physiological. The behaviors are similar: defective speech; deficient use of abstractions; poor visual and auditory discrimination; limited ability to express and comprehend ideas through spoken, written, and read language; social inadequacy; and personal vulnerability in self-esteem and family acceptance.

A Clarification of Terms

The prognosis for success in an integrated classroom setting is dependent not upon the degree of a student's hearing loss but on his "listening age," which dates from the day a hearing aid is prescribed and worn and auditory training is begun. The child who functions as hard of hearing—even though his audiogram may show him to be deaf—emerges from an environment offering rich auditory and language stimulation during the preschool years and, generally, from a home where parents have vigorously supported and reinforced his educational gains in a prescriptive program of early intervention (Pollack, 1970; Northcott, 1971b).

The Impact of Infant and Preschool Training

Results of effective infant education and home training during the sensitive periods of learning for a young child—and during the time that the psychological needs of his parents are at a peak—are evident at the kindergarten and first-grade levels. We find increased numbers of language-delayed children, in many instances hearing impaired, entering educational programs in their neighborhood schools. For them, certain supplemental services must be ensured and used appropriately. These may involve curriculum selection, teacher orientation, academic tutoring, speech correction and auditory training, and parent participation (Mulholland, 1968).

The Clinician's Role

The speech and hearing clinician's role in dealing with hearing impaired children in regular classes should be 1) to provide appropriate components of supplemental services directly to hearing impaired children; 2) to serve as a hearing consultant to teachers, administrators, and resource specialists, helping them make reasonable accommodations to meet the special needs of hearing impaired children in the integrated class setting; and 3) to serve as a member of an interdisciplinary team developing new components of comprehensive hearing services within the school district.

Questions To Ask Prior to Employment by a School District

It is important to work for agreement and clarity in defining the specific responsibilities of speech and hearing clinicians in a local school district. Some

Portions of this article appeared in Volume III of *Language, Speech and Hearing Services in Schools*, 1972, published by the American Speech and Hearing Association.

expected activities, relating to phonological problems, for example, may require little discussion. Diplomatically, the clinician should ask the following exploratory questions and expect affirmative answers:

1. Will I be expected to identify and evaluate children with speech, language, and hearing problems?
2. Will consultation with families of hearing handicapped children as part of an active program of parent education be considered an integral part of the work week?
3. Will I be permitted to schedule some time for coordination and cooperation with the classroom teacher, counselor, social worker, health representative, and academic tutor of the hearing impaired child? (This carries the implied assumption of membership on the professional team of resource specialists.)
4. Will I have opportunities to participate in developing school board and community support for the speech and hearing program?
5. Will I be expected to help provide a supportive climate in the community for expansion and improvement of services to hearing impaired children?

Direct Service to Hearing Impaired Children

The first responsibility of a speech clinician is the development of an individual diagnostic profile for each child, indicating his receptive, processing, and expressive language capabilities and performance. Only then can realistic behavioral objectives be written for each child and appropriate activities designed to meet them. Standardized tests such as the Peabody Picture Vocabulary Test, the Illinois Test of Psycholinguistic Abilities, and the Northwestern Syntax Screening Test, among many others, are valuable diagnostic tools (O'Neill, 1971).

In addition, a clinician should consider speech and language samples recorded by means of audio or video tape as valuable supplements. Examination of articulatory errors through precise recording is the basis for designing activities to remediate sound substitutions and omissions. Developmental logs and teacher-made tests are also sources of information for diagnosis and later evaluation and comparison.

Involvement of allied specialists in the diagnostic procedure is critical, and here one turns to "Current Clinical Practices in Language" (Stark, 1971) for a full delineation of the kinds of support specialists who may provide information: the audiologist, clinical psychologist, neurologist, otolaryngologist, pediatrician, reading specialist, classroom teacher, school psychologist, social worker, and special education teacher. Strangely, the school nurse, who is often the strongest link between home, school, and community resources, is not mentioned, nor are parents.

The clinician's credibility as a member of the team depends on the extent to which he contributes substantive diagnostic and educational information, communicates with team members in case conferences and in the hallways, and maintains quality records incorporating contributions from other members of the team. The child's social history, audiogram, specifications for proper fitting and use of a hearing aid, annual audiological assessment, general physical condition, and developmental log with speech and language time samples all belong in the clinician's file. However, the ASHA Committee on Language (Stark, 1971) found, in a sample of 2,184 clinicians, that the amount of time most frequently spent in language diagnosis ranged between 30 minutes and one hour per child and noted that available supportive resources were frequently untapped.

Language for the Hearing Impaired

The deafened student should be kept with his hearing peers initially in order to preserve his sophisticated language patterns. The trauma of his sudden deafness requires personal adjustment with trusted family and friends. Abruptly he misses the psychological cues and clues of his environment, previously available through the auditory channel. It is imperative that activities in the therapy room relate to such objectives as the maintenance of former rhythm, pitch, range, and fluency of speech.

The adventitiously deaf student will also need formal lessons in speechreading, with content drawn from his observed interests, attitudes, hobbies, and curricular assignments. There must be concentration on the gestalt of a sentence—or speechreading for ideas—rather than drill for recognition of isolated words. Emphasis should be given to the development of auditory attention, discrimination, and memory patterns, if appropriate.

For the congenitally hearing impaired child, the speech clinician's attention to articulatory problems begins after the child has developed sufficient content and substance in his expressive language patterns to warrant refinement of individual speech elements. At that point, expectations for language development should relate to 1) the mechanics of oral communication—voice quality, rate, rhythm, fluency, pronunciation, and grammatical use; 2) the content of oral communication—vocabulary, complexity of sentence structure, and clarity of thinking; and 3) applied skills in oral communication—skill in group discussion, conversation, and impromptu speaking (Marge, 1964).

At the junior and senior high school levels, emphasis is given to expansion of vocabulary rather than refinement and correction of individual phonemes. The challenge is to provide a social purpose to the language being developed, followed by remedial drill and positive instruction in word knowledge and usage, where linguistic forms take their proper place. The vocabulary lessons are related to a first job experience, to necessary phrases, and to characteristics by which others will judge the student—will he look sharp, how is his personality perceived, does he appear to be a willing worker? Speech correction is more meaningful if it relates to these goals.

The interlocking elements of language are phonology, syntax, morphology, and semantics. Drilling on individual speech sounds primarily involves the child's phonological system. Offering speech activities within a language environment is a different teaching process. The former process involves specific motoric skill with minimal carry-over through automatic transfer in academic expression. The latter is a way of life. Initially, the emphasis must be on comprehension of language, not correct articulation. Spontaneous verbal interaction is needed between clinician and child since rote responses to language or speech exercises do not guarantee informed language usage in everyday conversation. The weekly spelling list or science or social studies lesson vocabulary is a reasonable source for pertinent content on which speech and language lessons can be based and multiple meanings of words discussed.

Auditory Training

No standard set of acoustic cues can be assembled to help a child understand the conversation of others. Training is vital for his comprehension. The quality of education, auditory training, and linguistic environment (or lack of it) in the home dictate whether a child will remain deaf or become functionally hard of hearing. The auditory procedures themselves are diagnostic, giving indication of what a student hears and can discriminate, classify, and store (auditory memory) for later recall to give meaning in reading and conversation.

Academic content can be used appropriately in the training of residual hearing. This training may begin with identification of selected environmental sounds (farm animals only for children who live on a farm, please), localization of sound sources, and distance listening; then move gradually to discrimination of familiar words on the basis of vowel or consonant differences; and finally proceed to familiar and novel contrastive sentences. A clinician can thus evaluate the progress each hearing impaired student makes toward attaining the stated auditory objectives. Her evaluation leads to a reconsideration of expectations and appropriate modification of activities to reach them.

An Overview of the Speech and Language Lesson

The speech and language specialist is concerned not only with the development of the individual components of communication skill — speech production, auditory perception, speechreading, and language — but also with communication itself. Unless the student has the opportunity to exchange ideas, to share experiences, to develop an interest or transform an attitude, and to retain a memorable experience and want to transmit the stored memory pattern through spoken, written, or read language, the clinician's influence is negligible.

The child needs to know he belongs to his class and to his family; he needs to feel that people like him, to feel secure, and to feel good about himself. Often the hearing impaired child has difficulty developing these feelings of confidence. On a one-to-one basis, alone with the clinician, he dares to be himself, to see if he is liked as he is — not on the basis of how well he articulates a word, but on the basis of his ideas, his questions, and the attitudes his words reflect. Lessons for positive living relate to sharing, caring, belonging, and having responsibility. A clinician can build wholesome attitudes — or kill them — in the time spent alone with a hearing impaired child.

Inservice Training

The speech and language clinician may be able to develop a professional program for other staff members who relate directly to hearing impaired children in the public school setting (resource specialist, teacher, counselor, custodian, bus driver). One session might deal with the criteria for educational placement in the integrated setting, including such factors as 1) age at onset of loss; 2) age when hearing aid was fitted; 3) degree of loss in the speech range; 4) nature of preschool training; 5) professional guidance for parents during child's preschool years; 6) presence or absence of other handicapping conditions; 7) size of school district and classes; 8) distance child travels to school daily; 9) availability of speech services; 10) services of an academic tutor; 11) observed attitude of teacher, class; 12) personality of child; 13) social skills; 14) class participation; 15) clarity of speech; 16) speechreading ability; and 17) language patterns.

Another high priority topic is discussion of how hearing impaired students hear with and without a hearing aid. Subsequent meetings might consider additional needs of a hearing impaired student related to acoustic conditions for optimum hearing, appropriate electroacoustic implementation in the classroom, and accommodation to the homonyms and homophones of our language. We tend to take for granted that teachers know the conditions for optimum hearing: 1) a one-to-one ratio in a tutorial situation; 2) comfortable speechreading distance—three feet; 3) comfortable listening distance—18 inches; 4) normal tone of voice; 5) no touching, tapping—wait for normal interaction; 6) hearing aid turned on; 7) key words written on the boards; 8) revised wording for greater visibility on the lips; 9) warning cue for change of subject; 10) listening helper in classroom; and 11) personal adaptations for greater comfort.

Support for the Classroom Teacher

The average classroom teacher is often puzzled because the hearing impaired child gives uneven responses to conversation directed to him. When the clinician as a hearing consultant calls the teacher's attention to the noisy environment of the average classroom and the inadequate acoustic treatment of the room, the teacher recognizes these as confounding factors. In addition, the teacher must be aware that a hearing impaired child will frequently respond to familiar conversation but have trouble with new vocabulary in class recitation. He may function effectively when in good physical condition, but not when he has a cold. He may hear with amplification but not without it. The battery in his aid may be weak. In addition, hearing problems are greater when a child is unable to supplement the listening experience with speechreading and relies upon hearing alone. Fatigue may cause a child to hear better in the morning or to pay closer attention at some times. A teacher may not realize that her patience and humor or annoyance and testy ways in responding to the child's problems set the tone for the child's classmates, who are all too eager to take their cues from the teacher.

Periodically, the time that is normally devoted to therapy with a hearing impaired child should be spent observing that child in the classroom instead. Supplemental language therapy will probably be more relevant after such visits. Does the child shrug or nod when he doesn't understand? Perhaps he needs to learn such phrases as, "I don't understand. . . . Ask me again, please . . . . Is this correct?" Many hearing impaired children fail to understand the teacher's directions: "Begin on page five . . . . Do all examples except number five." *The Language of Directions,* a programmed workbook by Mary Lou Rush, may be helpful.

Classroom Hints

The clinician should encourage the teacher to appoint a "listening helper" for the hard of hearing child so that she can continue to teach the large group while accommodating individual needs. One the other hand, it is the responsibility of each child to write down homework assignments. Keeping a notebook to hand to the teacher at the end of the day with the question, "Is this our only homework for tonight?" should be the responsibility of the hearing impaired pupil, not the "helper."

Seating arrangements contribute to or detract from learning. The original placement should be evaluated after about a week. If there is a unilateral hearing loss, the pupil should be seated so that the ear that functions normally is toward the majority of the class. During the music period, the hearing impaired child may wish to stand near the piano, his hand resting lightly above the keyboard, facing the piano player and the rest of the class so that he can keep pace with the words and music.

The teacher should be reminded that it is helpful to use spelling words in sentences to provide additional clues for comprehension; that key words written on the blackboard are enormously helpful at times; that the hearing impaired pupil should be encouraged to contribute to some extent in oral daily discussions; that she should accept his imperfect expressive language, repeating the sentence correctly after him and making a note to discuss specific problems with his academic tutor; that a pat on the head or the shoulder now and then replaces the encouraging tone of voice she might use with a hearing child; and that she

---

Language of Directions, Mary Lou Rush. Available from the Alexander Graham Bell Association for the Deaf, 3417 Volta Place, N.W., Washington, D.C. 20007.

can enlist the parent's help, for example, in teaching the rules of the game newly learned in the physical education period. Clinicians should invite teacher appraisals of the student's progress.

Working with the Academic Tutor

The specific function of the academic tutor is to provide supplemental instruction in a particular subject area. However, with the assistance of the speech and hearing clinician, the tutor can develop an approach to the subject which will encompass such goals as improvement in the child's reading skills, growth of self-confidence (particularly when the child is confronting new assignments), development of pride in written work, expansion of vocabulary, comprehension and implementation of abstract concepts, and development of a sense of humor and spontaneous expression. The tutor should understand that the refinement of individual speech elements is not the primary emphasis; she should also be aware that asking questions which will stimulate cognition will also extend vocabulary and comprehension and enhance the quality of the pupil's spoken and written language. It is highly desirable that the tutor, speech clinician, and classroom teacher routinely schedule informal meetings to plan a unified program for the hearing impaired pupil.

The Role of the Parent

The parents of a hearing impaired child assigned to a regular class are often apprehensive about the attitudes of the school staff and students. They are frequently hesitant to inquire about the child's progress or to bring important new considerations to the attention of the teacher or principal. Sometimes the formal parent-teacher conference leaves both parties dissatisfied and the resolution of certain obvious deficiencies unsettled.

A great many activities relating to parent education are the responsibility of the speech and hearing specialist. Both parents should be invited to visit occasionally during therapy sessions. Later, in an informal meeting, the clinician can help explain the need for a mother and father to secure the weekly spelling list and weave those words into normal conversation with their child; to find the concepts covered in a reader, often listed at the back of the book, and to plan for home reinforcement in an informal way. Parents may listen to recently taped speech and language samples and compare them with those of a year earlier.

The clinician can encourage the classroom teacher and tutor to invite parents to spend a morning at school not only to observe the hearing impaired child's degree of comprehension and active participation in group and individual settings, but also to assess the ways in which his hearing classmates are functioning for generalized comparison.

Parents must be given a clear explanation of the school's grading system. It may be desirable to rate the hearing impaired child on his own potential, achievement, and effort rather than on the class curve. Any such adjustments should be explained in detail in parent conferences and on the report card itself.

Especially with younger hearing impaired students, parents should be encouraged to send notes to the school, such as, "Joe rode on a snowmobile for the first time last night." One parent was shocked because during "show and tell" his son didn't report his first trip to a museum. Actually, the boy didn't know the word *museum*. A simple note from home would have smoothed the way for his participation.

Of primary importance to parents is knowing whether or not the child is making more progress—academically and socially—in the local, integrated setting than he would if he were in a self-contained class. To give an informed opinion, the clinician must know firsthand what is happening at comparable grade levels in the part-time resource room or self-contained class.

The Annual Evaluation

The need for review of a hearing impaired pupil's achievement, as presented in traditional diagnostic and evaluative form, is well understood. During a case conference, at which the pupil's progress is being assessed to reach agreement on continuation, program modification, or demission to another educational setting, a speech clinician may volunteer to circulate questions to be answered during the meeting. Discussion of these questions may modify the judgments based on formal achievement tests. The questions relate to the roles and observations of individual supportive specialists as functional psychoeducational diagnosticians. The clinician can alter or expand the list according to the characteristics of the child and the particular program he is in.

1. Is the hearing impaired child performing at grade level in some subjects? (Remember, in the average sixth grade class one may find a span of at least six grades in reading ability.)
2. What is his general vocabulary level? Would he say, "I gave the slip of paper from the doctor to the man in the drugstore," when his classmates might say, "I gave the prescription to the druggist"?
3. Does he know words for categories, such as *money* for nickel, dime, penny?
4. Is he developing divergent thinking abilities with adequate semantic content for self-expression?
5. In reading, has he a systematic method of decoding with adequate word attack skills; does he make careful use of contextual clues; and does he have a functional knowledge of phonics?
6. What about the quality of his comprehension? Can he answer factual questions; is he able to "read between the lines" to answer inferential questions?

7. During discussion of a story just read, does he bring rich experience (for his age) to the situation; does he understand oral directions and questions; is his expressive vocabulary adequate for expressing his thoughts or replete with words like _thing_ and _like;_ does he benefit from exchange of ideas through individual and classroom discussion; and does he speak in quality sentences?

8. What is his level of independent operation? Does he need constant reassurance; does he follow written directions; what is his instructional level; and what is his frustration level?

9. What is his "free reading" level? Can he extract the main idea from a story?

10. Does he understand figurative language ("tied up in traffic," "schools of fish")?

11. Can he predict outcomes?

12. Can he use a dictionary? (upper grades)

13. What psychological cues are noticed in observation of the child: general tension, nail biting, frequent use of the bathroom, nervous habits, apprehension, poor self-image, or lack of social contacts in school and outside?

14. What is the degree of parental support and the quality of the home environment?

Summary

Often, it is not the hearing impaired child's inabilities which set his limitations, but rather the failure of the professionals directly involved in his educational program to set high enough standards for their own performance and to marshal the energy to maintain those standards.

The late Jack Bangs, as president of the American Speech and Hearing Association, stated in a guest editorial in _The Volta Review_ (1971) that the adoption of a commitment to provide individual and effective programs for the hearing impaired child will mean that traditional professional training programs in institutions of higher education will have to be modified to prepare individuals whose competencies span the fields of speech and hearing and special education.

How high do we set our standards? As high as our ambitions for the child based upon differential diagnosis and personal assessment; as high as our affection and involvement in his school-day programming; as high as our respect for the child as a thinking, sensitive, valuable person. The challenge and the charge to the speech and hearing specialist is to assume a catalytic role in providing direct services to the hearing impaired child, the classroom teachers and resource specialists who support the child during the school day, and his parents. As Linus said to Charlie Brown, "There is no heavier burden than great potential."

(See next page for references.)

REFERENCES

Bangs, J. L. Guest editorial. *The Volta Review*, 1971, 73, 210-211.

Calvert, D. R., Olshin, G. M., DeWeerd, M. J., & Berson, M. P. Office of Education describes model projects for young handicapped children. *Exceptional Children*, 1969, 36, 229-248.

David, H. (Ed.) The young deaf child: Identification and management. Proceedings, International Conference, Toronto, Canada, October 8-9, 1964. *Acta Otolaryngologica, Supplementum 206*, 1965.

Deno, E. L. Special education as developmental capital. *Exceptional Children*, 1970, 37, 229-240.

Lilly, M. S. A training-based model for special education. *Exceptional Children*, 1971, 37, 747-749.

Marge, M. Factor analysis of oral communication skills in older children. *Journal of Speech and Hearing Disorders*, 1964, 7, 291-309.

McConnell, F. L. (Ed.) Conference on current practices in the management of deaf infants (0-3 years). Proceedings, Vanderbilt University School of Medicine, Nashville, Tennessee, 1968.

Mulholland, A. (Ed.) *National research conference on day programs for hearing impaired children. Final Report.* Washington, D.C.: The Alexander Graham Bell Association for the Deaf, 1968.

Northcott, W. H. The integration of young deaf children into ordinary educational programs. *Exceptional Children*, 1971a, 38, 29-32.

Northcott, W. H. Infant education and home training. In L. E. Connor (Ed.), *Speech for the deaf child: Knowledge and use.* Washington, D.C.: The Alexander Graham Bell Association for the Deaf, 1971b.

O'Neill, J. J. The possible role and position of speech pathology and audiology in regard to language learning disabilities, and the hearing-impaired. *ASHA*, 1971, 13, 51-52.

Pollack, D. *Educational audiology for the limited hearing infant.* Springfield, Illinois: Charles C Thomas, 1970.

Stark, J. Current clinical practices in language. *ASHA*, 1971, 13, 217-220.

Wedenberg, E. Experience from 30 years of auditory training. Proceedings, International Conference on Oral Education of the Deaf, Northampton, Massachusetts, 1967. Pp. 2089-2100.

Have You Thought Of . . .

. . . encouraging parents to extend their role beyond expressing interest and appreciation to the teacher of an integrated class? They can and should participate in the full activities of the school, thus showing they are not simply the parent of a hearing impaired child but are willing to work for and do battle for *all* children in the school. Integration must work at ALL levels, not only at the level of the child in the classroom. — *Bruce Shepherd, Sydney, Australia.*

Part III
Organizational Patterns
And Evaluation Procedures

14

The Role of the Supervisor/Coordinator

The role of the supervisor-coordinator of an integrated day school program is described — from the coordinator's initial contact with the hearing impaired child to the child's final placement. Among her major responsibilities are: expanded and improved supportive services for pupils and staff; pupil placement, monitoring, and evaluation; development of a professional growth program; and community leadership. The importance of interaction with the regular classroom teacher is emphasized as one prerequisite to realistic integration of the hearing impaired child.

The Office of Special Education in the Denver Public Schools exists to provide services to pupils with special needs. Its basic function is to plan for, maintain, and improve existing special education programs and to organize and establish new programs as required by children's needs and in accordance with state regulations. The special education program and teachers are under the direct jurisdiction of the local school.

As the Coordinator in the Office of Special Education, I work with the individuals within the schools who are directly or indirectly involved with a hearing handicapped or visually impaired pupil. An open-ended list of my specific duties would include:

1. Interpreting and administering approved special education policies and directives to probationary and tenure teachers.

2. Planning and participating in inservice training programs.

3. Assisting the director in assigning pupils to programs that best meet their needs: receiving applications, soliciting pertinent information from various

Miss Chambers is Coordinator for the Hearing Handicapped and Visually Handicapped in the Denver Public Schools.

school sources, requesting information on the applicant from outside sources, compiling a report, evaluating the report with the director of special education, and on approval, transferring pupils to appropriate schools or providing itinerant services to the pupils within the school.

4. Visiting both probationary and tenure teachers to observe teaching methods and techniques and advising on ways to improve instructional materials and to ensure quality education for handicapped children.

5. Performing public relations functions to promote public understanding and endorsement of the programs for the hearing and visually handicapped children; attending conferences, serving on committees, speaking to PTA and other groups wishing to be informed on special education programs; counseling individuals seeking help in specialized fields and answering letters of inquiry.

6. Reviewing and making recommendations on teachers' requisitions for classroom materials, equipment, and supplies.

7. Collaborating with the director of special education and educators of the deaf in policy determination, program improvement, and preparation of instructional guides.

8. Maintaining membership in and participating in national, regional, and local professional organizations related to the coordinator's special field.

While the "job description" looks very orderly and specific, there may be a vast cavern separating the lines on the paper and the final disposition of those duties. A closer look at two of the most important functions may provide a better understanding of the coordinator's role and the conditions which influence it.

Interaction with Teachers

The coordinator's major responsibility is to work with the teachers of the deaf (both probationary and tenure) within the public schools where the classes for the hearing impaired are housed.* A great deal of time — although still not enough — is spent with the beginning teachers. The coordinator observes their teaching and takes notes on the observations; she then meets with them as soon as possible to discuss reactions and to make constructive suggestions for improvement or change when necessary. Often, demonstration teaching is offered, and occasionally the coordinator sits in on the new teacher's first parent conference. She must be well aware of the particular pupil's functioning in order to answer any questions the parent may direct to her.

The coordinator must do her best to assist teachers in providing the highest level of teaching to hearing handicapped youngsters. There are of course times

---

*Placement of the hearing handicapped pupils in the public school provides the opportunity for their integration into regular classes as their abilities allow. Itinerant teachers are provided for those pupils who are able to remain in their home schools and for those who have returned to home schools but still need support in language, auditory training, and speech.

when the teacher and coordinator will not agree on a method or opinion, but if both keep in mind that the primary concern is the child and his needs, the problem can generally be resolved. Working with the teachers is a challenge, for we must ever be on the lookout for new ways to approach a situation; if problems are not resolved, it is the child who suffers. Yet this interaction also offers me my greatest satisfaction: it is thrilling to see highly trained teachers using their knowledge and creativity to narrow the language gap of the hearing handicapped child; to be asked by teachers to share ideas; and, hopefully, to make excellent planning and instruction even more productive.

Three years ago a new procedure for teacher evaluation was developed by the Denver Public Schools. If the school principal wishes, the coordinators may be part of the evaluation team. This provides an opportunity for the teacher and coordinator to set down in writing the short-term and long-term goals for the classroom. There is thus a common understanding of what areas will be emphasized and observed during the evaluation process.

Pupil Placement

A second major function of the coordinator concerns placement of the hearing handicapped pupils in the special education programs. The coordinator is available to consult with public school personnel on questions regarding children with hearing or vision losses. After being contacted by the public school nurse or the Denver Public Schools Health Services Department, she makes arrangements to meet with the nurse to examine available medical and audiological information. She may observe the child in his classroom, talk with his teacher, find out if the speech therapist has had contact with the child, and relate all these findings to the principal. The principal or nurse then contacts the parents to discuss the concerns. If the child needs some assistance from the special education program, it is requested that the school make application.

According to state education department regulations, psychological testing must then be arranged, as well as a health evaluation. In the Denver Public Schools, there are two psychologists specifically trained in psychological testing for the hearing and visually handicapped; and the coordinator sometimes feels it is necessary to meet with the psychologist prior to testing. If we suspect that there are overlays of other problems, we request more definitive testing. When all information is gathered, a staffing is held on the child.

The parent is kept informed all along the way. If the pupil requires special education assistance, we meet with the parent to explain the kinds of programs available and the procedures we recommended. Parent permission is necessary before any child is placed in a special education program.

A Case Study

To illustrate how this process applies with an individual child, let us consider the case of 5-year-old Tina. She has a hearing loss of approximately 65 dB, which was not discovered until she was 4 years old. Her father, a military man, had been stationed overseas during her first three years, while the rest of the family resided in Denver. Because her mother does not speak English fluently, there has been little language stimulation in the home.

When Tina was enrolled in her home school kindergarten in September 1971, the special education office received a prompt SOS. It was decided that she should remain in her home school with itinerant service provided to supplement the classroom teaching. There were several reasons for this approach: Tina had an excellent kindergarten teacher and would be in a class of no more than 15 children; the kindergarten teacher was most cooperative in following suggestions of the itinerant teacher; also, she was able to give Tina the extra time and help she required. Before placing an exceptional child in a regular class, it is important to evaluate carefully the child's needs and to determine if the teacher has the time to meet those needs.

In the spring of 1972 we knew that a decision had to be made on the optimal placement for Tina the following September. Would first grade in her home school be best? Or, would she require more intensive help than the itinerant teacher could provide over the next few years — a crucial period academically? The itinerant teacher, the regular teacher, and I — the coordinator — each observed the home school first-grade classes individually and compared notes afterwards. Psychological testing indicated that Tina had above average ability, but there was a 50-point span between the verbal score and the performance score. It was the opinion of all concerned that she needed more intensive help than could be given by the itinerant teacher, and it was therefore recommended that Tina be placed in the *regular first grade* at the center school for the hearing handicapped and receive daily intensive help in language and auditory training.

These recommendations were discussed with Tina's father and the results of the psychological tests were interpreted to him. He agreed with our recommendation to place her in the regular class. When decisions have to be made concerning optimal placement of a child, it cannot be done by remote control, nor even by telephone. It can only be accomplished through personal contact, which necessarily requires a tremendous amount of time.

Liaison With Neighborhood Schools

In the case of a hearing handicapped pupil who is to be returned to his home school, certain procedures are followed. No pupil is merely returned. Conferences are arranged with the home school administrative staff and any others who will be involved with the pupil. Written reports, including a new psychological test and the most recent achievement test scores, are included. The administrative staff of the Denver elementary school where the classes for the hearing impaired are located are knowledgeable in deaf education and have developed a set of procedures for integrating a hearing impaired pupil into a regular classroom or returning him to his home school. When we are requesting the return of a pupil to his home school, it is imperative that we discuss his strengths and weaknesses openly and objectively with the administrators of the home school, for the educational planning now becomes largely the home school's responsibility with the coordinator serving as liaison between special education and the individual school.

Indeed the responsibilities of a coordinator in special education are not the same in every program, nor should they be the same. They must be adaptable to the situations and needs in the individual school district and will vary according to the orientation of the staff, state regulations, and the population of exceptional children who are served.

Have You Thought Of . . .

. . . encouraging parents to work with school authorities for reduction in class size to alleviate the teacher's added responsibility of helping an integrated hearing impaired child? — *Bruce Shepherd, Sydney, Australia.*

. . . providing resource room arrangements for certain children now fully integrated in regular classrooms? The average public school teacher seems to have an overly optimistic view of the performance of first and second grade hearing impaired children, based on the children's ability to complete the work sheets given to them in class. These often require multiple choice or matching type responses, and some hearing impaired children can perform deceptively well. If linguistic deficiencies are present, they become apparent at the end of the second grade and in third and higher grades, and reflect themselves in increasingly unsatisfactory academic work. In the resource room — a kind of "half-way house" — the hearing impaired student can be evaluated realistically to see if he can advance to status as a full-time student in a normal school. — *Mark Ross, Longmeadow, Massachusetts.*

(See page 108 for a discussion of the resource room.)

15

VERNA V. YATER

The Hearing Clinician Program

The Hearing Clinician Program of the Special School District of St. Louis County, Missouri, is designed to 1) encourage and facilitate the complete academic and social integration of children with moderate to profound bilateral sensorineural hearing losses into their regular neighborhood public schools and 2) to maintain students with less severe losses who are already integrated. Hearing clinicians provide a continuum of services including consultation with public school staff members, evaluation and/or needs assessment, individualized therapy, parent interaction, and curriculum assessment and modification.

The Role of the Hearing Clinician

At the Special School District of St. Louis County, Missouri, capable children with moderate to profound bilateral hearing losses are given an opportunity to advance and to compete with their normal-hearing peers as early in their educational careers as possible. The aim of a program for educating capable, normal children who have auditory impairments, we believe, should be total academic assimilation into regular neighborhood public schools. The child with a moderate, severe, or profound hearing loss, if totally integrated early, often requires some individualized help to function well in regular public school classes. Individualized placement, programming, and systematic indoctrination of the regular teaching staff is provided for this child within the framework of the Hearing Clinician Program.

A hearing clinician generally enters the program with a professional background as an audiologist, speech or language pathologist, or educator of the deaf.

Mrs. Yater is Supervisor of the Hearing Clinician Program of the Special School District of St. Louis County, Missouri.

Ideally, a hearing clinician would have a background of formal course work and practical experience in more than one of the above areas. At the Special District, hearing clinicians receive intensive and continuing inservice training. Clinicians need to interpret audiological and hearing aid evaluations to public school personnel and parents. They also need to know techniques of assessment and development of speech and language skills. Diagnostic assessment of developmental strengths and deficits in academic areas, particularly in reading, is conducted or reviewed. Parent counseling skills are developed or enhanced through participation in a program of continuing parental support. Skill and warmth in public relations activities designed to advance the needs and interests of each child are also fostered.

The hearing clinician is generally responsible for the coordination of the expertise of the entire school team — often in conjunction with a principal or guidance counselor — in case conferences and in analysis of necessary support services for each hearing impaired child. A team will be comprised of different people depending upon the particular school in which a child is enrolled. Possible team members include the principal, classroom teacher, guidance counselor, instructional specialist, reading consultant, language consultant, librarian, nurse, and volunteer student tutor. The hearing clinician is cognizant of the role of each of the specialists involved and acts to coordinate the utilization of their distinct skills for the benefit of the child.

A Functioning Total Integration Program

The Hearing Clinician Program* is designed to provide individualized programming for students enrolled in regular public school classes in more than 150 schools located in the 25 regular school districts of St. Louis County. All students in the program are totally integrated academically and socially. There are 179 students currently enrolled in active therapy. Thirteen students are attending the District's vocational-technical schools; approximately 50 other hearing impaired students are seen on an aperiodic observational basis. Students on observation and/or their parents are seen for counseling regarding required audiological services, for determination of classroom or teacher placement, or for minimal amounts of individual therapy.

---

*The Hearing Clinician Program is a part of the entire St. Louis County Special School District framework. The District provides the education for all handicapped children and youth and is responsible for the vocational-technical education of all 11th and 12th grade students in St. Louis County. Services are provided in 25 public school districts with a population of over 900,000 in the 495 square miles in the County. The Special District has its own elected Board of Education, a Superintendent, and a special tax rate. The District employs more than 500 full-time professional employees. Before a student enters any Special District program, he is evaluated by a staff which includes social workers, psychologists, speech pathologists, audiologists, educational consultants, and a pediatrician. Children who qualify are then assigned to the appropriate Special District program.

The Special District provides several options for hearing impaired children. They may be enrolled in a self-contained classroom program for children from age 3 through the high school level. Another option is the Hearing Clinician Program, or *total integration into the child's own neighborhood elementary or secondary school.* Of the students in this program, 85% are referred from classrooms for the deaf or hard of hearing in special schools including the Special District classes, Central Institute for the Deaf, and St. Joseph Institute for the Deaf. The remaining 15% come from the Special District Hearing Conservation Program. In 1972 more than 80,000 students in alternate grades (i.e., 1st, 3rd, and 5th) were screened in their neighborhood public schools through this service.

Criteria for acceptance into the Hearing Clinician Program include attendance in a regular public school or the Special District Vocational-Technical Schools, normal intelligence, a bilateral sensorineural hearing loss, and a need based on educational and/or social considerations. The areas requiring remediation are assessed by the hearing clinician on the basis of classroom observation, inspection of student work, teacher judgment, and objective measurement.

Operational Procedures

After a child is referred to the Hearing Clinician Program, the clinician makes an initial visit to the neighborhood public school which the child will be attending. During this and subsequent visits the clinician notes possible grade placements, types of class groupings, group and individual tests being used, textbooks, approaches to learning, kinds of instructional personnel and materials available, the physical environment of the school and classrooms, and the general quality of child-teacher interaction in formal and informal learning situations.

Since the complete cooperation of all school personnel is necessary to effect the best progress for each child, hearing clinicians serve as consultants to the child's classroom teachers or school administrative personnel, guidance counselors, social workers, psychologists, and other professional personnel. The enlistment of the cooperation of varied professionals is initiated during the first visit to the child's school.

A regular channel of communication between clinician and teacher is established to be used throughout the school year. Teachers are given information sheets with suggestions for accommodating to individual needs of the hearing impaired students in their classes. The written suggestions cover such topics as speechreading and auditory training; lighting, seating, and use of hearing aids; speech development; and teaching aids, oral homework correction, and class discussions.

In addition, teachers, counselors, and principals are invited to attend workshops planned by the hearing clinicians which are generally held in early October. These focus on topics related to hearing impairment and curriculum; i.e., hearing aids and training of residual hearing, speechreading, classroom modifications, speech, language, and reading skills. Teachers are also given an opportunity to discuss their particular problems and experiences. Generally, a public school teacher who has had at least a year's experience in working with hearing impaired children is invited to share her experiences with the other teachers at the workshop. The need and value of continual exchange of information throughout the academic year between teachers and clinicians cannot be overemphasized.

Teachers usually welcome this general orientation and encouragement; fellow students do, also. In September a demonstration is presented in classrooms in which a child with a hearing loss is enrolled to help the other students better understand the child's loss. A cartoon movie or filmstrip depicting the hearing process is shown; speechreading, the sounds the child can or cannot hear according to configuration of hearing loss, and hearing aids are explained. Concrete suggestions are given to hearing peers to improve their interaction with a hearing impaired child and to enhance their genuine understanding of the significance of a hearing loss. They are also given ideas about what they individually can do to create a positive learning environment for a child with a hearing impairment. The child with a hearing loss often helps to plan and execute this valuable session with his classmates. Students in the class are encouraged to comment and ask questions.

Secondary Students and Their Activities

Most of the secondary level students who are enrolled in the Hearing Clinician Program are audiometrically deaf.* While many students in the St. Louis County area now enter public schools at the elementary level, some secondary students do not enter public schools until ninth grade. These students then have the simultaneous adjustments of making new friends, moving from the relatively sheltered environment of a school or class for the deaf to a large high school, and learning new study approaches and habits.

Once a high school student has been referred to the program, a hearing clinician begins to work with the director of the guidance department or the specific counselor to whom the student has been assigned in the school where he will be enrolled. Teachers of all academic and nonacademic subjects as well as the guidance counselor, principal, librarian, nurse, and other professionals who might work with the student are included in a staffing to familiarize them with matters regarding the deaf student's integration and to encourage positive attitudes.

During the first month of school the hearing clinician meets with student notetakers, who have been selected by the hearing impaired student or his teacher. Hearing losses and their educational significance are explained to the notetakers. They are encouraged to talk to the deaf student and are guided in the mechanics of taking good notes through discussions and written suggestions.

Generally, a hearing impaired student should have two notetakers for each academic subject so that there is an alternate to take notes if the regular note-taker is absent or unavailable. In carrying out the actual job of notetaking these students also often become knowledgeable regarding the implications of hearing loss for daily functioning and can educate other students informally about hearing impairment as well.

Curriculum Preparation

Certain facets of communication skills development frequently present problems for hearing impaired students. For greater efficiency in helping students improve in these skill areas, packets have been assembled or modified from previously existing materials or new materials have been written as needed. The hearing clinicians have prepared units in vocabulary, with pre- and post-tests, exercise materials, written directions, language units, and dictionary usage units. When a child is seen to have difficulties in a particular area of receptive or expressive language or vocabulary development, these units can be drawn on for use as a pre-programmed aid to regular classroom teaching.

Because of the volume of work which high school students are often required to complete, units in literature and social studies have also been prepared for student and/or parent use. These units include outlines, study guides, quizzes, and summaries of text material. These units have been developed and revised from materials and tests generally being used in school districts in St. Louis County.

Therapy

Hearing impaired students take all academic courses which their normal-hearing peers take. Generally, they are also seen for individual therapy sessions. Therapy needs are programmed individually in terms of both content and number of sessions per week. The main skill areas usually considered for inclusion in therapy sessions are: vocabulary and language building, speech development, improvement of listening skills, temporary academic assistance, study skills, and reading. The areas of greater deficit are usually considered first for inclusion in therapy. Therapy goals and behavioral objectives are planned and written to move the student efficiently toward greater competency. The clinician attempts to pinpoint deficit areas in relation to present and future-needed competencies; he does not act as an academic tutor.

If it is the opinion of the hearing clinician and/or the child's classroom teacher that he has more than a partial difficulty or misunderstanding in some subject areas, additional help is sought for the child. This might involve referral to a reading consultant, a resource or coaching teacher, a tutor, or a psychologist. A tutor may be a paid, private professional or, more often, a capable student who will provide short-term explanations in an area of temporary difficulty.

Summary

The overall purpose of the Special District Hearing Clinician Program is to facilitate total academic and social integration of children with hearing impairments into their regular neighborhood public schools. In St. Louis County, it is the framework for achieving the working cooperation of all school personnel and parents in the education of the hearing impaired student and for ensuring the provision of required individualized therapy for the student.

The role of the hearing clinician is multifaceted. He acts as a consultant, teacher educator, indoctrinator, diagnostician, interpreter of audiological assessments, skills assessor and developer of academic, speech, and language skills, parent counselor, and skilled public relations liaison with regular public school personnel. He draws together the competencies of many professionals to help shape the total student.

Have You Thought Of . . .

. . . letting parents know what kinds of extracurricular activities are going on at school and/or supplying the hearing impaired child with a brief schedule of activities so that he knows what's happening? Sometimes children integrated in a hearing classroom miss out on afterschool activities simply because they do not hear the announcement. Teachers should be alerted to this: there is no more excluded feeling for the hearing impaired child than to have all the kids in the class rush to sign up for some activity after school when he doesn't even know where they are running! — *Virginia Stern, Stamford, Connecticut.*

. . . asking a child to act as a "buddy" to the hearing impaired child? Seated next to him, the "buddy" can be sure that the newcomer turns to the right page during lessons and has details of assignments. On the playground or in the lunch room, the "buddy" can help include the hearing impaired child in games and explain rules. — *Elizabeth Frick, St. Louis, Missouri.*

16

A Resource Room Program
For Hearing Impaired Students

A resource room located within a regular public school provides a setting where integrated hearing impaired pupils can receive tutoring and support from a trained teacher of the deaf to supplement their daily participation in regular classes. The students, who come from many areas within the county to the resource room in a central location, enjoy all the facilities of a large elementary school while benefiting from the individualized assistance and companionship in the resource room at the opening and close of the day and for one additional 50-minute period of daily instruction.

Integration into a regular elementary school in a progressive school district offers many dividends and widens educational and social horizons for hearing impaired children. In analyzing the problems of educating handicapped children in New York State, the Fleischmann Commission Report (1972) deplores the fact that so many children have been "left out or behind in the educational process because of physical, mental, or emotional deficiencies, or because they are in state and private institutions or foster homes where educational opportunities are scarce or nonexistent." It mentions the inadequate placement and programming and the inability of many public schools to educate these children. Among the specific recommendations for improvement is this:

Give overall fiscal and administrative authority for educating all handicapped children, including those in state-supported child-caring institutions, to regional

Dr. Bowman is Supervisor of Resource Room Programming for the Board of Cooperative Educational Services for Hearing Impaired Students (BOCES #3), Suffolk County, New York.

representatives who would be deputies to the Commissioner of Education, with the expectation that most of the children would be educated in local public school districts.*

A resource room program provides special education services for hearing impaired students in line with the proposals of the Fleischmann Commission, and even goes beyond the recommendations by not segregating the children into a class for the hearing impaired within the local school district, but by placing them, according to their ability, in various classes throughout the elementary school program. Further support is at hand from New York State legislators who are sponsoring a bill of rights for handicapped people, insisting that they be given equal opportunities to fulfill their individual potential. Growing public interest and government support will demand a more determined educational thrust to place hearing handicapped children in a regular school system.

The resource room program herein described is a service of the Board of Cooperative Educational Services, Supervisory District #3, Suffolk County, New York, which administers 18 school districts. The resource room teacher, a certified teacher of the deaf with many years' experience in teaching hearing impaired children from nursery school through senior high school, is employed by the BOCES Board of Education. The 10 hearing impaired children, from 6 to 12 years of age, are referred to the program from their home districts in Suffolk County and are served by the resource room located at Countrywood Elementary School, Huntington Station, New York.

Rationale for Integration

The hearing impaired students are integrated into regular classes from grades 1-6 at Countrywood School, where the entire staff welcomes the program and contributes to its continuing success in every possible way. Students have access to a fine school library and the supervision of a library teacher. There is a well-equipped gymnasium, which affords an opportunity for the children to take part in team sports along with hearing classmates. The music and drama departments develop special concerts, and families can experience the joy of having their hearing impaired children participate in the chorus, orchestra, and school plays. Hearing impaired students are included in reading enrichment programs under the tutelage of the reading specialist. The art program helps develop personal confidence, for the children can work on their own projects and enter district competitions along with hearing classmates. Often they experience the pleasure of having their drawings chosen for display on the corridor bulletin boards. Classroom mother helpers, college education majors, and student volunteers are involved in the program at Countrywood School and give generously of their services so that the hearing impaired child is not left

---

*Fleischmann Commission Report, Volume 3, Chapter 9. Children with Special Needs. October, 1972.

behind. All these encounters with different people, possible only in a regular school situation, provide opportunities for the child to speechread and communicate freely in a lively and interesting environment.

A Transitional Stage

The well-staffed resource room, located in a large, well-equipped elementary school, offers a transitional level of service between the one-teacher contained classroom and full-time integration with hearing students. Current educational developments — the "open classroom," modular scheduling, rotating classes (even in elementary grades), team teaching, and the use of audio-visual equipment such as educational television and videotapes — make strong demands on children's adaptability and listening skills. Informal learning through class projects with little emphasis on formal textbook instruction can create a virtual nightmare for the auditorily handicapped child. The assistance of a resource room specialist to interpret this progressive educational system for the hearing impaired child, his regular classroom teacher, and administrative personnel is imperative.

The resource room program provides comfort and security for its members in countless ways. A battery tester and new hearing aid batteries are always available. Since the hearing impaired children do not live in the immediate vicinity of their classmates, they are encouraged to bring their new friends to the resource room with its homelike atmosphere, where they can have a private chat or enjoy a favorite game or hobby at recess. The child who has been struggling alone with his hearing handicap in his home district is usually thrilled to have the companionship of the others in the resource room when he is referred to the program. So often these children have no image of a hearing impaired child to relate to, other than themselves — and at first it is helpful for them to be exposed during the day to other hearing impaired children. Even the most reticent new pupil is drawn out and coaxed to participate in activities, first in the shelter of the resource room and then in the regular classroom to which he is assigned. The resource room pupils vie with each other for success in their respective classrooms. They see that being hearing impaired is no excuse for not achieving, and they realize that they must try harder. Through their own intuition, these children know the most meaningful way to comfort and help each other when they are in special need of understanding. There are few discipline problems, for group pressure reproves the pupil who is sent back to the resource room for misconduct in class.

The Facility

BOCES #3 placed the resource room by renting a classroom in a regular elementary school. A central location within the county facilitates bus routing. Extra planning is required at Countrywood School as primary and intermediate classes have different schedules for arrival and dismissal. Since fluctuating school populations on Long Island can interfere with available classroom space, it is important to locate a facility where the program can continue from year to year; for both students and resource room teacher need the continuity of school progress and relationships.

The resource room at Countrywood School is of regular classroom size and is attractively furnished with reading tables, chairs, and mementos of school activities. There is space for the children to store personal articles and to display their best classroom papers; praise from the resource room teacher as well as the classroom teacher helps give coherence to the pupil's academic program.

Functions and Competencies of the Resource Room Teacher

The understanding and guidance of the resource room teacher are sought when academic and social problems pertaining to hearing impaired students need to be resolved. Beyond required academic training, the personalities of the classroom teachers and the resource room specialist are vital to the success of the program. The selected classroom teachers must be compassionate, understanding, and willing to accept hearing handicapped children in the classroom and throughout the school. The resource specialist must be realistically aware of each classroom situation and make every effort to smooth the way for a pleasant relationship between the hearing impaired child, his teacher, and classmates.

The Fleischmann Report acknowledges the necessity for special training for teachers of hearing impaired children. The resource room teacher must be familiar with the academic curriculum for both elementary and secondary schools and cognizant of how each teacher in the program presents material. In addition to supplemental academic instruction, the resource room teacher should be a trained teacher of the deaf so that instruction in speechreading, language development, and speech correction is given by a specialist.

The screening of candidates for a resource room is done with care and expertise, for students must have potential to benefit from such a program. Determinants are the age at which the child became hearing impaired, degree of hearing loss in the speech range, speechreading skill, use of an individual hearing aid, the amount of supportive help from home, and the child's own personality. Placement is finalized by the end of the spring semester, permitting the pupil to enter his assigned class along with the hearing children on the first day of the new school year, thus avoiding any embarrassing delay and late placement from the resource room. Preparatory planning gives the resource room teacher an opportunity to meet in advance with the school staff for an orientation session during which the special needs of the children are explained. An annual evaluation, taking into consideration the child's academic achievement, intellectual potential, and social maturity, is made by a committee including the classroom teacher, the resource room teacher, the school principal, and members of supportive services. They determine if the child is properly placed, if he can return to his home school, or if he should continue in the program for a longer period of time.

Schedule Adjustment for Individual Children

All instruction is oral and the children are immersed in a hearing environment throughout the day. On arrival at school, the hearing impaired children report first to the resource room teacher. If any of the pupils are concerned about a homework assignment, a health problem, or a misunderstanding with another teacher or pupil, the resource room teacher is alerted and responds to the situation immediately. All students return to the resource room at the end of the school day and are dismissed by the resource room teacher; this is another time to find out if all has gone well during the day. In addition, each student comes to the resource room teacher daily for an instruction period of 40 minutes or more. Scheduling is assigned at the classroom teacher's recommendation, so that the pupil is not in the resource room when new material is presented. No more than two students, preferably on the same grade level, come for instruction at the same time. If a student is absent, the resource room teacher checks on the lessons that he missed and tutors him accordingly.

Liaison with Regular Classroom Teacher

The classroom teacher uses the official school report card for evaluating the hearing impaired child. The resource room teacher writes an additional report which is also part of the pupil's cumulative record. At the end of the year a comprehensive report is sent to the home district for each pupil.

Every effort is made to concentrate on the grade curriculum, and a copy of the course outline is given to the resource teacher every week. Daily briefings are arranged, when needed. New vocabulary is studied in advance, especially for science and social studies. Mathematics and language principles which are not grasped in the classroom are reinforced in the resource room. The value of a specialist's expertise in speechreading, speech, and language development is enhanced by modifying the classroom material to ensure greater comprehension and relating it to the child's daily activities. There is opportunity in the resource room to dramatize a mathematical problem, do added research for a social studies project, or demonstrate again a science experiment in order that the meaning and related concepts are completely understood. For example, in a sixth-grade science project on sound, a hearing impaired student chose as her project "The Mechanics of Hearing." This gave her an opportunity to explain to the science teacher and peers her unique position in the classroom.

Teachers and other pupils should be reminded that the hearing impaired child may experience difficulty in relying on speechreading and partial hearing for information. Suggestions such as these — 1) keep hands away from the face when talking, and 2) enunciate clearly, but do not exaggerate or "mouth" words — make speechreading easier for the pupil. Comprehension is aided if the classroom teacher writes vocabulary words and key phrases on the blackboard and uses spelling words in sentences. Flexible seating improves the pupil's position for better speechreading and listening. The teachers at Countrywood School report that the whole class, indeed the entire school, benefits from the experience of working and interacting with the hearing impaired children. In turn, total immersion in a hearing environment is the best possible learning situation for the hearing handicapped child, for it increases his self-reliance and his confidence in oral communication.

Working Together

Key figures in the success of the program at Countrywood School are the principal and assistant principal. Without their support and the cooperation of the staff, the resource room teacher could not develop and maintain a functional and useful program.

The parents meet with the classroom teacher and resource room teacher for scheduled conferences. They are encouraged to attend PTA meetings and become identified with the school. The Meet-Your-Teacher-Night, a covered-dish supper, and a Saturday work session offer occasions for family involvement and conversations with the grade teachers and other parents.

The future for hearing impaired children is largely dependent on the child's own inner drive, the encouragement and training given to him by parents, and the education and accommodation of the regular classroom teacher initiated by the resource room specialist. The elementary school provides the physical plant and sets the climate for learning, with support of the administration and staff. The goal of the resource room is to help the children experience the thrill of learning and the pleasure that comes with personal accomplishment. Using this interdisciplinary approach, the school, parents, and community can offer a more unified educational and social program for hearing impaired children.

Have You Thought Of . . .

. . . writing the new vocabulary and concepts introduced during the week in the blank space at the left-hand side of the teacher's weekly plan book? These can also be listed on the board in the tutoring room. When there are a few minutes left just before the bell rings, I ask the pupils I am tutoring to: "Write a funny sentence with _____." Or, "Ask a question using _____," etc. — *Dorothy Hedgecock, Rochester, Minnesota.*

17

LOIS BELL GERMAIN

Inservice Training: Mini-Model

Educating the Hearing To Educate the Hearing Impaired

Successful integration of a hearing impaired student is dependent upon a dynamic working relationship between the teacher of the hearing impaired and the regular teacher. Assuring a responsive climate in the regular classroom is largely the responsibility of the "special teacher" but it is important that the regular teacher feel competent to undertake her own responsibilities. Increased numbers of hearing impaired children can enter into the mainstream program if the traditional interpretation of integration is expanded. Suggestions for educating hearing teachers and students informally are delineated as ways of reaching the desired goal.

Classes for the hearing impaired in a relatively small public school system have inherent problems which are not present in a large, established setting. The smaller system does not justify having the personnel to handle the administrative and supervisory aspects of public day classes; consequently the teacher of the hearing impaired is faced with complex, varied responsibilities. She must educate her hearing impaired youngsters, counsel parents, act as a resource teacher, perform public relations functions, and handle miscellaneous administrative duties such as bookkeeping, devising evaluation forms, and selecting books.

In addition, the teacher must constantly be concerned with integration — a process which, in itself, is quite involved. Understandably, her main concern is

---

Mrs. Germain is Head Teacher in the Program for the Hearing Impaired, Fayette County Public Schools, Lexington, Kentucky.

usually focused on determining who should be integrated — and for what. In Lexington, Kentucky*, we have found this to be an oversimplification of a very complex process. In fact, we have found that two often overlooked aspects of integration — expanding integration opportunities and educating the hearing — are so vital to the total program that they should be uppermost in the teacher's mind. Indeed, every aspect of her job is directly influenced by these two concerns.

Expanding Integration

"Integration" generally refers to the placement of a given child in a regular (hearing) classroom for whichever subjects he can handle. Various factors determine whether a particular child can be integrated at all and, if so, to what extent. We have found that traditional programs for partial or full-time integration are often inadequate because they exclude the child who would benefit from a public school environment yet cannot keep up with a regular class due to social, emotional, or academic reasons. Thus, meaningful integration would seem unattainable for many children.

We feel that integration is so valuable that it should not be restricted to merely a few children. To overcome this limitation and to enable all of our students to benefit, we expanded the integration concept to encompass the following variations:

1. *Full-time integration*

> The child is able to function independently in a regular classroom. He returns to the class for the hearing impaired only for speech and supplementary tutoring when necessary.

2. *Part-time integration*

> a. Traditional: The child is integrated for those subjects he can handle. Math and science are usually the first subjects involved.
> b. Individual nonacademic: The child is integrated into a specific class on specific days in nonacademic areas such as art, gym, lunch, special programs, homeroom, free play, story time. (For example, one of our students regularly goes to lunch with a fifth-grade class.)
> c. Group nonacademic: The child is integrated for specific activities (as noted above) along with a group of his hearing impaired classmates. This differs from individual nonacademic integration in that the child is involved as a member of a group and is sometimes accompanied by his own

---

*Presently the two classes for hearing impaired children, which serve the entire county, are housed in a neighborhood school. These classes are taught by two special education teachers who are the only persons in the system with special knowledge in the area of hearing impairment. The children range in age from 6 to 15; most previously attended the Lexington Deaf Oral School, the local private preschool.

teacher; therefore, less independence is required of him. (For example, six of our children attend gym with a second-grade class.)

d. Informal: The child is integrated individually or within a group for short-term projects; the special teacher may or may not be present. The occasions arise spontaneously as a result of a close working relationship between the regular teacher and the teacher for the hearing impaired. This differs from the other forms of integration in its temporary nature and constant flexibility. (For example, two hearing impaired children participate in a first-grade science experiment; the hearing impaired class plans a party with a regular class.)

e. Reverse: Normally hearing children are brought into the classroom for the hearing impaired to participate in activities such as art and free play on a limited, short-term basis.

Through the use of these expanded forms of integration, *every* child in our program is able to interact in some way with hearing children. The benefits of expanding integration have been exciting and worthwhile. The hearing impaired children have gained independence through participation in large classes. They have more contact with hearing peers, which is especially important when the number of hearing impaired children is small and interaction with children of the same age would otherwise be very limited. The hearing impaired children are exposed to the diversified, stimulating atmosphere of a regular classroom and are also bombarded with normal, meaningful language. Equally important, the hearing children learn open-mindedness and understanding at an early age — a lesson that can remain with them the rest of their lives.

Educating the Hearing

Another aspect of integration which affects the entire program is public relations — educating the hearing about deafness and its varied effects on children. This is the indispensable foundation of a public day-class program. While the teacher of the hearing impaired in a small system often subordinates public relations to her many other responsibilities, we have found that a well-planned, positive approach to this component greatly improves the quality of our educational program.

Education of the hearing involves various groups: teachers, students, administrators, parents, and the community. In our program we've been especially pleased with the responsiveness of teachers and students to our efforts and achievements and offer our ideas for possible incorporation in other systems.

The Teachers

Our goal is to help the classroom teachers view the hearing impaired students as a *challenge* rather than a burden and as an *asset to the school*. In other words, we hope to do more than educate the teachers about hearing loss; we want to build positive attitudes. Our original plan which provided for inservice workshops was overambitious and lacking in perspective; based on experiences at private schools for the hearing impaired, it was not well-suited to the focus and personality of the faculty at a public school where hearing impaired children are few in number. Over a period of time we gathered some insights into the teachers' attitudes which have since served as guidelines for our revised program.

First, we found that most classroom teachers are conscientious and hardworking in their jobs; but they may feel burdened. Salaries (compared to those of other professionals) are low; clerical work is time-consuming; and classroom responsibilities, while stimulating, are emotionally and physically exhausting. It increases the teacher's work load to place a handicapped child in her class and schedule after-school workshops for orientation. This practice, therefore, may not initially be well received.

We've also learned that individual differences are as important in teachers as in children. Attitudes, interests, and personalities vary widely among adults; some of these traits can be effectively altered, but others cannot. It is helpful to remember this in selecting and educating teachers to work with our hearing impaired students.

Finally, teachers often seem to have misconceptions about special classes. They may resent the implication of superiority that the term "special" suggests. They may not understand how seven children in a "special" class can be as much work as thirty in a regular classroom. They may be uncomfortable with the unperfected voices or other noticeable differences in children from special classes.

Any approach for orienting teachers to children from special classes should reflect an awareness of these attitudes. Teachers who are selected must be those who are interested and who enjoy the diversity of their jobs. We mustn't burden them with extracurricular workshops and meetings; yet we should try to erase any fears or confusion by helping them understand more about hearing loss, convincing them that a specialist will always be available to help, and assuring them that they and their other students will have something to gain.

The Orientation Program

Our program for teacher orientation evolved over the period of one year. Although it may seem informal, loosely organized, and very simple, it represents a great deal of careful planning. It is based on these principles.:

1. The teacher of the hearing impaired must win respect as a person and as a professional. She should not set herself apart as a "special" teacher, but should strive to be friendly, sociable, and hard-working.

2. When a regular teacher initially receives a hearing impaired child, there should be a brief orientation session. It should include discussion of: a) ways to communicate with the child without embarrassment; b) the implications of language vs. speech and how language affects communication; c) special considerations relating to a particular child; and d) questions raised by the

teacher. Most important, the classroom teacher must understand that she will have full support and guidance from the special teacher whenever she wants it.

3. The regular teacher must always feel free to ask for help and advice. In addition, the special teacher should always be aware of how things are going. Their exchanges of information should be informal and can occur in the lounge, at lunch, and casually after school.

4. The teacher of the hearing impaired should periodically share meaningful written information (excerpts from journals, suggestions, etc.) with the regular classroom teachers. In this way, much information can be transmitted without consuming a great deal of time.

5. Formal meetings to discuss common problems are useful but should not be compulsory.

6. One of the greatest concerns of the classroom teacher is communication. She needs guidelines to follow in speaking to the child (facing him, using simple language, etc.) and in understanding him (being patient, asking him to repeat, etc.). She can learn best by watching the teacher for the hearing impaired communicate with the children.

7. The classroom teacher should be invited to observe hearing impaired children in their own classroom during her free time. She should not be made to feel guilty if she does not take advantage of each opportunity to visit, but should be encouraged to observe informally whenever she can.

8. The teacher of the hearing impaired should offer to observe the regular teacher, making it clear that she is there to help, not to judge.

9. The teacher of the hearing impaired and the regular teacher should periodically plan joint activities such as art lessons and combined games and sports at recess. The hearing impaired class should invite the regular classes to participate in a project or party. Once again, this is an opportunity for the regular teacher to observe the hearing impaired children with their specially trained teacher.

10. The classroom teacher must receive constant encouragement and assurance.

In summary, we suggest an informal but thorough program, the success of which largely depends on the efforts and interest of the teacher of the hearing impaired. One goal must serve as a constant guideline: to foster the attitude that a hearing impaired child is a challenge and an asset, not a burden.

The Students

By building knowledge and encouraging positive attitudes among the teachers, a large step can be taken toward educating the hearing students. However, a second technique — "rap sessions" — has been so effective that it has become a highlight of our program. The special teacher schedules these sessions with individual classes throughout the year. The "rap sessions" are informal, relaxing times for questions and answers between hearing students and the teacher of the hearing impaired. A session might begin with the teacher's describing to the children a particular area of interest (e.g., how hearing aids help, why the deaf children speak as they do, etc.), but usually the students' questions direct the rest of the session. The classroom teacher is urged to attend and picks up a great deal of information with a minimum expenditure of time. This is especially valuable when she hears the answers to questions she herself might not have wanted to ask.

Conclusion

Experimenting with different forms of integration has been a valuable experience for everyone in our program. The emphasis on establishing good relations with the regular teachers and students — as well as educating them about the hearing impaired — has been extremely rewarding. The attitude in our school toward hearing impaired youngsters is excellent now, and integration is becoming a more successful and enjoyable experience for all involved.

Have You Thought Of . . .

. . . using physical education classes to help start new friendships between hearing and hearing impaired students through personal relations in games and mutual enjoyment of sports? — *Linda McArthur, Arcadia, California.*

. . . reminding students, teachers, and others that the deaf child can speechread natural, slightly slowed speech better than *exaggerated* slow speech and may find it hard to speechread people with sunglasses, beards, or mustaches? — *Linda McArthur, Arcadia, California.*

18

ANNE SELTZ

Inservice Training: Maxi-Model

This Title III interdistrict inservice training program is part of an ongoing consultative project designed to demonstrate that hearing impaired students can successfully attend neighborhood schools when administrators, teachers, support staff, and peers are comfortable with the idea and have the potential for acquiring competencies to meet the students' needs. The inservice program attempts to acquaint mainstream educators with the implications of hearing and hearing loss, the use of hearing aids, and the capabilities of hearing impaired students. Descriptions of specific inservice sessions for specific audiences are furnished.

"Would you accept a hearing impaired student in your classroom?"
"I think that would be devastating."
"For whom?"
"For the child, the other students, and for ME!"

This conversation took place between a hearing consultant from our staff and an elementary teacher who had had no experience with hearing impaired students.

When planning inservice training for a school district, you must recognize this attitude, *respect it,* remember it, and develop materials to change it. Classroom teachers *can* become comfortable about hearing impaired students. And when they do, their attitude will pervade the classroom, set the model of behavior for students, and positively influence the hearing impaired student's learning environment for an entire school year.

Ms. Seltz is Project Director for the Title III Interdistrict Project for Hearing Impaired Children in the Minneapolis, Minnesota, Metropolitan Public Schools.

Students with varying degrees of hearing and auditory discrimination ability are attending regular schools throughout the United States in increasing numbers. These students include children who wear hearing aids. Yet, few teachers in regular schools have had experience either with hearing impaired students or with hearing aids; likewise, psychologists, counselors, social workers, tutors, principals, special education directors, nurses, reading specialists, and even some speech pathologists have minimal knowledge about and experience with hearing impaired students. All of these professionals have skills which can benefit hearing impaired students, and all can learn to adapt their professional behavior to accommodate these students when they are given additional knowledge, understanding, guidance, and ongoing support. Inservice programs can effectively begin to alter attitudes, provide knowledge, and encourage change.

An inservice program may be prepared by a hearing consultant in a district or by a team of consultants serving many districts on a regional level. In 1971 a Title III grant was awarded to Minneapolis to develop a demonstration consultative project for 28 school districts. The project focus has been on support to the hearing impaired child's teachers and supplemental personnel rather than on provision of direct services to the student himself. The diverse backgrounds of the Title III staff — including audiology, speech pathology, regular education, and education of the hearing impaired — permit program input from each area of specialty. The regional aspect allows the staff to share a variety of district-initiated ideas among all the participating districts. As part of this ongoing consultative effort, a general inservice program was developed.

Prior to a specific case management session with the staff for each hearing impaired student, a general inservice program can improve the comfort level of the mainstream staff, teach some working vocabulary, provide general teaching guidelines, and familiarize the staff with implications of hearing impairment and hearing aid usage. With this introduction, local school staff members can better attend to the particular child or children with whom they are to work.

Identifying Target Audiences for Inservicing

It is imperative to determine the audience for whom a program of inservice training is designed and to outline the objectives of each meeting. While an entire school staff can be included in a first general orientation, certain subgroups are appropriate when exploring the role of the individual members of the inter-disciplinary team who work with the hearing impaired child and his family. These include 1. special and regular educators/administrators (principal, classroom teacher, school nurse); 2. special education resource specialists (academic tutor, learning disabilities tutor, speech clinician; 3. general education specialists (developmental reading teacher, behavior management specialists); 4. social and vocational specialists (psychologists, social workers, school counselors); and other special groups such as parents or community audiologists.

Inservice training should be provided whenever necessary. Many districts find sessions during the first week of school or late in spring particularly useful. Inservice training permits an introduction to principles and techniques with the opportunity for feedback and subsequent program modification. The goal is to maximize the potential of the student's educational environment through staff education.

The frequency of inservice sessions depends on the needs of the particular system. Some determining factors may be the strength of the supportive staff in a particular school, changeover of staff from year to year, or the number of special students in a school or district. Sessions may be of varying lengths and may be organized to include several districts, individual schools, or even particular sections within one school.

What Should the Hearing Consultant Know Before the Inservice?

The consultant should be familiar with the number of hearing impaired students in the school or district and the students' abilities to use their residual hearing. He should know who make up the supportive staff, what is the school's attitude toward change, what is the quality of intra-staff communication, and what local deaf education programs have to offer. He should also be personally familiar with at least one member of the support staff — usually the speech pathologist or the nurse — who can serve as liaison at the inservice session.

Content and Format of an Inservice

Efforts should be made to provide as interesting an inservice as possible. Use the best available advice and resources of audio-visual experts. Think about previous inservices — remember what put you to sleep and don't duplicate it. Multi-media programs are usually more interesting than a straight lecture, regardless of the interest level of the audience.

We have prepared materials in the form of slide-tape shows and films to ensure that major topics are covered. A consultant can individualize the program for each group with a discussion session and comments while presenting these basic materials consistently. You can use movies, records, videotapes, slide-tape programs, transparencies on an overhead projector, the blackboard — anything to keep the audience visually, auditorily, and intellectually interested.

The following is a summary of our 2½-hour inservice program, which is often presented in two sessions. (The materials described are also listed at the end of this article with information about availability and cost.)

I. Film — Lisa, Pay Attention!

This 30-minute film of a second-grade classroom shows Lisa, the hearing impaired student, in trouble because the teacher is unaware of her needs. The film describes the effect of a hearing loss on language acquisition and inter-personal communication, the listening problems a hearing impaired student has in the acoustic environment of a classroom, the effect of glare and other physical conditions on the hearing impaired student's use of visual information, and the obvious disparity between intelligence and linguistic competencies. In short, it covers almost every situation in a classroom that would be potentially difficult for a hearing impaired student and has a high interest value for teachers. With the film, we provide a written hand-out for each member of the audience that summarizes the main points of the movie.

II. How Speech Sounds Through a Hearing Aid

This tape recording of a gentleman speaking into a hearing aid demonstrates effects of distance, noise, and reverberation or echo on speech understanding. Slides of cartoons visually demonstrating the narration accompany the tape. The presentation provides a fairly good coverage of strengths and weaknesses of hearing aid usage and is a good experience for almost any audience.

III. How They Hear

Teaching behaviors and strategies have been observed to change radically after teachers have been exposed to audio and visual materials demonstrating what their hearing impaired children do or do not hear. Although no audio-visual program has been designed which can duplicate the experience of an individual student who needs to combine auditory, visual, kinesthetic, contextual, and syntactic information to interpret his environment, there *are* materials which demonstrate the effects of various degrees and patterns of hearing loss on speech and language intelligibility. The Gordon Stowe record, *How They Hear*, is probably the best.

In addition, the anatomy of hearing is also discussed during this portion of the inservice. Attention is given to causes of hearing loss and available medical, surgical, and audiological treatment.

IV. The Team Approach

A slide-tape presentation, developed by the Title III staff, demonstrates the need for the team approach. It defines responsibilities of the Core Team (the teacher, tutor, clinician), the need for parent-school interaction, the importance of preview-review tutoring, and the crucial need for team interaction. The hearing impaired student benefits most when those working with him are working toward the same goal and are continually monitoring his progress. A teacher-tutor communication form is provided as a hand-out.

V. PACT: Procedural Adaptations for Classroom Teachers, Tutors, Therapists

This slide-tape show describes procedures which are easily adaptable to indi-vidual educational situations by a regular school staff. It emphasizes hearing aid monitoring by the staff, demonstrates variations in preferential seating patterns, and illustrates effective use of the blackboard, overhead projectors, and the buddy system. It describes how to provide the best visual and acoustic environment in the classroom. Pictures of hearing aids, cords, and batteries are shown to familiarize the audience with this equipment. A hand-out detailing each procedural adaptation is provided for every member of the audience.

These above segments compose the prepared portion of the 2½-hour inservice program which has been presented to over 2000 mainstream staff members in the Minnesota area during the past two years. The response from classroom teachers and other staff has indicated that the program has been effective in changing attitudes, teaching new vocabulary, providing an introduction to new skills, and promoting an ongoing interest in improvement of programs for hearing impaired students.

When the inservice audience begins to interact regarding their mutual concerns and uses the hearing consultant as the resource, we feel the inservice program has been successful. Anticipating that some audiences may be reluctant to ask questions, we have collected a variety of questions from teachers and included them in the hand-out package so that we can then ask the audience to choose a question they'd like answered. Our consultants know their inservice audience will have direct involvement with hearing impaired students and are eager to promote maximum learning through a lively discussion period. The presence of parents usually guarantees audience interaction.

The inservice program presents general information to a school staff; follow-up concentrates on individual staff members who are working with a specific student. The hearing consultant schedules classroom observations so that she knows the child well, helps develop a competent support team for each student, and assists the team with program planning, monitoring, and evaluation. To ensure follow-up service to each inservice participant, we circulate an attendance sheet to obtain each person's name, professional title, and school address.

Specialized Inservice Sessions

In addition to provision of the inservice to a local school staff, these same prepared materials can be used with a variety of audiences who will have a future impact on funding, regional planning, preparation of teachers, public acceptance, and legislation relating to the hearing impaired. By changing the focus of the introductory remarks and discussion and by choosing parts or all of the prepared materials, the hearing consultant can present an appropriate program to groups such as school nurses, state nursing organizations, superintendents, boards of education, parents, physicians, college students, audiologists, university staffs, diagnostic centers, speech pathologists, state departments of education, community action groups, legislators, etc. The materials we have developed combined with those you prepare can make the inservicing task much easier and more flexible. Here are some examples:

I. Nurses' Inservice

At a district level, school nurses may discuss their role in identification, referral, and follow-up. The sessions will emphasize monitoring of students with permanent hearing loss, frequent hearing aid checks, and promotion of annual audiological evaluation.* Hearing aids are distributed among the audience to familiarize the nurses with their operation and design. Selected portions of the general inservice may be presented.

In Minnesota, as in many other states, there is a high incidence of ear infection and associated disorders which affect a student's ability to hear in the classroom, at least on a temporary basis. Audiological as well as medical referral are encouraged.

The greatest need, as we see it, is to convince school nurses of the educational value of normal hearing, the educational significance of even a 30-40 dB bilateral hearing loss, and their responsibility to monitor hearing.

II. Audiologists' Inservice

Creating an active liaison with clinical audiologists through an inservice has resulted in good working relationships and strengthening of professional concern for hearing impaired students. This is a must in every community. Share with audiologists the materials you present to mainstream staff and ask for suggestions and advice. In turn, offer your advice on ways to improve their communication with the schools.

III. Parents' Inservice

Present your inservice sessions to parents whenever possible and let them help you develop materials. We have found it useful to include parents among the school inservice audiences, too. They need to know what you are telling the schools about their children and they want to be able to convey correct information when they discuss in parent meetings the ways they can be more effective in their role as child advocate. Support from parents in times of need can have a powerful effect on the child and the school.

IV. Students' Inservice

In describing various types of inservice programs, we have saved the best for last. The "student inservice" is our staff's favorite.

---

*This last is especially important in Minnesota, where hearing impaired students are integrating at the first-grade level. As a result of the family-oriented infant program for hearing impaired children 0-3½ in Minneapolis public schools and in community agency programs prior to 1958, a great many children with severe and profound losses are integrated in the primary grades. The Minneapolis preprimary program also serves as the laboratory facility of the UNISTAPS Model Demonstration Project for Hearing-Impaired Children, 0-6, and their Parents, Minnesota Department of Education, St. Paul (P.L.91-230, Title VI, Part C, Section 623).

Normal-hearing peers can be the hearing impaired student's greatest support or severest handicap. The curiosity of hearing children must be respected and satisfied. Too often, well-meaning adults, including parents, try to keep the hearing aid and the hearing loss a secret from the classroom, fearful that the hearing impaired student might feel "different." But the child *is* different, and the other children know this: the important thing is that they understand and keep this difference in proper perspective. If we as adults continue to treat the hearing impairment and the hearing aids as something to be ashamed of and embarrassed about, we will promote that very attitude among the child's peers — and it is the hearing impaired student who suffers. The more his friends know about the hearing impaired child in their classroom, what his hearing aid looks and sounds like, and what things can help him hear better, the better able they will be to understand, accept, and help the child. Understanding and acceptance make integration work. Differences are O.K.

The hearing consultant should meet with the hearing impaired child prior to the inservice session, and they should plan it together. As much responsibility as possible is given to the child. He teaches the class about his aid, how it works, what it costs, how it is put on, what its limitations are, why it whistles, and how he takes care of it. The consultant acts as the back-up expert. Working hearing aids are passed around for a touch and listen session. Children are fortunately uninhibited about asking questions, and when they quickly realize that *you* think it is all right to talk about the aid — they do the same. The adults in the room (teachers and parents are invited) learn a great deal, too, for many of the questions they are reluctant to ask may be answered.

Conclusion

Suggestions have been given for general and specific inservicing of mainstream staff, parents, nurses, audiologists, and students. These, of course, are merely guidelines and rationale around which each district can develop its own materials or make use of prepared items. No matter what is included in an inservice session — no matter what the content or format — the focus should be on developing a healthy, knowledgeable, accepting attitude toward hearing, hearing loss, hearing aids, and hearing impaired students. Hopefully, the effect will be the provision of a realistic educational environment in which hearing impaired children *can* function effectively because the staff and students accept and respect them as regular members of the student body in their neighborhood schools.

Suggested Guidelines for School Staff Preparation
Prior to Case Management Conference with Title III Itinerant Consultant

1. School team should clarify problem and define solutions already attempted.
2. Member of staff should review cumulative file, including health and screening records, and have information available.

3. Team should have knowledge of parents' awareness of and feelings about child's problem (also their attitude toward school).
4. Tutor and speech pathologist can bring their files, including any test results obtained by either.
5. Speech pathologist can bring tape recording of child's spontaneous speech if consultant cannot observe child directly.
6. Teacher can bring child's classroom folder (including samples of classroom work) to discuss performance over time.
7. Teacher can provide a sample of an uncorrected creative writing exercise (if available) so that she can describe written language level.
8. If social problem is a concern, a sociogram would be helpful prior to conference.
9. To serve your district most efficiently, we strongly suggest inviting other staff as *observers*. It would be a good learning experience and make good use of the consultant's time.

(Note: See also pages 271 and 272 for teacher and administrator questionnaires used in inservice training and preparation for integration.)

LIST OF RESOURCES

Film—*Lisa, Pay Attention!*
For information write: Bono Film Service, Inc., 1042 Wisconsin Avenue, N.W., Washington, D.C. 20007.

Hearing Aid Demonstration
Audio tape, $3.00 per tape.
Write to: A.V. Resources, Engineering Division, Room 70, Shops Building, 319 15 Ave., S.E., Minneapolis, Minnesota 55455.

How They Hear
Long play record.
Write to: Gordon Stowe Assts., Custom Records Dept., RCA Victor, Northbrook, Illinois.

Title III Interdistrict Project for Hearing Impaired Children.
Available materials and slide-tape programs:

Team Approach slide-tape program
PACT-Procedural Adaptations for Classroom Teachers, Tutors, and Therapists.
(A slide-tape program)
Hand-outs for Team and PACT
List of questions to promote discussion
Teacher-Tutor communication form
Guidelines for preparing for Case Management Conference
Entire packet of materials for hand-out to staff.

Write to: Anne Seltz, Project Director, Title III Interdistrict Project for Hearing Impaired Children, Minneapolis Public Schools, Special Education Division, 807 N.E. Broadway, Minneapolis, Minnesota 55413.

J. PAUL RUDY
JOHN G. NACE

19

A Transitional Instrument

Selection of Hearing Impaired Students for Integration

To assist those responsible for referring and placing hearing impaired students into schools and classes for the hearing, a transitional instrument was developed at the Sterck School. Using quantitative scores in the areas of intelligence, achievement, social maturity, and hearing loss, this instrument may be employed as a predictor of a student's potential success or failure in a regular school.

A review of literature on integration suggests that students have been selected for placement in integrated programs largely on the basis of their intelligence, achievement, communication, and coping skills. Although these criteria or guidelines are fairly consistent in their content among the various schools where they are used, they are usually not assigned values which might lend themselves to measurement and quantitative comparison. In response to this need, the Sterck School for the Hearing Impaired (Newark, Delaware) has devised an instrument to be used for quantitatively measuring integrative (transitional) potentials of hearing impaired students.

When the integration program of Sterck School was first initiated in 1969, the selection of participating students was made in much the same manner as in most other schools. The students' records were examined, staff meetings were conducted, and administrative decisions were made. To provide supportive help for the students in the Sterck transitional program, an appropriation was made through Title III of the Elementary and Secondary Education Act of 1965 to

---

Mr. Rudy is the former Director and Principal of the Sterck School for the Hearing Impaired, Newark, Delaware. Dr. Nace is Coordinator of Special Projects at the School.

implement a project entitled, "Modified Staffing for the Education of the Deaf." When, after a year's trial period, the 1970-71 program was being planned, modifications were made in the requirements and responsibilities of these supportive staff members (Learning Counselors); among their functions, they were to assist in the development of a Transitional Instrument for evaluating students' potential adjustment to integration. This was to be done under the guidance of Mr. Willis Proctor, consulting psychologist.

To carry out the evaluation of individual students prior to placement, a committee was formed consisting of the psychologist, guidance counselor, Learning Counselor, nurse, classroom teacher, and others concerned with a particular student. The committee functioned with information assembled by the guidance counselor on a profile sheet. These data concerned the areas of intelligence, achievement, social adjustment, and hearing loss. Arbitrary values were assigned to each of the four areas based on the means and standard deviations of the Sterck population. Individual placement was determined on the probability of success as reflected by the cumulative quotient a student received when the Transitional Instrument was applied to his test scores and evaluations. The guideline quotients for the program are shown in Figure 1.

The areas of intelligence, achievement, and hearing loss (in most instances) provide objective means of measurement; the various tests provide quantitative scores. Thus, few problems are encountered in assembling evaluative information in these areas. However, the area of social adjustment is not as readily assessable — it is more subjective in nature, and test scores are not as easily available. Members of the Sterck staff thus developed a Social Adjustment Scale (Figure 2). It presents 25 characteristics to be evaluated by the teachers on a point system. The result is a quantitative score which can then be used along with the scores in intelligence, achievement, and hearing loss.

Applying the Transitional Instrument

The following might be the procedure used with a student being considered for a transitional program. His records show an IQ of 115, which according to the instrument (Figure 1) gives him 20 points toward a transitional quotient (TQ). In achievement, he has a quotient of 88, which adds 20 points to his TQ. His score on the Social Adjustment Scale totals 70, adding 20 more points; and his hearing loss is 65 dB, entitling him to 20 additional points. Summarized, his profile work sheet would look like this.

	AREA	SCORE	TQ
I.	Intelligence	115 quotient	20 points
II.	Achievement	88 quotient	20 points
III.	Social Adjustment	70 points	20 points
IV.	Hearing Loss (ISO)	65 db loss	20 points
		Transitional Quotient	80 points

Figure 1

Guideline Quotients for Transitional Program

I. Intelligence
    Quotients 125 and above   - 25 points
    Quotients 110-124   - 20 points
    Quotients 95-109   - 15 points
    Quotients 80-94   - 10 points

II. Achievement*
    1. Ginn Vocabulary Survey
    2. Wide Range Achievement Test Reading, Spelling, Arithmetic
    3. Stanford Achievement Test
       Word Meaning, Paragraph Meaning. Science and Social Studies, Spelling, Word Study
       Skills, Language, Arithmetic Computation, Arithmetic Concepts.
    Quotients 100 and above   - 25 points
    Quotients 88-99   - 20 points
    Quotients 76-87   - 15 points
    Quotients 64-75   - 10 points

III. Social Adjustment Scale (Teacher's evaluation)
    Scores 80-100   - 25 points
    Scores 69-79   - 20 points
    Scores 59-68   - 15 points
    Below 58-   - 10 points

IV. ISO Standards, 1964 - Pure Tones
    Mild Hearing Loss (20-40 dB)   - 25 points
    Moderate Hearing Loss (41-65 dB)   - 20 points
    Severe Hearing Loss (66-80 dB)   - 15 points
    Profound Hearing Loss (81-100 dB)   - 10 points

Intelligence + Achievement* + Social Adjustment Score + Hearing Level = Cumulative Quotient:
    75 and above   - Success Probable
    50-74   - Success Borderline
    49-25   - Success Improbable
    24 and below   - Transition not advised

*Quotient used in the achievement testing is the highest figure attained in any area and *not* an average of the quotients.

When the TQ of 80 points is compared with the "standards" on the guideline outline, it is found that the student qualifies for a transitional program on a "success probable" level.

At the conclusion of the second year of the integration project, evaluations of the transitional students were conducted by the Learning Counselors. These were in the form of teachers' marks and questionnaires directed to the co-operating teachers, homeroom teachers, Learning Counselors, hearing peers, the hearing impaired students themselves, and their parents. On the basis of the results of these evaluations, the transitional program was considered successful.

Figure 2

Social Adjustment Scale

Characteristics	Above Average	Average	Below Average
Self-concept			
Accepts others			
Is sensitive			
Understands others			
Accepts criticism			
Conformist			
Behaviorally agreeable			
Completes assignments			
Is attentive			
Uses time well			
Is competitive			
Sedentary in interests			
Is physically skillful			
Completes written work			
Work is organized			
Reacts positively to success			
Independent			
Makes decisions			
Plans well, is logical			
Is relevant and appropriate			
Organizes ideas			
Draws conclusions			
Makes inferences			
Generalizes			
Pays attention to detail			
	4 points for each factor	2 points for each factor	0 points for each factor

Validation of the Instrument

During the third year of the integration program (1971-72), it was considered appropriate to evaluate the Transitional Instrument to determine its validity. The research design for the validation was developed by Mr. Neil F. Walzl, statistician. As a first step in the validation, 10 teachers of hearing impaired students in the cooperating elementary school (Jennie Smith School in Newark) were asked to list observable criteria which they felt were important factors in *any* student's becoming a successful learner. Factors were identified and grouped, and it was found that no characteristics were listed that could not be included in one or another of these four headings: ability, prior achievement, social maturity, and communication skills. A rating scale was then developed from the frequency distribution of the factors and weighted accordingly (Fig.3).

Before using this second set of criteria to evaluate the Transitional Instrument, the reliability of the second system had to be determined. To this end, 25 students were selected at random from the fifth grade of Jennie Smith School.

Figure 3

Rating Scale for Factors Contributing to Educational Adjustment

Teacher _____

Subject _____

Name of Student _____

	High	Above Average	Average	Below Average	Low

ABILITY
Can organize knowledge and make it functional
Sorts out relevant and important facts from opinion
Can classify, categorize and understand relationships
Has sufficient ability to proceed at rate comparable
    to group
Can form generalizations, draw conclusions, based on
    known facts

PRIOR ACHIEVEMENT
Adjusts to learning level of group
Is cognitively ready to work at level assigned
Has sufficient experiential background to succeed at
    assigned level
Uses previously learned facts, concepts, in a new context
Can apply newly learned facts to a previous situation
Finds some success in any learning situation

SOCIAL MATURITY
Works and plays well with other children
Has completed socialization process in recess as well as
    classroom
Shows interest and is motivated to participate in class-
    room activities
Copes with problems, new or strange situations,
    appropriate to age level
Has self-confidence to work on own
Does not manifest anxiety due to outside pressures
Appears to have a well-developed self-concept
Is aware of others around him
Shows adequate self-control
Takes correction well
Relates well to teachers and adults

COMMUNICATION SKILLS
Pays attention
Adds useful information in informal discussion
Strives to communicate with peers and adults
Asks for help when it is needed
Writes legibly
Comprehends what is being said
Expresses ideas effectively in more than one media
(Speaking, drawing, demonstrating)

Each of the five teachers responsible for their instruction was asked to rate the students independently using the second system. After one month, they were asked to repeat the task, and tests were performed on the data following each rating period. 1) The mean, standard deviation, and range were computed for each set of teacher's scores, and an average score was computed for each student. 2) An analysis of variance (one-way) was conducted to determine if the variation among teacher means could not reasonably be attributed to chance. 3) The Pearson product moment correlation coefficient was computed between ratings of the teachers and between each teacher's rating and the average ratings. 4) After the second rating, the Pearson product correlation was computed between the first and second rating for each teacher. Based on the outcome of these tests*, it was the conclusion of the investigators that the second evaluation system would be used to investigate the validity of the Transitional Instrument.

At the completion of the school year, the hearing impaired students who had been placed in regular classrooms for hearing students were rated by their regular classroom teachers using the second system to evaluate their success. A study was then done to determine whether there was a correlation between the teachers' ratings and the total value obtained from the Transitional Instrument. Correlations were also found using the teachers' ratings and the partial scores of the predictor scale.

The conclusions drawn by the investigators, based upon the above procedures and data, were that the Transitional Instrument can be used effectively for placement of hearing impaired students into classes for the hearing, but that the correlation of this instrument with the actual achievement of the students needs further investigation. It is recommended that the study be replicated, placing hearing impaired students whose transitional quotients predict success, as well as those whose quotients do not predict success, into regular classrooms. This type of comparative study would be necessary to confirm or deny the conclusions presented.

*The data showed that teachers' ratings (means) did not vary greatly between the first and second administrations, and there were small differences in the standard deviations and the ranges, also. The coefficients of correlation between the ratings of the teachers, and those between individual teachers and the average ratings, were high. When the correlations between the first and second ratings for each teacher were computed, they were also high, with an average of .98. These data, in table form, with a more complete description and discussion can be obtained from the authors at Sterck School.

REFERENCES

Cruickshank, W.M., & Johnson, G.O. (Eds.) *Education of exceptional children and youth.* (2nd ed.) Englewood Cliffs, N.J.: Prentice Hall, Inc., 1968.

Directory of services for the deaf in the United States. *American Annals of the Deaf,* 1970, **115,** 324-364.

Yearsley, M. The education of the deaf: Its present state, with suggestions as to its future modifications and development. *American Annals of the Deaf,* 1911, **56** (3,5), 284-323, 484-499.

Part IV

The Preprimary Years

Finger Paint on the Hearing Aid

Written by his mother, this is an account of a young deaf boy's experiences and growth while attending a private nursery with hearing children. His contacts with the children offered the opportunity for social interaction with peers and gave him the chance to listen to normal speech of children his own age. It also provided a challenge to compete for attention by using his own voice and exposed him to conversation involved with child-centered activities.

"You mean you send him down the street to school with regular children?" asked my curious neighbor. "But how does he manage? How do they understand him? Are the teachers specially trained? How do they ever know what to do?"

When our little boy was 3 years old he attended a program for deaf preschool children. It was an excellent program, offering the best in language stimulation and auditory training. However, as is the case in every special school following the rubella epidemic, there were too many children for the number of available teachers and classrooms; each child could only attend two half-days a week. Mark was extremely active, raring to go, and wanting to learn.

We "talked, talked, talked" as much as we could at home about Mark's experiences as they occurred, but we felt he could use more school than the two half-days available at the time. The hearing center and our pediatrician agreed. Also, we were committed to an oral education; we wanted as much oral stimulation as possible, and we felt that Mark would be encouraged to talk if he could spend some time in an organized group of hearing children.

Mrs. Stern is the Editor of Ideas for Families, *a publication for parents at the Lexington School for the Deaf. She is the mother of four children, one of whom is deaf, and resides in Westport, Connecticut.*

It happened that there was a nursery school located at the end of our street. It was well-equipped and offered a wide variety of indoor and outdoor activities. After talking to neighbors and friends who had children enrolled in the school, I went to visit the director.

Only the mother of a deaf child will understand my feelings as I approached this perfectly ordinary school on our own street and sat in the waiting room. That was the whole point. This school was for ordinary children and our child was different. These children could hear and ours was profoundly deaf. These children could speak, and Mark, although he understood a lot through speechreading, as yet had no speech at all. Did I have the courage to ask this school to take our child; and if I asked, what would they say?

Fortunately, the director of the nursery school was a person of unusual understanding. She wasn't afraid of a child who was different; in fact, she was most encouraging. There had never been a deaf child in the school, but there were some children who had other special problems. She believed that Mark could make it.

We discussed various practicalities, and it was agreed that Mark would attend school in a class of children his own age, three afternoons a week. Before he started, however, the director went with me to visit Mark's class of deaf children, and we had a conference with the principal of the hearing center. They discussed what help they could give the teachers of Mark's new class in the nursery school (there were two teachers for a class of 18 children).

The principal of the hearing center advised that we be as simple as possible: "Tell the nursery school teacher to treat Mark like any other child, but to remember two things — get down at his level if you want to give him the most chance of understanding; don't talk to his back because he simply won't hear."

The instructions seemed a little too brief to me at the time, but I was to learn that they represented excellent advice. With 18 other children in a class, you cannot expect a teacher, no matter how interested, to learn all the information that we, as parents of deaf children, had been absorbing for two, three, or four years. It was best to give the simplest, most important directions and let the rest take care of itself. Later we added, "Accept whatever Mark tries to say, and repeat it in full sentences."

The rest *has* taken care of itself. When Mark first came home, smiling from ear to ear, with bright green finger paint smeared on his shoes, his nose, his hair, and his earmolds, I gasped. But the finger paint wiped right off the earmolds, and the smile stayed on.

The First Few Months

The teachers admitted they were nervous at first. Why not — they had never known a deaf child before, and here was one in their class. Nevertheless, they treated Mark normally and did not pass their early nervousness on to the children. With only a few suggestions, the children quickly learned that they had to walk around in front of Mark to get his attention; if they were impatient, they tugged his overall strap, and he turned right around to see what was going on. There were a few comments about his hearing aids. One child said: "Well, he could hear better if only they'd take those plugs out of his ears." Within a week or so, however, the aids were accepted as part of his clothing.

Mark had to watch a great deal to see what people were doing; no one was more anxious than he to be part of the system. He learned to leave his jacket and snow boots in the right little locker, to put the blocks away on the shelf, to find a plastic smock if he wanted to paint.

He was not interested in sitting in a circle during story time; he couldn't hear the story and he saw no reason to sit still. The teacher solved that by giving him the job of laying out paper napkins and milk straws while the others were listening to the book; it made him feel important and useful and stopped a potential discipline problem. (When he was older, he could sit still longer and did join the group.)

In the first months, he seemed always to be a half-beat behind the others — when they went to get their coats, wash their hands, etc. After a while he picked up enough visual clues so that he no longer seemed behind. He was first to grab the bird seed when it was time to feed the parakeet. He was right out the door when it was time for outside play. When the children made a choo-choo train with their chairs, he was there. When they pretended to be airplanes, going down the slide, he was an airplane, too. When they were playing house, he was happy to push the carriage as the mama or to climb right in and be the baby. He had melted into the group, as one of them, a perfectly ordinary child who happened to be wearing hearing aids.

Developing Communication Skills

One day over a year later, when Mark was just beginning to use expressive language, he was seated at the table during milk time and turned to hold up his empty cup toward the teacher, saying "Mo mil!" (more milk). The little 4-year-old girl sitting next to him drained her own milk container, crumpled the cup, and then commented matter-of-factly to nobody in particular: "Oh, Mark talks now. When did they teach him — yesterday?"

It is impossible to measure the value of having a deaf child attend nursery school with hearing children. First of all, the parents should not delude themselves into believing that such an experience will take the place of the specific language and speech training a deaf child needs. But as a supplementary education, its worth is inestimable. You are giving your child a chance to listen to children talk as they dig, eat, rest, play house, paint, swing, slide, hammer, pound, cut, paste, push, pull, laugh, tickle, climb, and fall. These children are speaking in full sentences using normal inflection. Because they are his size, they are automatically talking at your child's level. They are talking about things he is interested in because they are children his own age.

Did Mark learn to lipread the word "carrot" because we repeated it to him every time he looked at a picture of a carrot, or because the nursery class had a rabbit in the room and the children crowded around the cage every day, clamoring, "Let me hold the carrot!"? Does he recognize the word "blue" because he was introduced to it formally in a speechreading lesson, or because we pointed it out to him when he put on his blue socks in the morning, or because one of the children in the class wiggled next to him at the painting easel and said, "Give me the blue paint. It's my turn to use blue!"? We will never know. But being exposed to language in these meaningful situations has been a great enrichment for Mark and a stimulus for him to be oral.

Preschool programs designed for deaf children *can* include all of these creative activities; some of them do. However, there is no childish conversation for the children to imitate. The facilities are not available. Moreover, it is difficult for any teacher of the deaf whose first job is to encourage language and teach speechreading to clean up finger paint from the floor at the same time.

Whatever the availability of special education facilities, there is a lot to be said for allowing a deaf child to mix with hearing children at an early age. No matter what form his future education might take, this early exposure is bound to have a positive effect on his social adjustment and his motivation to talk. The deaf child in the hearing nursery will observe hundreds of objects and experiment with dozens of materials. He will expand his social horizons on many levels by watching as well as participating. Two, three, or five years later, when he has acquired the language he could not possibly have had during the nursery years, he will draw on the bank of his preschool experiences and fit the language to the impressions he has absorbed and stored.

Alternatives to the Nursery School

If there isn't a nursery school in your community, or you cannot make an arrangement with one, there are other alternatives that will give your child some of the same benefits. You might be able to organize a play group with mothers in your neighborhood that would rotate from house to house. If you are the innovator and do the beginning organization, the mothers of hearing children will probably be glad to join. If there is a summer recreation program for preschoolers at the local playground, you might speak to the director, offering to brief the counselors on how to help your child fit in. If you are near a church that has a preschool or play group, it may be particularly interested in including your child. Church preschools usually make an effort to serve the residents of the neighborhood surrounding them.

In Mark's case, he was extremely lucky to have the added social advantage of a school in our own neighborhood, attended by a number of neighborhood children. Mark was able to make friends in school with the children he saw naturally after school and during vacation. We were happy that some of the teachers from the hearing center and nursery school exchanged visits and ideas, which everyone felt were most worthwhile. But in a wider sense, the greatest, though unmeasurable, value of the whole experience may have been to the hearing children. If we're ever going to break down the barriers against the "deaf and dumb," the early years are the years in which to do it. If a child has played next to a deaf child in a sandbox, has built a castle with him, and has spoken to him, won't he find it more natural one day, when he is grown, to speak to a deaf adult? Or even before that, won't he be more willing to accept another child who may be different in some other way?

Suggestions for Parents

Any parent interested in enrolling a little deaf child in a nursery school with hearing children might find these suggestions helpful:

Don't telephone a school with which you have had no prior contact and ask the million-dollar question, "Will you take a deaf child?" It's a disconcerting and unexpected question. The easiest answer is, "No." Chances are the person who answers the phone has nothing to do with admission policies anyway.

Do telephone and ask to visit the school at a convenient time. Look and see if it is the kind of school you would want a child of yours to attend. Are there enough teachers? Enough space, light, and air? Is there a sympathetic, interested atmosphere? Do you have friends with children enrolled who might be able to give further information? Sit down and speak to the director when she has enough time for you. Tell her about your child. Let her ask questions. Try to explain, without too many technicalities, what you mean by exposing your child to an oral atmosphere.

Don't expect your child to receive all sorts of special considerations just because he has a handicap. It may be possible to arrange some exceptions (in Mark's case he was allowed to attend only three days a week instead of the usual five because he was in the hearing center school for the other two days); but generally your child should be able to follow any reasonable program planned for children his own age. If you request too many concessions you will not be taking full advantage of the situation.

Do demonstrate your child's abilities to follow simple directions and to mix with other children. Your own positive attitude toward his abilities and his limitations will be transmitted to the teacher, to the children, and, ultimately, to their parents. Acceptance by all these people will put your child at ease and help him get more out of the experience. If you show your doubts, everyone else will feel them, and your child will surely feel "out."

Don't tell the teacher every bit of information that you've ever read in *The Volta Review* and other publications dealing with hearing impairment. She is neither a trained teacher of the deaf nor the parent of a child with a handicap. She cannot possibly absorb it all at once. If she feels somewhat inadequate with this different child, a flood of strange information will only make her feel more so.

Do be ready to "clue in" the teacher about some of the experiences your child may be having outside of school. If your child has begun to speechread, perhaps you can supply her with a list of the words he recognizes. If he has begun to acquire speech, yóu might point out to her what some of his expressive sounds mean. She will probably become interested and ask you further questions. Try not to squeeze in these discussions during class time. She has responsibilities to the other children. Also, remember they can overhear conversations about your child's "specialness."

Don't think that once your child is enrolled in the school, all your participation is over.

Do remember that there has to be a continuing, sometimes changing relationship between you, the teachers, and the director. Ideally, the hearing center or whatever special education institution you use should be brought into the relationship, too. There are bound to be some snags. A change of teachers, a change of classrooms, or schedule alterations can be disconcerting to your deaf child and cause behavior problems. It is your job as parent to be sure the communication lines are kept open — to maintain a spirit of cooperation and an openness to change.

Don't fool yourself into thinking that just because your preschool deaf child can integrate with hearing children he will not need many years of special work in language, speech, and auditory training. Think of the nursery school experience as an additional, perhaps very important part of his early education, but not as a substitute for specific language training.

And, finally, **do** remember that much of what your child gains from the integrated experience may be difficult to see, at first. When everybody wants integration to work, they may want too much too soon. Parents of *young* hearing impaired children, especially, are often pressured into feeling that there is not a day to lose in saturating their child with language and meaningful experiences, and they anxiously measure all progress in bits of language produced. It helps to think of the integrated nursery experience not only as a situation to stimulate immediate language, but also as an opportunity to build a storehouse of information for *the language that is to come.*

EDITOR'S NOTE: An official in the Department of Education of the State of Minnesota informs us that state aids encourage local school districts to underwrite the cost of tuition for deaf and hard of hearing children in private nursery schools, provided the nursery school teacher in the private school is certified at the nursery, kindergarten, and primary level by the Minnesota Department of Education. In the regional programs offered by the Minneapolis, St. Paul, and Duluth public schools, for instance, deaf children around 3 years of age are in regular nursery schools, with tuition being paid by the local district where the child's family resides. The nursery school experience supplements individual and group parent guidance and child tutoring supplied by the teachers of the deaf in the preschool program of the public schools.

The author wishes to express appreciation for the time, interest, and effort contributed by Miss Eleanor Taussig, formerly the Principal of Children's Hearing and Speech Center, Washington, D.C.; Miss Barbara-Jeanne Seabury, formerly the Director of the nursery school; and the staffs of the schools for their assistance in making this article possible. Miss Taussig is presently Instructional Advisor, Delaware County, Pennsylvania, Speech-Hearing Unit; and Miss Seabury is now Director of Children's Activities Services, Children's Hospital Medical Center, Washington, D.C.

21

WINIFRED H. NORTHCOTT

Candidate for Integration

A Hearing Impaired Child in a Regular Nursery School

A description is furnished of techniques which can be employed by the nursery school teacher during music, story time, and free play to increase a hearing impaired child's comprehension of language and to model and expand his attempts at verbal self-expression. The goal is the dynamic use of residual hearing and motivation of the hearing impaired child to use well-inflected jargon and natural sentences in play and in communication with others. The child's adjustment to a regular nursery school will be aided by periodic visits of a special educator to orient the nursery school staff to the child's special needs through demonstration and discussion.

Preprimary teachers are seeking increased support in working effectively with hearing impaired children presently enrolling in today's nursery schools and kindergartens. Following an epidemic of German measles (rubella) which produced nearly 30,000 newborn infants with handicaps, the nation responded by enactment of the Handicapped Children's Early Education Assistance Act of 1968 (P.L. 90-538). Nursery school experience with normal children is an integral component of the exemplary preschool programs presently funded under this law. They address to the child development and special education needs of the 0-5 group while serving to encourage replication by local and state agencies assigning a high priority to preprimary programs (Calvert, 1969).

When a hearing impaired child enters a nursery school for hearing children he is enveloped by an absorbing world of action and thought and creativity gaily

Dr. Northcott is Consultant, Early Childhood Education Program for Hearing Impaired Children, 0–6, Minnesota State Department of Education, St. Paul.

wrapped in color and sound. Here he is offered the valuable experience of listening to the natural speech of children his own age and interest level presented with a wide range of pitch and lively intonation patterns.

Since the language concepts presented are linked with child-centered activities at the moment of occurrence, the deaf or hard of hearing child begins to think, to reason, and to conceptualize in terms of words. He gradually becomes word-minded although his expressive vocabulary may be extremely limited. This early bombardment of auditory experience and language encourages the child's dynamic use of residual hearing. It makes him a more effective hearing aid user with resulting improvement in speech and development of more normal language patterns (Simmons, 1968; Pollack, 1967).

In nursery school the hearing impaired child also gains vital impressions about appropriate behavior options for coping with the pressures and challenges of daily living. Here he learns concepts of size, color, and relationships. The explosion of child-oriented experience and teacher-directed instruction encourages him to become a better learner and problem-solver. It develops his coping skills, allowing him to devise strategies for organizing and storing information logically. Through the exercise of initiative, curiosity, and persistence he becomes self-disciplined.

An integrated nursery program furnishes parents with the first opportunity to realistically assess and appreciate their hearing impaired child's abilities and assets as well as his limitations. Frequently, it serves the important purpose of decreasing an excessively dependent relationship which may have developed between a mother and her young hearing handicapped child.

As for the children in the nursery group who have normal hearing, Dr. Evaline Omwake, President of NAEYC* and professor of child development at Connecticut College, draws from observation of physically handicapped children enrolled in the New London campus nursery to assure us that "children take little notice of a playmate's handicap. Acceptance of the group hinges largely upon constructive contribution to the group's activity."

A Cascade of Services

Perhaps the challenge of integrating a child who may still be an infant linguistically but sophisticated about the business of living will seem less formidable if we examine the cascade of services presently available at the preschool level for a hearing impaired child and his family. The instructional program is directed by a specialist in speech and hearing, and includes:

- parent counseling and guidance in group and individual therapy sessions
- individual tutoring (acoustic and language stimulation)
- home visitation
- preschool group educational activities with hearing children.

*National Association for the Education of Young Children

The placement of a hearing impaired child in a nursery for hearing children is not automatic. It is not suitable if 1) the hearing loss was recently diagnosed and there has been no parent guidance to ensure transfer and maintenance of educational gains through home stimulation, and 2) the child is not yet aware that his hearing aid brings in meaningful environmental sounds, including speech, or that he must look at faces to gain understanding from moving lips and facial expression. The degree of parent and special education involvement and cooperation is the primary determinant rather than the severity of the hearing loss.

Upon admission, the child's interests and abilities rather than his linguistic level should determine his assignment to a suitable group of hearing children. The presence of a single deaf or hard of hearing child in a nursery school would ensure optimum conditions for his cognitive development, but practical experience indicates an effective ratio to be one hearing impaired child to four with normal hearing.

Goals for the Hearing Impaired Child

It is expected that the child will wear his hearing aid daily, with confidence, monitoring the volume of his voice as the situation requires and using his voice purposively to get attention either with or without the presence of meaningful speech. The primary goal, however, is comprehension of language, although we delight in spontaneous speech, accept it, and expand it. At this age we are not concerned with the *quality* of speech produced by a child whose expressive language may range from babbling to telegraphic speech or more complex transformations. Since the body-type hearing aids worn today can deliver linguistic significance to even a profoundly deaf child, the challenge is to give him sufficient listening and speaking experience so that he can build up a large receptive vocabulary and begin to generate his own sentences by inducing the rules of his language. For a child with normal hearing this requires months of absorption of speech before he comprehends its meaning without situational clues or says his first words spontaneously.

Welcoming the Newcomer

When a newcomer enters a nursery group, its members look to the teacher for guidance. Is he a new friend or an interloper? In subtle ways your facial expression, muscle tone, the distance between you and the child, and even posture will convey your feelings about him. Let these aspects of meta-communication be consistent with your welcoming greeting.

If the children indicate a natural curiosity about the hearing aid during the first week, you may wish to talk about it briefly and describe the need for protecting it, but not the wearer, from rough-and-tumble play.

Children who talk to the hearing impaired playmate are already at his eye level and they soon learn to face him so he can "hear better." Their sentences are short and pertinent to the situation: "Here's a big one." "See what I made?" "That's mine!" and they are delivered with zestful force. It would not occur to these children to put their hands on the friend's cheek, chest, or throat to coax sounds from him nor to speak without voice (which exaggerates all lip movements) nor shout (the hearing aid does the magnifying). Adults can learn much from observing the naturalness of children.

Early observation of a child's verbal and behavioral response to familiar language will indicate whether he is able to respond by listening alone or whether he requires additional clues from speechreading. It is imperative that a child who has functional residual hearing, regardless of the severity of loss as indicated on an audiogram, make dynamic use of this hearing and be encouraged to listen in order to gain information. You can ensure this by talking to him from a position behind or alongside the child at a distance of approximately 18 inches. "Your turn to feed the fish," you might say, and wait for him to get the fish food. Perhaps he will glance up, not responding, and require a repetition of the phrase. In the same manner, you can reinforce a child's attention to environmental sounds when he looks to you for interpretation. Crash! "The easel tipped over," or, "Billy dropped his truck." Gradually, he will turn in the direction of the sounds and begin to localize their source.

When you are speaking to a child who relies primarily on speechreading, use the same natural, clear voice and normal facial animation but face the light or window so that your lips are easily visible. Lipstick helps, too! The ideal speechreading distance is a deep-knee bend and three feet from the child. Since it is a strain to listen and watch steadily you may want to remind a parent to provide a rest period at home for the toddler who seems fatigued at the close of the nursery day.

These guidelines won't seem formidable once you have put them into practice for a few days. In fact, you'll soon find they dovetail with that line from "Annie Get Your Gun!" — "Doin' what comes naturally." Remember, too, that children are extremely resilient. You can make a lot of mistakes and they will forgive you.

Stimulating Language Comprehension

A child of 3 who has worn his hearing aid for one year has a "listening age" of only one year. In the nursery where everyone talks to him in sentences, circumstances help him to understand the meaning of language related to his play, guided instruction, and observations. "You dropped your book." "It's too big." "That's funny." "You cut your finger."

There is meaningful repetition of verbs such as "pull," for example, associated with action involving the child's toys, clothing, and the games he plays with others. The concept "soft" unfolds in a myriad of dimensions relating to walking, talking, eating ice cream, listening to music, or patting a rabbit.

While the child's expressive language is limited, you will notice a longer auditory attention span and a deepening interest in the situational clues provided by the speaker's eyes and facial expression. Often his behavior is the best evidence of comprehension. Prior to the time a child discriminates in terms of the actual meaning of the words themselves, normal changes in the speaker's pitch, intonation, and stress patterns will furnish him with valuable linguistic information.

If necessary, use your eyes to furnish added meaning to spoken words. You might say, "Throw it in the wastebasket," and if there is no response, glance at it. Give the direction, pause to allow a child time to respond, then add an eye clue if needed. Directions should be given only once. If there is no evidence of understanding through listening or speechreading, do the activity yourself and explain in a simple sentence what you are doing. To illustrate: "Turn the water off, please." Pause for response . . . . then a simple, "I'll turn the water off," and a subsequent turn of the faucet.

Hearing impaired children feel more secure when they know the sequential routine of nursery school. The accompanying language is understood more easily if the same phrases are used for activities which occur daily. "It's time to wash up." "Let's get ready to go outside." "Get your rug for nap time." "It's time to go home." After the child gives evidence of understanding your directions without glancing at his playmates for reassurance, the phrases can be varied for added depth of meaning.

Encouraging Expressive Language

As a hearing impaired child begins the search for a basic phrase structure in an attempt to unlock the linguistic code (Brown & Bellugi, 1964; McNeill, 1966) he will find his first information in the prosodic patterns (rhythm, pitch, stress) of the speech he hears. Later he will respond to the content or lexical words which have higher acoustic power and carry the primary stress.

At the same time he will be using jargon with increasingly normal quality and inflection in order to make his wishes known. Accept the child's gestures, pointing, facial expressions, soundless speech, as well as his words and phrases however inadequately they convey his ideas.

The important point to remember is that at each stage he depends upon appropriate verbal reinforcement and expansion to supplement his imperfect audition and sufficient experience to give it meaning.

To illustrate:

> Child: "eeeeeeeeee" (Holding up a paper pumpkin ripped in two)
> Teacher: "It tore. Too bad!"
> Child: "dudududud" (Holding out a pair of scissors and paper)
> Teacher: "Help me, please."
> Child: "Mell" (Offering a flower)
> Teacher: "Mmmmm. It smells good!"
> Child: "moh-pee" (Holding out his cup)
> Teacher: "I want some more juice, please."

Child: "Paint fell over"

Teacher: "The paint spilled. Wipe it up." (Handing him a cloth)

A child should be held responsible for the well-inflected jargon, words, or phrases he can express independently. He will only learn to use them in appropriate situations if you wait for his vocal expressions rather than anticipate his needs; otherwise, you will destroy his motivation to talk. If you ask, "Do you want a turn?" and the child nods, your response should be, "Tell me, 'It's my turn,' " then wait for him to imitate the phrase before he is permitted to begin the action.

Behavior Management

While you can probably operate on a "double standard" of expectations in the development of communication skills in a hearing impaired child, it is reasonable to expect his behavior, perseverence, and initiative to be comparable to that of others in his group. The concepts, "Yes," "No," "Wait," "After a while," and "Not now," are in natural use daily and must be respected by all members of the group.

Be gentle and consistent in your discipline, but above all be honest. If the hearing impaired child's actions are unsatisfactory, say so. If he doesn't understand your specific verbal scolding, he is reading a great deal from the provoked expression on your face. When you are enthusiastic about his show of independence or verbal expression, let your acknowledgment be a delighted smile, a pat on the head, or an affectionate squeeze along with spoken praise. After all, he cannot extract sufficient comfort and pleasure from an endearing tone of voice.

Music and Story Time

Story time can be a very joyful or frustrating period for a hearing impaired child depending upon his auditory and visual attention span and the extent of his receptive vocabulary. After a reasonable period of experimentation, you will know whether he should be excused to follow a more meaningful activity. If the child stays, his seat should be "front and center," where he can comfortably see and hear the teacher without craning while enjoying the picture shown after each page is read.

The value of music in developing patterns of concentration and listening in young children has long been recognized. All preschoolers learn to enjoy the lively rhythm and movement connected with music and to move freely and expressively in response.

Hard of hearing children will enjoy the actual tones of music while the deaf child responds to the vibrations produced by high and low notes. When children hear or "feel" music describing a leaf falling or an airplane taking off and can translate the sound into motion, it enriches the concepts of high and low, up and down, while providing an opportunity for creative expression (Birkenshaw,

1967). It is helpful to show appropriate pictures to the hearing impaired child to assure correct impressions.

When the children are singing and the teacher is at the piano, let the hearing impaired child stand alongside the piano, resting his arm lightly on the frame above the keyboard so he can see the face of the player and follow the tempo and words being sung by the group.

What Might You Expect of Others?

"Show and Tell" is a sound intellectual exercise for adults as well as children. In developing this presentation, there has been more "tell" than "show." The smooth adjustment of a deaf or hard of hearing child into a regular nursery school will require an early visit from the specialist in speech and hearing (a teacher of the deaf, speech and hearing clinician, or audiologist) who has assumed the leadership role in comprehensive special education planning and can describe the child's special needs through demonstration and discussion. At this time, the substance of prior medical, otological, and audiological evaluations should be shared with you.

A nursery school staff should expect an invitation to periodic inservice meetings where they can gain added knowledge about the auditory defect itself and the implications for training of residual hearing, the developmental stages of language growth in children, and the care and management of an individual hearing aid.

All parents should be welcomed as occasional visitors to ensure carry-over of nursery school experiences into the home and observation of their child's interaction with others. Notes pinned to the hearing impaired child's collar by his teacher and parent make certain both home and school appreciate and reinforce the important events in a child's life. (I'm reminded of the child who appeared in school with her best party dress on, all ruffles and bows, over blue jeans. Mother's note read, "This certainly wasn't *my* idea!") The child's favorite songs and stories can be repeated at home and by the tutor if there is a routine three-way exchange of information.

Transfer of the hearing impaired child to a more appropriate educational setting requires a comprehensive case conference to which the nursery teacher is invited as well as specialists who provide additional components of diagnostic and rehabilitative services to the preschooler and his family. In this way a consensus can be reached which ensures congruence of realistic objectives and subsequent educational programming.

A few hearing impaired children will advance to their neighborhood kindergarten with supplemental instruction in speech and language while the child who has made minimal language gains and is functionally deaf will move to a class taught by an appropriate specialist in a day or residential program for the deaf.

Thus we encourage the placement of a hearing impaired child in a nursery school for children with normal hearing. Completely absorbed in the sights, sounds, and experiences of the moment, and surrounded by children whose laughter and chatter are spontaneous, he becomes a child whose ideas and interests far exceed his ability to express them but who regards speech as a natural outlet for expression of his creative intelligence and imagination.

REFERENCES

Bereiter, C., & Engelmann, S. *Teaching disadvantaged children in the preschool.* Englewood Cliffs, New Jersey: Prentice Hall, 1966.

Birkenshaw, L. A suggested programme for using music in teaching deaf children. *Proceedings, International Congress on Oral Education of the Deaf,* New York, 1967. Washington, D.C.: The Alexander Graham Bell Association for the Deaf, 1967. Pp. 1233-1244.

Brown, R. & Bellugi, U. Three processes in the child's acquisition of syntax. In E.H. Lenneberg(Ed.), *New directions in the study of language.* Cambridge, Mass.: MIT Press, 1964.

Cazden, C. Environmental assistances to the child's acquisition of grammar. Unpublished doctoral dissertation, Harvard University, 1965.

Karnes, M., Hodgins, A., & Teska, J.A. An evaluation of two preschool programs for disadvantaged children: A traditional and highly structured experimental preschool. *Exceptional Children,* 1968, 35(5), 667-676.

McNeill, D. The capacity for language acquisition. *The Volta Review,* 1966, 68(1), 17-33.

Moore, O.K., & Anderson, A.R. The responsive environments project. In R.D. Hess, & R. Bear (Ed.), *Early education: Current theory, research, and practice.* Chicago: Aldine Pub. Co., 1967.

Pollack, D. The crucial year: A time to listen. *International Audiology,* 1967, 6(2), 243-247.

Simmons, A. Teaching aural language. *The Volta Review,* 1968, 70(1), 26-30.

(Note: See also pages 268 and 269 for criteria for admission to, continuance in, and demission from an integrated nursery school for 3-year-old hearing impaired children.)

22

THOMAS J. WATSON

Integration of Hearing Impaired Children
In Nursery Schools in England

The term "integration" is discussed with the suggestion that "assimilation" might be a better expression of the desired goal. The present arrangements for "integration" of preschool children in regular classes in England are summarized, with distinction between regular class assignments which are likely to be temporary and those which may be permanent. Criteria for determining the different placements are suggested and illustrative cases are quoted. The effects that full-time placement at this stage may have on both the parents and the child are noted, and it is emphasized that the objectives of any particular placement must be clearly understood by all involved.

Educational provision for hearing impaired children of nursery school age in England is made in a variety of ways. Many residential schools for deaf children have nursery departments; some day schools for deaf and partially hearing children have nursery classes; there are special classes for partially hearing pupils in some ordinary nursery and infant schools; and some hearing impaired children are "integrated" into regular nursery classes. This last-named arrangement is one that has been developed during the past 20 years; the purposes for which it has been made have been varied and have depended on the interpretation of the term "integration." It may therefore be useful at this point to look at the term itself since we cannot determine how effective the placement is unless we know to what end it is being made.

Dr. Watson is a Reader in Audiology and Education of the Deaf, Manchester University, England.

One sociological definition of integration is "the unification of the increasingly diverse and multiple elements in a society." This use of the term assumes that hearing impaired children are a separate group and that the group can come together with the main body of society into a unified whole. However, sociologists use two other terms to describe changes in a relationship of this kind. One is *absorption*, which may be defined as the process of "causing to disappear, as if by swallowing up"; and the other is *assimilation*, which is the act of "rendering alike by environmental influences."* Discounting the further possibility that the groups will remain segregated, there are then three possible relationships between the minority group of the hearing impaired and society in general: integration, absorption, and assimilation. It could be argued from the definitions quoted that the concept of assimilation is a more fruitful goal than the others since it assumes the ability to be a fully participating member of the group interaction processes — at work, at play, and in interpersonal verbal communication.

In reports on integration in the elementary grades, there frequently seems to be a differentiation between what is described as "academic" integration and "social" integration. These two terms reflect the two important aspects of a hearing impaired child's attendance at an ordinary class: his ability to cope with the work or subject matter and his acceptance by and of the hearing members of the class. They further suggest the need to have two scales of reference: a scale of *adaption*, indicating the extent to which the individual from the minority group has adapted to the ways of the majority; and a scale of *acceptance*, indicating how fully the majority accepts the candidate for integration.

Expectations for Integration

When special classes for hearing impaired pupils (known as units) were being established in ordinary schools in England in the 1940's, the intention was that the pupils should progressively integrate into regular classes so that by the time they had reached the end of the primary stage (11+ years of age), they would be completely integrated. In a report on units published in 1967 by the Department of Education and Science, it was noted that "it has become increasingly clear that many pupils will not be able to take their place in the normal classes of an ordinary school when the secondary stage is reached, and units for partially hearing pupils of secondary age have therefore been established."** This change in the character of units has not met with unanimous approval and raises the question of what should be expected from a policy of integration. Should it involve complete or partial adaption in relation to school work; should it require 100% acceptance on the part of the hearing pupils; or does either really matter as long as the child is exposed to normal language and social situations? To some

---

*All definitions taken from *Webster's New International Dictionary, 2nd Edition, 1934.*

**Department of Education and Science, *Units for Partially Hearing Children.* H.M.S.O. London, 1967.

extent the answers to these questions will depend upon the stage of development that the child has reached. This discussion will focus on the preschool stage which, for the present purposes, will be taken to be the period between the ages of 3 and 6.

Those responsible for the management of preschool hearing impaired children in England — be they in local education authorities, school health services, maternity and child welfare services, or audiology clinics — generally have one of three possibilities in mind when they recommend children for placement in ordinary nursery schools or classes. They may hope, or even feel confident, that at the end of this period the child will be able to continue in a normal school environment. They may be reasonably certain that at the age of 4, 5, or 6 the child will need to be placed in a special school. Or, they may consider that the child will probably need to attend a unit for hearing impaired children for a period, but will gradually be able to integrate into the classes of normally hearing pupils in that school and ultimately will receive full-time education there. Their expectations of the extent to which a child is likely to integrate — or to be assimilated — into the nursery class will therefore vary according to the progress of the child.

Achieving Assimilation

Children in the first category — that is, those who have in fact been sufficiently assimilated into the ordinary nursery class to enable them to progress to a regular class in a primary school — are generally those with considerable residual hearing. An example is a boy with the following pure tone thresholds (decibel loss, ISO):

	250 Hz	500 Hz	1000 Hz	2000 Hz	4000 Hz
R. Ear	30	50	65	75	80
L. Ear	25	50	60	65	70

On the other hand, some more severely deaf children, such as the child with the following configuration, have also been successful:

	250 Hz	500 Hz	1000 Hz	2000 Hz	4000 Hz
R. Ear	70	70	75	80	70
L. Ear	70	70	85	85	90

This particular child, however, was above average in intellectual ability and, at age 4½, was only one year below the norm for his chronological age in verbal ability. It should also be pointed out, of course, that hearing loss was by no means the sole criterion upon which placement was determined. The information about hearing thresholds is provided solely as a means of identifying the kind of child under discussion. In these two cases, parental training had been excellent, and support was still first-rate.

It seems likely that for success in this first category, the essential factors are early diagnosis, good early training, continuing home support, a high level of ability, and, perhaps, a flair for language. With these advantages, a child whose hearing loss is severe can be successfully assimilated into an ordinary nursery class. With regard to children with lesser degrees of hearing loss, we would expect assimilation at the nursery stage to be followed by attendance at regular schools in a larger proportion of cases. But it must be stressed that continuing parental support is as important for them as it is for severely deaf children.

In general, with children who have severe and profound losses*, their attendance at ordinary nursery schools or classes is considered to be only temporary. Peripatetic teachers who work with these preschool children and their parents generally visit the children in the nursery school environment to give the regular teachers advice on management. Their expectations for a particular child are related to his stage of communication and linguistic development when he enters the nursery class, and also to the efficiency with which he has learned to use a hearing aid. Most teachers comment that the social play experience is probably the most valuable result of the placement for these children. Exposure to normal language can be valuable for partially hearing children as well as to those who are more severely deaf since the average hearing aid offers a 40-45 dB gain. One large local education authority arranges for a specialist teacher of the deaf and an extra nursery assistant to be on the staff of any nursery which admits a group of hearing impaired pupils. The specialist teacher withdraws the children individually for special help and the additional nursery assistant takes special responsibility for them in group activities, particularly by relating language patterns to their play.

Determining Individual Placement

There is a strong body of opinion in England that placement of a young hearing impaired child in a regular nursery school should be only on a part-time basis. One of the main reasons for this belief is that full-time attendance removes the young child from the influence of and functional interaction with parents for too long a period. Parents may feel that they no longer have any responsibility for the development of communication skills and behavior patterns and may therefore opt out of their contribution to the child's training. Apart from the immediate effect of this on social development and communication in the home, there can be long-term effects in the growth of feelings of isolation in the child. On the other hand, social workers agree that there are cases where full-time attendance can ameliorate a difficult situation — for example, if the mother is overworked, under great stress, or expecting another child.

The decision as to future placement of hearing impaired children who have been integrated into nursery classes or "play groups" must depend upon many facets of demonstrated growth and development: personal and social behavior;

---

*91 dB = profound hearing loss; 71-90 dB - severe hearing loss.

level of receptive and expressive language; contribution to group activity; relationships with adults. For many, the future placement will be attendance at a unit or school for partially hearing children; for some it will be a school or day class for the deaf. If the latter is to be the next stage, the attendance at an ordinary nursery school serves the useful purpose of motivating the hearing impaired child to use verbal expression, however primitive, in imitation of his hearing peers. If the child is not given this opportunity, the issue is prejudged.

Conclusion

From the opening discussion on integration and the subsequent description of the purposes of placement in an ordinary school, it would seem that in this context the term "integration" is a misnomer. At the preprimary level, when the interactions of all children relate primarily to group play, there is a wide range in the degree of acceptance by hearing children. While assimilation is the desired goal, its lack of attainment by some children, for a variety of contributing reasons, does not mean that the placement in an ordinary nursery school is without merit, nor yet that attendance is valueless. It does, however, suggest that purposes must be flexible and that practices must relate closely to the needs of the child and his family. This qualified approval of the custom would seem to be a fair assessment of professional opinion in England. Levels of aspiration must be realistic, and the goals for each child clearly set. On these bases, the concept of integration — or, more specifically, potential assimilation — for preschool hearing impaired children receives wide support.

Have You Thought Of . . .

. . . visiting a self-contained class for the deaf to obtain added information for comparison judgment about the academic and social performance of a hearing impaired child in your classroom? — *Winifred Northcott, St. Paul, Minnesota.*

. . . teaching the awareness of and ability to report the difference between: "I didn't hear," and "I don't understand," or "I don't know," as a first and very important goal for the hearing impaired child? — *Jack Lundgren, Bloomington, Minnesota.*

DOREEN POLLACK
MARIAN ERNST

23

Don't Set Limits:
Expectations for Preschool Children

When hearing impaired preschoolers are fitted with hearing aids at an early age, they should be given the opportunity to learn speech and language through listening. The nursery school is an ideal environment to acquire a basis for interpersonal communication if parents and teachers do not set limits upon their expectations for the child. The development of listening skills with a nearing aid is described, and suggestions are given to the teacher for structuring the auditory environment of the nursery school so that the hearing impaired child can learn to interact and communicate verbally with others.

A young child goes through specific stages in his development when it is easier to acquire certain types of learning than it will ever be again. This applies to auditory and verbal communication almost more than to any other skill; but, until the advent of equipment to test infant hearing and the manufacture of the modern wearable hearing aid, the opportunity to learn speech and language in the early years — by listening, as do normal-hearing children — was denied to the youngster with a hearing loss.

Most hearing impaired infants today can be fitted with hearing aids which, at the very least, offer the opportunity to hear speech at a conversational level. Unfortunately, some professionals, no less than lay people, have been guilty of setting limits on what the hearing impaired child can do, instead of giving him the benefit of the doubt — the opportunity and support to try and succeed! Too

---

Mrs. Pollack is Director of Speech and Hearing Services at Porter Memorial Hospital, Denver, Colorado. Mrs. Ernst is an Educational Audiologist at the Hospital.

often we have overprotected and set our expectation levels low. This is especially true with respect to the child's listening capabilities.

Recently, however, the educational pendulum has begun to swing away from segregation in a special learning environment. It is now felt that the preschooler with a severe hearing loss should go to a regular preschool where he will be encouraged to use his hearing and to have the opportunity for listening to the natural speech and language of his peers. In an environment where everyone else talks, he will be motivated to speak himself. Even if his speech is extremely limited, he will be exposed to the functional language connected with normal child-centered activities; and this will aid his own conceptual development. Ideally, there should be only one hearing impaired child in a preschool class, and his age should be within two years of the average chronological age of the group. Unfortunately, if there are too many "special" preschoolers in one room, they tend to form their own nonverbal group — and very rapidly, too.

The Role of the Teacher

Although the role of the teacher does not really change when a hearing impaired child enters her class, she may find that she has to assume a more active role in structuring the auditory and verbal environment.

Understanding the Hearing Aid

It is the responsibility of the clinician or the parent to demonstrate to the teacher the working of a hearing aid. Worn either behind the ear or in a special harness on the chest, a modern hearing aid is easy to handle. The parent should test the battery or batteries for power before the child leaves home, and it is helpful to leave a spare at school in case the aid stops working. A small wheel on the hearing aid controls the volume: a slight turn, and sound is amplified for the child, just as the volume of a radio is increased with a turn of the dial. Sometimes there is a separate on-off switch, too. The sound is conducted into the ear from the aid through a cord or tube attached to an earmold which must fit snugly into the ear. If the mold slips out a little, a squealing or whistling sound will be heard, but it easy to push the mold back without hurting the ear. The aids should be worn at all times. During water or sandbox play, the aids can be covered with a piece of plastic. If, because of a change in the child's responses to sound, the teacher suspects that the aids are not working, she should alert the parent as soon as possible.

What Can the Teacher Tell the Other Children?

Remembering that youngsters adapt easily to each other, the teacher really need not bring up the subject of a hearing aid until someone notices it and asks questions. It may be days or weeks before this happens unless the aid is worn conspicuously in a large harness outside the clothes. The easiest way to explain the aid is the most direct way. You might choose to say: "Some of us do not see well. Our eyes do not work the way they should, so we have to wear glasses. Bobby's ears do not work the way they should so he has to wear a hearing aid. It makes everything louder so Bobby can hear better. Do you want to listen to it?"

The teacher should explain to the other children that a pull on a cord may cause it to break easily and that a bump on the earmold may hurt Bobby's ears; everyone should be reminded not to shout at Bobby but to talk naturally and close by him so that they can be heard clearly. It is not unusual for some of the other children to want a hearing aid, too!.

How Much Does He Hear?

The questions which most puzzle the first-time teacher of a child with a hearing loss (especially if the child does not respond immediately) are: "Can he really hear me? How much can he hear? Will he talk clearly? Do I have to wait until he looks at me before I speak to him?"

For too long, the word *deafness* has been understood as a total, irreversible condition; that is, you can either hear or not hear. In reality, there are all degrees of hearing loss, from mild to profound, and most children labeled "deaf" do possess residual hearing. This hearing can be actively utilized if the child is fitted with hearing aids at an early age and is given the training necessary to make optimal use of his aided hearing. The deaf child of today does not have to grow in silence. Although a hearing aid does not give him normal hearing, he can develop auditory skills, following a normal sequence, and these can be supplemented with visual clues.

Learning To Listen–The Development of Auditory Skills

All children move through several levels of listening before reaching a conversational level.* The first level involves *awareness* of and *attention* to sound. Children become aware — as they are stimulated by noisemakers, music, environmental sounds, and the human voice — that sound is on or off, loud or quiet, high or low pitched, rhythmic or noisy, near or distant, indoors or outdoors. The teacher can help the young child with a hearing loss develop better awareness and attention if she puts her hands over her ears and says, "I hear that. Listen! What's that?" (Pause for child's response.) "That's an airplane. Oh, I don't hear it anymore. It's all gone."

Learning to listen is reinforced when a nursery teacher encourages the child to participate. For example, he may enjoy helping to turn the record player on and off. Rhythmic activities become meaningful when he rides the rocking boat or horse to music, joins in a game of "Here we go round the mulberry bush," or dances around when the guitar is played. If he does not move, the teacher can take his hands and gently rock him to and fro in time to the music.

*Educational Audiology for the Limited Hearing Infant, Doreen Pollack. Springfield, Illinois: Charles C Thomas, 1970.

Integration in Action

Danny Norling, crossing guard at his neighborhood school, is a profoundly deaf fully-integrated sixth-grader doing well in his classes with only minimal supplementary tutoring.

Mrs. Shirley Burge, kindergarten teacher in Berrien Springs (Mich.) Public School, gives math directions to her class. Three hearing impaired children, some with profound losses, sit in front.

Linda Briney

In a school where staff and students are adequately oriented, integration naturally extends beyond the classroom into playground activities. (*See pages 114-119.*)

William Lyth, education major at Nazareth College (Kalamazoo, Mich.), tutors a younger student. Despite his severe hearing loss, he attends all college classes with hearing students and participates in numerous volunteer service activities. (*See pages 231-36.*)

Linda Briney

In the cafeteria, hearing impaired Edmund Viega has the opportunity to socialize with his hearing friends at the elementary school where he participates in a resource room program. (*See pages 108-113.*)

George Siegel

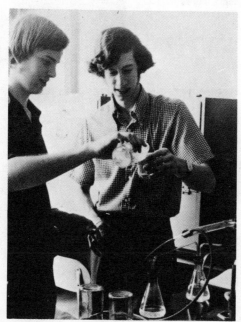

Steven Rattner (right), graduate of Montgomery Blair High School (Silver Spring, Md.), did not let his profound hearing loss interfere with his progress at school, where he earned honor roll marks. Chemistry was a favorite subject. (*See pages 196-205.*)

Suez Kehl

Moving from a self-contained classroom to a regular third-grade class for Pat Fish (profound hearing loss) is a specific team transition involving Mrs. Rae Holman, the third-grade teacher, and the teacher of the hearing impaired, Berrien County (Mich.) Day Program for Hearing Impaired Children. (*See pages 57-60.*)

Third-graders at Rock Lake Elementary School (Orlando, Fla.) learned about the similarities in the telephone and a hearing aid receiver worn by classmate Dan Hunter when Dan's father, a cable repairman for Southern Bell Telephone Co., presented a demonstration at the integrated school.

13-year-old Victor Phillips examines a soil sample at an outdoor school in Portland, Ore., where he is the only hearing impaired student. Victor attended a rugged YMCA mountain camp for two weeks during the summer through contributions from Delta Kappa Gamma. Encouraging extracurricular activities in integrated settings is one function of the social worker in Portland's Regional Facility for the Deaf. (*See pages 71-76.*)

C. Seithel

Gradually, young hearing impaired children can develop the ability to *localize* the source of sounds; this is the second level of listening. As sounds come from different distances and different directions, it helps to turn the hearing impaired child in the right direction if he does not do so himself, especially when someone calls his name. A preschooler will have fun hunting for a music box which has been hidden, or finding a child who is hiding and calling out, "Here I am!"

The third level of auditory perception involves *discrimination,* or the ability to sort out all the stimuli and organize them into meaningful classifications (or categories): this sound means a dog is nearby; that sound means daddy is home. This learning takes place only after much stimulation, and early understanding is often accompanied by gestures, such as *waving* goodbye or *extending the hand* for "give it to me." One must be careful not to use too many gestures which will divert attention away from listening.

The child's awakening realization that sound is used for contact and communication is of great significance in the early development of listening skills. Parent and infant make sounds to each other, but what is said is not as important as the inflection and tone of the voice. Even if the child does not seem to understand, it is very important for the adult to talk to him as much as possible.

On the fourth level, the child learns the appropriate *response* to sound. If we hear the door bell, we open the door. If our name is called, we turn around and say, "What?" In the nursery school, the children may enjoy playing games which involve different responses: marching when the music is played and sitting down when it stops; standing in a circle, closing the eyes, and guessing who is calling their names.

Hopefully, by the time the child with a hearing loss enters preschool he has been taught not only to listen but also to imitate (even if it sounds like jargon) what he hears so that speaking will accompany his growth in understanding language. Imitation should be encouraged whenever possible. The child who is listening wants to be like his peers, do what they do, and make the same sounds. At first, a hearing impaired preschooler may only imitate the laughter, clapping to music, and so on. He may have progressed only to the vocal level of speech, during which stage he is acquiring the prelinguistic skills of blowing and babbling consonant and vowel sounds. He is, however, also developing an auditory feedback system so that he can begin to monitor his own speech through listening. All of these skills can be incorporated into the nursery activities: blowing bubbles; whispering during quiet time; humming when the children pretend to be airplanes; saying "ch, ch, oooo" when they form a line for a train; singing "E-I-E-I-O" for Old MacDonald's Farm; and so on.

It is only a matter of time before the child who wears a hearing aid will move on to the verbal level of communication and try to imitate the words which are used to name people, actions, and objects in school. Auditory learning and verbal learning can then develop simultaneously; but it must never be forgotten that all children spend thousands of hours just listening before they understand language and begin to talk. The teacher can be most helpful at this time if she routinely and separately verbalizes the child's experiences as they occur daily.

Unless proved otherwise, the hearing impaired child also has the innate ability to perceive the structure or syntax of his native language through his hearing aids, provided he receives enough auditory input. He must, however, first increase his *auditory memory span* and his *ability to recall the correct sequence* of words in a sentence. Once a child can use one-word phrases, the adult should begin to say very short sentences naturally and encourage him to imitate one word at a time; then she should again say the word group naturally to him. From a two-unit span, such as: "Help me," "My turn," "I'm tired," the child can be urged on to a three-unit span: "Put it back," "I want more," "Where's my ball?"; and then to a four-word span: "I want a ride," "That's a funny hat."

Activities which develop good listening skills will benefit the whole group. Rhythm bands, dance and song, nursery rhymes to act out, finger-plays such as "Itsy-Bitsy Spider," puppet shows, and counting rhymes are some of the many activities for which there are attractive materials available today.* The children must also learn to follow directions, answer questions, and associate sounds with printed symbols.

Some inattention may be anticipated if the hearing impaired child is required to sit for a long period of time listening to a story, a recording, or group discussion without any visual aids. He should be seated next to the teacher where he can see the pictures in a book, or be "cued into" the subject under discussion. If the child has very little speech or language comprehension, it may be necessary to arrange another activity for him, but it is not wise to make too many exceptions.

Structuring the Auditory Environment of the Nursery School

The development of listening skills is among the most important learning experiences for young children during preschool years. Virtually all academic skills which children encounter during their first years of formal education are based upon the assumption that they know how to listen well, know what to listen for, and are able to identify the presence of significant information within the changing auditory milieu. The following suggestions intended to aid the hearing impaired child in this phase of his development are also helpful for all children.

1. Develop an attitude of readiness to listen.

Anticipation is an important aspect of readiness. With young children it is often necessary to prepare them for listening activities by telling them to quiet hands and feet before the activity begins. Teaching the child to say, "I'm ready,"

Auditory Perception, T. Oakland and F. Williams. Seattle: Special Child Publications, 1971.

will help him assume a listening attitude. The use of a pause or a contrasting auditory pattern helps children direct their attention to the next activity. The auditory drama present in the nursery school can take many forms, but it is greatly enhanced by vocal inflection, particularly in story-telling.

2. Use auditory signals.

Many preschool teachers use a variety of auditory clues to help children move from activity to activity. A ringing bell may signify snack time, chords on the piano may mean rest time. If the hearing impaired child fails to respond appropriately to these signals, tell him to "listen, it's time for something to happen." With experience and improved awareness he will begin to respond. The use of auditory signals also helps children begin to identify the significant foreground (meaningful) sounds from the background milieu (which he must learn to inhibit). In the same way, significant speech communication is perceived against a background of environmental sounds.

3. Use the voice to get attention.

Rather than touching the child to get his attention, always call his name until he turns around. If an adult acts as though she expects the child to hear, he will become conditioned to listening.

4. Allow sufficient time for auditory processing.

Give the child time to process what he has heard and do not rush an answer if you feel that the child can respond by himself. However, if he has difficulty, offer the correct response as a model and then encourage him to imitate the word or phrase.

5. Keep within close range when speaking.

The child who wears a hearing aid will hear most clearly when you speak within 12 inches from the aid and at ear level. Sit beside the child when giving individualized instruction.

6. Use a normal conversational tone of voice.

Voices which are too quiet are difficult to hear, but if they are too loud they become distorted. Verbal messages are best perceived through short sentences used in conjunction with the appropriate activity.

7. Provide good speech models.

Use interesting, animated inflections and short, clear phrases. Speak a little more slowly than usual and do not gesture too much.

8. Use frequent repetitions.

Talk more, not less, to the hearing impaired child and reinforce with the same phrases. When the child responds appropriately to a phrase, expand it: "Put it back. Put it in the box. Put it on the shelf." "He's soft. Feel it. He's soft like your hair. He's soft like the bunny."

9. Orient the child to the activity or discussion.

When a child joins a group, he may fail to understand what is being said unless he is clued in to the discussion taking place. "Mary is talking about her new dog. His name is Tippy."

10. Encourage the parents to expand the work of the nursery school.

Pin a note on the child or talk to his mother about the school day. Provide her with the words to songs and finger-plays. A knowledgeable parent can do a great deal to help a child reconstruct verbally his school day and reinforce vocabulary and concepts. Some parents work with the child to record his experiences at school in a notebook or daily journal with pictures partially drawn by the child.

Helping the Child To Interact Verbally

Speech is the natural outgrowth of learning to listen. The development of verbal communication can be stimulated by 1) providing the child with the appropriate verbal patterns which are incorporated into the activity itself, or 2) expanding upon the child's own utterances.

Teaching verbal communication is usually more successful when the teacher and one normally hearing child participate with the hearing impaired child. In activities which stimulate social and emotional growth — such as tea parties, washing dishes, planting seeds, or teaching a dog to "sit" — the teacher should take an active role initially in establishing the verbal patterns which become an integral part of the activity. "Would you like a cookie? Yes, please. Would you like some tea? Pour! Pour! Thank you." Most games for young children have very simple rules, which can be translated into simple verbal expressions. "My turn" and "your turn" become expressions he will soon learn to use in playing with other children. Knowledge of the child's vocabulary can also be helpful. For example, if the child knows the names of colors, a game which uses color words offers the child an opportunity for active verbal participation. The teacher can help the child expand on his own experiences by supplying new information to use with the familiar words in short phrases.

Once the child begins to interact verbally with others (intelligibility not always being a requirement), he begins to add another dimension to his listening skill, that of self-monitoring. As he listens more and more to others he begins unconsciously to match the sounds he hears others speak, and his cycle of communication then becomes complete.

Nursery school is an ideal environment for the hearing impaired child to acquire the basis for this interpersonal communication. It can happen — naturally and spontaneously — if parents and teachers don't set limits.

SHIRLEY G. PARKER

Observation by Parents:
The Preprimary Hearing Impaired Child

Parents and teachers who are guided by a recorded observation of a hearing impaired child in his classroom are better equipped to confer and make decisions regarding his development and educational needs.

After spending several hours observing a young hearing impaired child in his regular school setting, most parents return home content with a visual picture of the way Junior spends his morning. However, if asked about some of the specifics of his behavior and adjustment, they would be at a loss to pinpoint his interests, attitudes, and personal relationships in the classroom. Parents often lack an awareness of the enlightening details of class performance and tend to reflect merely on obvious generalities. To obtain a more knowledgeable and detailed picture of the child's involvement in class, some guidelines should be kept in mind during the visit.

The recording of responses, reactions, and general behavior patterns of a young child during a school experience is an important reminder to parents of what they have seen and what progress could be made in the future. The significance of their child's hearing loss often gets in the way of parents' judgment of his behavior. They lose sight of chronological age characteristics. With an outline in hand the parents can more realistically evaluate their child's behavior in the light of interaction with a peer group.

The following observation form designed for use by parents in a regular school setting has been a useful tool in the preprimary program for hearing

Mrs. Parker is a nursery school teacher for the hearing impaired in the Minneapolis, Minnesota, Public Schools.

impaired children in the Minneapolis Public Schools. An integral component of this program is parent guidance through appropriate means — phone calls, home visits, and invitations to the school during class sessions. Use of this outline is helpful during parent-teacher conferences. When individually prescriptive objectives are written for each child, the completed observational report serves as a valuable reference.

Structured Observation of a Child in School
— For Parents —

Please respond with a check in the appropriate space or with a few words, as appropriate.

1. **Choice of Activities**

   A. How much time does your child spend in large muscle activities such as running, jumping, climbing, building with large blocks, or other physically strenuous activities that call for the use of his entire body? A lot of play time____; a moderate amount of time____; very little time____.

   B. Does he do these things easily, gracefully, and fearlessly?____Or, are his movements hesitant, tentative, or clumsy?____

   C. How much time does he spend in quiet activities such as sitting at a table or on the floor playing with manipulative toys and games like puzzles, lego, stringing beads, building with small blocks, dominoes and lotto games? A lot of play time____; a moderate amount of time____; very little time____.

   D. Does he participate voluntarily____ or must he be encouraged____ in the more unstructured media such as paints, clay or Play Doh, fingerpainting, or whatever kind of art activity is provided?

   E. How does he use these materials: freely without restraint____ or anxiously as if fearful of getting dirty or not being able to do what he wants with them?____

   F. Does he get deeply engrossed in the activity he is engaged in?____Does he give it a fairly long attention span and personal involvement?____Does he seem to only "dabble" for very short periods of time?____Is he easily distracted by other activities or children in the room so that he rarely really "sinks his teeth" into what he is doing?____

   G. Does he spend much time watching others do things?____Does he get involved himself fairly quickly in projects and activities?____

2. **Social and Emotional Behavior**

   A. Relationships with other children
      a. How much time does he spend in
      Solitary play — being by himself, or playing entirely alone? A lot of time____; a reasonable amount____; very little____.
      Parallel play — being in close physical proximity to other children but playing

side by side rather than actually playing with them. A lot of time____; a reasonable amount ____; very little____.

Cooperative play — playing and interacting with others in pairs or in groups such as cooperative block building, dramatic play in the housekeeping corner and in group games?

A lot of time____; a reasonable amount____; very little____.

B. When he is playing with other children, how does he get along with them? Is he a leader, organizing the activity, supplying the ideas and seeing that they get implemented?____Does he spend some time observing other children at their activities before joining them?____Does he tend to be more a follower doing what others suggest and taking their directions?____Or, does he tend to do some of both leading and following?____

(It is helpful to think of this along a scale from extreme leader to extreme follower. After observing, where do you see your child on this line?)

( )   ( )   ( )   ( )   ( )

Leader — more a leader — part leader and part follower — more a follower — follower

C. Does he get along well with other children?____ Or, is there frequent friction and conflict?____In either case, what kind of children does he seem to get along with best and least well? What type of child is he attracted to and what type is attracted to him?

Active and outgoing____; passive and shy____; children between the two extremes____.

Is he generally accepting____ or rejecting of other children____ and they of him?

D. What effect does his behavior seem to have on the group and what effect does the group have on him? Is he over-stimulated or easily distracted by the other children? ____ Is he disruptive?____Or, is he generally cooperative and constructively involved with others?____

3. **Relationships with Adults**

A. Does he interact with the teachers frequently?____ Or, do they interact infrequently? ____What is the nature of his interaction? Conversation ____; play____; work ____. Does he initiate this interaction?____Or, do the teachers?_____

B. Does he seem excessively dependent on the teachers for attention and for help? ____Or, is he relatively independent? _____

C. Is he able to give and receive affection and to relate warmly to his teachers?____ Or, does he maintain some emotional distance from them?_____

D. Does he take directions easily and usually follow them? ____ Is he able to adhere to the usual classroom routine without constant reminding?____Do changes in routine seem to confuse or distress him?_____

4. **Communication**

A. Does he seem alert and aware of things that are happening around and to him?_____

                                  (yes)   (no)

B. Does he attempt any verbal communication?   ____   ____

Actual speech in sentences? (sample) _____

Sentence fragments? _____

Single words? _____

Clear or garbled enunciation? _____

Grunts and/or babbling? _____

C. If he does talk, does he talk more to adults? ____ To other children? ____ To himself? ____ Does he talk more during one type of activity than another? ____

D. What forms of nonverbal communication does he use?

Hand and body gestures? _____

Facial expressions? _____

Crying and/or temper tantrums? _____

Anything else? _____

E. Does he express his emotions and ideas through any forms other than those mentioned above, such as through play or through physical acts? Give example ____

_____

F. Does he display a wide range of emotions? ____ Only a few? ____ Or, practically none? ____ Which feelings does he show most and how? Describe in a sentence or two. _____

_____

G. Considering his age, do you feel he is finding and using constructive outlets for his feelings and ideas in the classroom? ____ If so, what are those outlets? ____ If not, what other ways would you like him to behave to show his feelings and ideas now? _____

_____

How do you think you and the school can be helpful to him in this area?

_____

_____

_____

Part V

The Elementary Years

25

CAROLE BLUMBERG

A School for the Deaf Facilitates Integration

At the Lexington School integration of deaf and hearing children is thought of as a way of life. The deaf students have many opportunities to interact with hearing students in school and community recreational and social programs. In addition, a systematic approach is used to ensure the successful integration of selected students into regular school classes. This includes application of an Integration Profile for each pupil, preparation of the host school, and follow-up by special education personnel after placement.

Students at the Lexington School for the Deaf are given the opportunity to integrate with hearing children in a number of ways: hearing students often attend their classes and may participate in recreational, social, and athletic programs; and the Lexington pupils may be involved in community activities such as the Young Men's Hebrew Association, the YMCA, scout troops, or other extracurricular associations. One of the main thrusts of Lexington's program for integrating deaf and hearing children deals with preparation of hearing impaired students for later placement in regular schools. While Lexington has carried on this integration program for many years, some of the concepts may be new to other systems. We have therefore endeavored to develop some guidelines based on the questions most frequently asked by educators, parents, deaf persons, and the community.

What Is Integration at the Lexington School?

Integration is a way of living which provides an opportunity for a child with a hearing loss to achieve his maximum potential in an educational and social

Mrs. Blumberg is Liaison to Outside Programs at the Lexington School for the Deaf in Jackson Heights, Queens, New York.

environment which *demands* his functional communication and interaction with other individuals. This concept of integration is possible only when the hearing impaired child is constantly associated with normally hearing children.

When Is the Optimum Time for Integration?

Each deaf child is unique; thus the best time for integration is when he, as an individual, is ready. We encourage early integration, for we believe that once it is initiated, integration is a life-long learning experience providing stimulation for the hearing impaired person to meet the challenges and joys inherent in living.

How Do We Integrate?

Anyone may refer a child as a candidate for integration. All referrals are considered carefully by the integration department staff, which consists of the Director and the Liaison to Outside Programs. The following procedures are used:

1. The child's teacher submits a written summary indicating the student's strengths and weaknesses.

2. Educational faculty members, child care staff, and pupil personnel specialists submit Integration Profiles (Figure 1) designed to provide an objective and more accurate evaluation of the qualities necessary for successful integration. These include academic capability, effective communication skills, functional use of hearing and consistent use of hearing aids, reading level, social development, and parental support.

3. The integration department staff observes the student in his classroom.

4. Staff members from the audiology, psychology, health, education, and child care departments hold an Integration Conference, and their conclusions and recommendations are submitted to the Executive Director for final approval.

5. Parents then attend a conference with the integration staff to discuss parental support, expectation level for the child, projected problem areas, viable solutions, and the selection of a school. They also discuss with the student his proposed attendance at a "hearing" school.

6. The Lexington staff evaluates public, private, and parochial educational facilities available to each student. The schools receive information about Lexington's philosophy and attitudes toward integration and have an opportunity to discuss expectations, levels of performance, and areas of particular concern for the integrating student. The type of program into which the deaf youngster is placed is mutually determined by the parent and the Lexington staff, but all programs considered must have one thing in common: the desire on the part of those who work with the child to help him in whatever ways are necessary to ensure a good education. We generally look for a program which offers experienced teachers, small classes, various

supportive services in the speech and academic areas, and a staff of educators eager to work with the hearing impaired child.

How Do We Prepare the Host School?

The integration staff makes an initial visit to the host school in the spring to provide orientation for the host staff. The discussion includes:

1. the child's hearing loss
2. the particular hearing aids he wears and how they help him receive sound and speech
3. language achievement
4. speech skills
5. social needs
6. academic capabilities
7. personality characteristics
8. motivational patterns
9. practical suggestions for everyday classroom teaching (to supplement this discussion, we distribute copies of "Lexington Guidelines for Classroom Teachers"). While the concerns of classroom teachers about hearing impaired children vary greatly, five basic questions are generally asked about the students integrating into regular classes. These questions follow, with some of our answers:

A. What general considerations are important when having a hearing impaired youngster in my class?

1. Recognize and accept the child as an integral part of the class.
2. Establish realistic goals and expect him to meet the same standards of behavior, promptness, and courtesy as his hearing classmates.
3. Foster feelings of independence by giving him responsibilities.
4. Maintain high standards so that the child has goals to achieve. Don't let him use his hearing impairment as an excuse for not completing his work.
5. Remember that he has a hearing loss. This has affected his reception of speech and language as well as his oral and written expression.
6. Establish and maintain contact with his parents. They will provide the vital support necessary outside of school.
7. Maintain close communication with the resource or itinerant teacher who works with the child. She will reinforce and supplement class work and help you with any special problems should they arise.

B. What about hearing?

1. Most children have some useful residual hearing. Children at the Lexington School have been trained to use their residual hearing. This training enables them to listen. When listening is combined with looking, the child utilizes the two senses to receive a spoken message.

2. Hearing aids do not cure deafness; they only make sounds louder. Certain sounds may not be heard by the hearing impaired child regardless of how loud they are.

3. No hearing aid is free from distortion. No matter what degree of residual hearing the child has, he will never hear as you do.

4. The child should be encouraged to *use* his hearing. (Call his name — don't tap him to get his attention.)

This information is given in conjunction with an explanation of the individual child's hearing loss and of what his particular aids do for him.

C. *What about speech?*

1. Hearing impaired children often do not hear many of the speech sounds we hear. Sounds such as *s, t, h, f,* and *th* are difficult for them to hear because they are voiceless. In addition, some sounds are not clearly visible on the lips — *k, g, ng*. Because the child does not see and/or hear many of these sounds, he may omit them in his speech, mispronounce them, or substitute other sounds. His understandability is thus affected.

2. The child's voice may sound a bit strained because he has difficulty hearing himself.

3. The child's hearing loss will affect his rhythm, intonation, and inflection patterns.

4. The hearing impaired child may receive tutoring either during the school day or after school. Contact the tutor to find out more about his particular speech work. If you observe any carry-over in class, report it to the speech tutor.

5. Praise the child when his speech is good, but don't be afraid to tell him if you don't understand him. Generally his classmates will get to know his speech patterns quickly — perhaps more quickly than you.

6. Remember that this child is amazing in that he is able to express with varying degrees of intelligibility much that he cannot hear.

D. *What is lipreading or speechreading?*

1. This term refers to the ability to understand movement made by the mouth as the speaker articulates or talks. It is a skill which hearing impaired children rely on for a great deal of information. Ideally it is used in combination with hearing so that the child receives the spoken message in the fullest possible manner.

2. It is necessary for a hearing impaired child to have an unobstructed view of the speaker in order to speechread. Speaking to the blackboard or into a book held in front of your face will make speechreading impossible.

3. It is difficult to speechread an isolated word because so many sounds look alike on the lips. Therefore, all new vocabulary and any words in question should be used in context.

4. If the child does not understand after repetition, rephrase your message or

question. You may be using words that look or sound alike to him.

5. When you write new vocabulary words on the board, say them to the child so that he can see what they look like on the lips. It's good practice for the hearing students, too.

6. Speechreading can only be achieved at close range. Seat the child where he will get the best view of you and of the other members of the class. This may necessitate changing his seat for certain activities.

E. How about some helpful hints?

1. Make sure the child is attending, not merely watching. Ask him an open-ended question or two about the subject to be sure he is alert to the content.

2. Use visual aids whenever possible to supplement a presentation.

3. Substitute a filmstrip for a movie or recording, and allow the deaf child to use this aid independently.

4. Institute a "buddy system." This usually works well for many subjects and activities, especially with children who need help taking notes.

5. Write homework assignments on the board.

6. Outline the lesson on the board as you proceed.

7. Provide the class with supplementary written materials.

8. Keep your hands away from your face when speaking and try to stand fairly still.

9. Speak in a well modulated voice, at a normal rate, without exaggerated mouth movements.

10. Encourage the hearing children to speak clearly, not to mumble. (Their parents will really appreciate you for this.)

11. Be patient if the hearing impaired child asks you to repeat. He wants to make sure he knows what's going on.

12. Don't ask the child to memorize long lists of items presented orally; his auditory memory span may be shorter than his hearing classmates'.

After the initial orientation by the integration staff, arrangements are made for the child to spend a few days with his prospective classmates. This is done at the end of the school year, although full-time placement will not begin until the fall term. At the elementary level, an orientation is also provided for the class prior to the hearing impaired child's visit. This includes an explanation of hearing loss, hearing aids, and speech patterns and gives the children an opportunity to listen through a hearing aid and to ask questions. We suggest that the parent of the hearing impaired child also meet with the teacher of the new class and with the guidance counselor; they should maintain close contact throughout the year.

What Happens After the Child Is Integrated?

The integration staff at Lexington arranges early in the year to visit the classes of all newly integrated students. In addition, conferences are held with the child's new teacher and other personnel to discuss his progress. Issues unique to each child are carefully viewed along with suggestions for workable solutions. The hearing impaired child's parents are informed of the results of the visit.

To supplement the personal observations, follow-up questionnaires are sent annually to schools which have enrolled former Lexington pupils prior to the current school year. These supply data on use of speech and hearing, academic, social, and emotional progress, type of special tutoring, and standing in class.

The integration staff is available to any parent, student, staff member, or school at all times on a consulting basis.

Are All Placements Permanent?

In addition to the regular integration program, Lexington has developed another type of educational integration which involves temporary placement. Public and private schools in the immediate area may accept Lexington students (one per class at various grade levels) on a "trial" basis. This arrangement enables us to maintain constant communication with the staffs of these schools to assist in programming and to facilitate the adjustment of an individual hearing impaired child. Placement is for a full day in the regular class over a one-month or a one-year period; it is a major means of ascertaining whether a child can function effectively in a regular school.

The Lexington School invites classes from these neighborhood schools to visit our campus for a day and our staff plans a varied program for them. The hearing impaired children's parents also take an active part in their youngsters' "trial" placement by meeting with both the regular school teachers and the Lexington staff and by observing the children in their new classrooms. This helps them develop a better understanding of what to expect when the time comes for permanent transfer.

What Supportive Services Are Provided by Lexington?

The Lexington Hearing and Speech Center provides diagnostic, educational, and therapeutic services for infants, children, and adults. Individual and group instruction in all hearing and speech problems is available, as well as academic tutoring. Parental guidance is provided by the integration staff, school psychologists, and social workers.

Why Bother?

It may be asked — with these difficult challenges to the child, the parent, and the school — why we consider integration at all. The answer lies in the fact that it is the only way to provide the hearing impaired child with what he cannot gain from his ordinary "deaf" environmental experiences. Social, business, and professional contacts in life cannot be fully achieved without effective language and communication. Therefore, integration is designed first to build speech and language skills, and second to strengthen the self-concept of the deaf child as an integral part of the hearing world.

Integration is one of the logical steps in the chain of events which will prepare a child with a hearing loss to take his place in society as a contributing individual. Integration by itself is not a bold, new step. The boldness of the Lexington School concept is in the timing and the methods, so that the child moves forward as early in life as possible to develop his personality and his communication skills. In this way, he is not isolated from his family, neighbors, and the community. The results *speak* for themselves.

Figure 1.
Integration Profile

Foreword

The integration program at Lexington has broadened considerably during the past several years. It has become essential to develop a profile in order to provide an objective definition of the qualities which are necessary for consideration of any potential integration candidate. *Please consider each child in relation to his peers* (i.e. all children at his age level at the Lexington School) and check the appropriate column.

The following variables must be considered before placement is made: the type of educational programs available (outside of Lexington); willingness of that staff to accept the child; supportive services; and grade placement.

Respondents should omit any areas with which they are unfamiliar.

Name of child   D.O.B.

Current Class   Respondent

Date of report

Consideration	Rating Scale				
	Supr.	Above Avg.	Avg.	Below Avg.	Infr.
I. Academic Skills					
Reading ability					
Math ability					
Work habits					
Ability to work independently					
Overall academic capability					

(Continued on next page.)

(Continued from preceding page.)
 	
II. Communication
  Skills
  Intelligibility of speech
  Spontaneity of speech
  Receptive language
    ability
  Spoken language
    ability
  Written language ability
  Speechreading
 	
III. Auditory Skills
  Functional use of hearing
  Consistent use of hearing
    aid
 	
IV. Social Skills
  Peer relationships
  Adult relationships
  Leadership ability
  Independence
  Awareness of environ-
    ment
 	
V. Parent Support
  Attitude toward integra-
    tion
  Interest in school work
  Ability to assist the
    child at home
 	
VI. Personality
  Creativity
  Curiosity
  Assertiveness
  Emotional Stability
  Maturity					

A note of appreciation is expressed to Mr. Vincent Aniello, Director of the Lexington School Integration Department, for his guidance and assistance.

(Note: See also pages 271 and 272 for teacher and administrator questionnaires used in inservice training and preparation for integration.)

26

ELIZABETH FRICK

Ensuring Successful Adjustment
To Integration

Hearing impaired children in St. Louis County, Missouri, are integrated into public school at all levels. Typically they come from two private oral schools or the Special School District's classes and are seen for individual therapy by the Special School District hearing clinicians serving the county's 25 districts. The major difficulties these children have at different levels in public school (first grade through twelfth) and ways they can be avoided or alleviated are discussed in the light of information from members of the hearing clinician staff, parents, public school teachers, and the children themselves.

Few hearing impaired children who are integrated into St. Louis County public school classes have difficulties just getting along with their hearing class-mates; they have good study habits; they generally continue to wear their hearing aids; and the language and speech training they have received enables them to get along satisfactorily.

There are, however, problems that arise. This paper will deal with some of the most obvious, most troublesome difficulties. Although they have been divided into several categories, overlap from one category to another is unavoidable — seldom does a problem confine itself to one area alone. The problems are dealt with generally, and not all are discussed. Where a problem affects both deaf and hard of hearing children, the term *hearing impaired* is used; where the difficulty is more specific to one group, the term *deaf* or *hard of hearing* is used.

Mrs. Frick is a hearing clinician in the Special School District of St. Louis County, Missouri.

The statements presented are based mainly on my personal observations as a classroom teacher of older children at Central Institute for the Deaf and a hearing clinician for the Special District of St. Louis County since September 1969. In the capacity of hearing clinician I have worked with hearing impaired children from kindergarten through twelfth grade in four of the school districts in St. Louis County.* The children have losses varying from slight to profound. Although most have been in special classes at some time, a few have always been in public school.

What's Going on in the Public School?

One of the best ways teachers of hearing impaired children can prepare their pupils for public school is to know firsthand what's happening in public schools. It is essential to observe and discuss things with public school personnel to learn what is going on *today*, not five or ten years ago when the teacher herself was still in school. It isn't necessary to have a specific outline of points to look for — you don't know what you will see until you actually see it. The best guideline is to be prepared to take in lots of information and then just jump in and get your feet wet. A week in the fall and another in the spring every year or so is not too much time. Visits should include schools in different districts and classrooms where the children are the same age and function at about the same level as your pupils. Seeing classes at levels above that of your students is advisable, too, to give you an idea of where your children should be going academically and socially. Also important are visits to curriculum centers and attendance at teachers' meetings.

As you visit, you will undoubtedly see things that your hearing impaired children can do better than the hearing children can. For instance:

1. Older hearing impaired children are sometimes better in grammar work.

2. Frequently, hearing impaired children have better study habits than hearing children. Fourth grade hearing children are just beginning to develop study habits, while a hearing impaired child integrating at this level has usually been trained to study, to complete seatwork assignments, and to do homework. Older hearing impaired children should be well organized, able to use their study time well, able to work with their parents, and accustomed to having almost

---

*The St. Louis area is served by several facilities for hearing impaired children. Central Institute for the Deaf and St. Joseph Institute for the Deaf are oral private residential and day schools for children through eighth grade level. Gallaudet School is a public elementary school for hearing impaired children living within the city limits of St. Louis. The Special School District of St. Louis County provides public school facilities for oral education of hearing impaired children, from age 6 through high school, who live in the County's 25 school districts. A preschool program for children through age 4 was instituted in September 1972 in the Special School District, and preschool programs are in effect at CID and St. Joseph.

While most children in St. Louis County attending CID or St. Joseph are integrated at ninth grade level, some children from these private schools and many from the Special District's classes are integrated into public school at lower grade levels.

daily homework. In fact, students and parents are often surprised by the lack of homework assigned in public schools. Pupils are often given class time or study halls and can complete most of their work during the day.

3. Children who integrate at first grade level usually read *much* more and know more about the motor skills of handwriting than do their first grade class-mates.

Seeing such things should not encourage teachers to "slack up" in their classrooms. To the contrary, they should keep up in these areas because hearing impaired children need all the "bonuses" they can get to be successful in public school. Teachers of the deaf will also see things that their pupils cannot handle as well as hearing children can; some specific problem areas will be dealt with in the next section.

Audiological Considerations — Speechreading

In public school, speechreading becomes more necessary for the hard of hearing child than it was in the school for the deaf. A child who has been taught primarily with an auditory approach, and who functions well in a special class of six to seven children in a sound-treated room where a group aid helps the teacher's voice override noise, finds that these advantageous listening circum-stances do not exist in a public school classroom. Instead, the child is usually faced with an uncarpeted room, a fan, and 25 other children who move around, whisper, talk in small groups, and *very* effectively mask out the teacher's voice unless she is right next to him. He must supplement what he is able to hear with speechreading. If this skill has been neglected, the child will have great difficulty getting along.

The public school teacher should keep in mind that she needs to face the hearing impaired child, with light from windows falling on her face to prevent shadows. The child will have difficulty speechreading his teacher when she is across the room from him or when she moves around while talking. Repetition and rewording are helpful when the child doesn't understand what has been said.

Hearing impaired children tend to be "nodders" and "smilers"; that is, whether or not they really understand what has been said, they may nod "yes" or smile at the speaker. Classroom teachers need to be alerted to this charac-teristic so that they habitually question the child directly ("How many planets are larger than the Earth?" is better than, "Do you understand what I said about the planets?"). Another check on speechreading is to have the child repeat directions or demonstrate understanding by doing an example while the teacher watches.

Auditory Training — Group and Individual Aids

After observing classrooms during a 1970 workshop in the Special District, a public school teacher asked how great an adjustment a child must make when he no longer uses a group aid (that is, when he enters a public school classroom).

The more the matter was considered the more apparent it became that the child must indeed make a big adjustment.

1. He can rely only on his individual aid in academic situations when he was accustomed formerly to having stronger amplification.

2. He is usually on a monaural system (one receiver).

3. The teacher's voice no longer overrides other signals.

4. The child hears whatever sound source is closest to him — the teacher, other students, himself, clothing noise, chairs and people moving about, and so on.

During the workshop recommendations were made for a spring program of "transition auditory training" for children scheduled to enter public school the next year. These children should be given more opportunities to use their individual aids during the school day. They should be given training in what they can and cannot expect from their individual aids in different situations, especially during actual academic teaching time. Group amplification should *not* be discarded for these children but should be alternated with the use of individual aids. It was felt that the children would make the adjustment more easily if they began to do this while still in a setting with people trained to work with them and familiar with the capabilities of hearing aids.

Classroom teachers should be advised that no matter how powerful the child's hearing aid is, it is not effective beyond a distance of a few feet, even in a quiet situation. A severely deaf child may respond to his name through aided hearing, but understanding of speech through hearing alone is very limited. The teacher should call on the deaf child to get his attention, then should proceed with instructions or questions when the child is looking at her. The more hearing the child has, the more he may actually understand through hearing alone — the teacher will discover the child's abilities as she works with him.

Academic Considerations — The Child Entering First Grade

Presently most of these children come from the Special District Program and are hard of hearing or partially deaf; that is, they have been taught with an auditory approach. Up until 1971 they had used "ita" (the Initial Teaching Alphabet), which sometimes caused confusion in the transfer to traditional orthography.

Often these children are ahead of their classmates in reading and writing. Some of them are so far ahead that their teachers remark that a second-grade placement would have been better (especially since the children are often old enough for second grade). However, sometime during the first grade or early in second grade the hearing impaired child's classmates often catch up and pass him. Reasons may be that hearing children's vocabularies grow faster; they seem to get more from phonics work and thus can attack words better; and they learn great quantities of information from outside sources.

At some time in the year the teacher may report that the hearing impaired child in her class seems to have stopped listening, has become a behavior problem, and isn't trying. What has probably happened is that the child is no longer reviewing what he had in his special class. Now he is being presented with new material and is having difficulty understanding the new concepts and new words that are presented so rapidly.

The main burden of helping these children to be successful lies in a good relationship among the teacher, the parents, and the hearing clinician so that difficulties can be spotted quickly and something can be done about them. Teachers need to be educated on how to help the child overcome his problems.

The Child Who Enters Third or Fourth Grade

Here we encounter children from all of the special schools and children with all types of hearing losses, although the majority are hard of hearing. In general, teachers at this level comment that hearing impaired children have better study habits than their hearing classmates and that they have few social difficulties—they are accepted by their peers and get along well.

Problems at this level do occur, however. Hearing impaired children need to use speechreading in the classroom and need to have an understanding of what their hearing aids can and cannot do for them. They need to know how to manipulate their classroom so that they can operate most successfully in listening and speechreading situations.

Many of the hearing impaired children have had little experience in writing. While they may be able to talk in sentences, they may not be able to write a straight, simple sentence in response to a question or as a part of a story or composition as hearing children at these grade levels are expected to do. The classroom teacher can help the hearing impaired pupil improve his written language skills by providing materials such as newspaper cartoons for which the child writes dialogue, language master cards with recorded sentences for the child to listen to and write, and packs of sentence parts (subjects, verbs, endings) which the child constructs into sentences. It will also help a child at this stage to tell a story to his teacher before he writes it. A brief "outline" supplying key words and phrases in chronological order will also help him in writing stories. Written work should be checked and discussed with the child so that he becomes aware of his errors and has an opportunity to correct them.

Some public schools are using linguistic approaches to grammar, such as *Roberts English Series.* Hearing children have a good start at analyzing sentences—picking out parts of speech, changing verb forms, etc.—by third or fourth grade. Even classes using a standard grammar are ahead of hearing impaired children in structured use of language.

Hearing impaired children who enter public school at this level are behind in the type of phonics skills taught in public schools. Because some of them have been taught with an auditory approach, they may have had very little exposure to phonics (vowel sounds, consonant sounds, sound combinations and spellings, syllabication, accents)—all covered in first, second, and third grades. The older children do get phonics training along with speech and dictionary work, but by the time they enter public school phonics is no longer taught. (The training is vital to older hearing impaired children in helping them sound out words, and it is not being suggested that it be dropped.)

Achievement in Academic Subjects at Third-Fourth Grade Level

Third and fourth grade public school children have quite a fund of knowledge in academic areas. The older they get, the more deeply you can probe for detailed understanding. Academic work may not be more than started in special schools by the time a hearing impaired child is 9 or 10 years of age. This puts hearing impaired children at a disadvantage in that they have so few concepts upon which to hang facts. Material is presented so rapidly in public school that the hearing impaired child may never catch up.

Math is an area of particular difficulty; in third and fourth grade public school children are multiplying, dividing, and using quite sophisticated concepts and vocabulary in modern math. Textbooks in science and social studies have advanced vocabularies and are becoming more and more difficult as new editions are published. The language structures used in the texts and the types of questions asked are very complex. Simple *who, when, where* questions are seldom asked. Literature (poetry, plays, classics) is included in some reading and grammar series such as *The Roberts English Series* (Harcourt, Brace, and World) and *New Directions in English* (Harper and Row).

The Child Who Enters Eighth or Ninth Grade

At this level hearing impaired children have different academic problems. The written language of many children from the special schools is generally quite accurate, if not very imaginative. The child's speech and language may undergo a rather amazing improvement during his first year in public school. Hearing impaired students realize that if they are to be understood, their speech must be as nearly perfect as possible and that there will be no one to remind or correct them all the time. There are, of course, exceptions; but I have noticed improvement among many children. In the long run, the speech and language training pays off.

At the eighth to ninth grade level, vocabularies of hearing impaired children are usually further behind those of their peers than at lower levels. Three factors contribute to this problem: 1) general vocabulary development is slow; 2) vocabulary specialized to one subject becomes important, e.g., Missouri Constitution, biology, civics, literature; and 3) abstract concepts and aspects of vocabulary are stressed in classroom work.

According to parents and students, as well as hearing clinicians and teachers, the greatest problem for hearing impaired students at eighth and ninth grade levels is lack of exposure to the study of various academic topics.

Math. Work in new math is needed. A student entering eighth or ninth grade algebra is expected to have a background of several years' experience in modern math. The hearing impaired student with no background has an almost insurmountable task in making up what he has missed before he can get started.

Social studies. More American history, world history, and geography are needed. Hearing impaired students cannot be expected to understand current events without knowledge about their own and other countries. Most public school children have been through a complete course in American and world history at least once by the time they reach ninth grade.

Every student in Missouri must pass a test on the federal and state constitutions before he leaves high school. Usually these are covered in seventh to tenth grades. The concepts in the constitutions are complicated and the volume of vocabulary is quite large — on the order of 300 words. If hearing impaired students were given some previous exposure to these constitutions, they would at least be able to follow some of what the teacher says in discussions and would have an idea about what they are studying.

Literature. For a hearing impaired student entering eighth or ninth grade, literature is largely an unexplored territory. Students who have recently come from CID or St. Joseph know what plays are and are familiar with some of the specialized vocabulary; they may know that poems have rhyme or rhythm, understand what rhymes are, and know the names of a few classics and their authors. In public school they are expected to read, understand, discuss, and write about the complex concepts of characterization, plot, the climax of a story, narrative, symbolism, rhythm patterns, and so on, all while dealing with these new words as well as with the vocabulary inherent in whatever they are reading — short stories, novels, plays, poetry, drama, tragedy, comedy, and so on.

In special classes, additional vocabulary development and exposure to a wide variety of literature forms would enhance the chances of a hearing impaired student's success in public school. Former students have told me that more vocabulary work would have helped them. Stress on developing study habits, teaching students how to read textbooks (which could be done better), and teaching language and speech skills are all important and should not be shortchanged.

Gaining Information from Outside Sources

The ability to use outside sources to acquire information is important in the development of independence. Three factors play an important role in this area:

1. Hearing impaired children as a group tend to learn little from sources other than their classrooms. Gaps occur in their knowledge; they lack everyday vocabulary not taught in the school; they are relatively unaware of current events.

2. From subject to subject there seems to be little generalization or carry-over of learning. What is learned in speech class *stays* there. Math stays in the math room and isn't applied to science.

3. Teachers of the deaf sometimes "spoonfeed" and overprotect their pupils. They may tell them answers or give them so much information that the students aren't required to think. They check closely on homework and other assignments and do not always demand responsibility and independence.

From an early age hearing impaired children develop characteristics of dependence on others—largely because they have been overprotected and taught to be dependent — to the extent that when they reach the upper elementary level in a school for the deaf or enter public school at third or fourth grade level, they are unable to work independently. Granted, it is an effort for most hearing impaired children to get information from sources such as TV, newspapers, magazines, the family, peers, and strangers. Since it is a natural inclination of children to take the easy way, they don't learn from outside sources unless they are required to. The older they become, the less practice they have and the more their desire to learn from outside areas dwindles.

Early stimulation to utilize all possible sources for vocabulary, concepts, and general information should be encouraged. This should be started long before the hearing impaired child enters school. He needn't be protected from the world. Instead, he needs to be shown that the world is there and can teach him things. Hearing impaired children must *want* to find out about things. They need to be aggressive and curious.

Encouraging Independent Study

Teachers of hearing impaired children can start encouraging independence early by creating situations in which current events are discussed and children are stimulated to find out more about something that happens. The children should use the library, use resource books in the classroom, ask questions of parents or brothers and sisters, find pictures in magazines, and so on. In other words, instead of the teacher staying up all night preparing materials on what happens to a cocoon, let the children do it—they will learn more in the long run and may even pick up some additional related information. They will learn how to use reference books and how to read pictures, and they will learn that people other than their teacher know about things.

At the upper level in a school for the deaf, pupils need to learn to utilize outside sources and to rely on themselves even more than at lower levels. These two skills are necessities in public school and in later life. Before their last year, pupils at the upper level need to be taught skills that help make them independent learners, such as: 1) how to read pictures, tables, graphs, and diagrams; 2) how to read a text and to take notes on it; 3) how to locate information in a reference book and to use more than just *World Book;* 4) how to write a report, a composition, a book report. While still in a special class, pupils would profit from frequent experience in writing short research reports, books reports, etc., without close supervision, but with help after they have finished the assignments.

Social Considerations — Social Graces and General Naivete

Along with the tendency of hearing impaired children to be dependent and inexperienced in using outside sources for learning, we often find a general lack of social graces and an overall naivete. These are understandable weaknesses, but they cause the children and others embarrassment and hurt feelings as well as leaving the children "out of it" and occasionally even in danger.

While it is true that the hearing impaired students from St. Louis' special schools usually have few problems getting along socially, we still see children at fourth grade level and above who ask their teachers embarrassing personal questions or make remarks, quite innocently, that hurt people's feelings. They are tactless. In public schools there are hearing impaired children who know virtually nothing about drugs, smoking, handling their sexual feelings, racial differences, dating, the hippie culture, athletic events, politics, the economy, local events, ecology, and so on. Some of these topics take on new importance since the voting age has been lowered to 18.

Many older pupils do not know how to weigh what people tell them before making a decision; they are followers who may go along with few opinions of their own. In this day of drug abuse, riots, and the like, this is downright dangerous. Some older children have definite opinions but no reasons to back them up. For example, one girl said that she would never date a hearing boy. When asked why, she replied, "Because," and that was the only explanation she had.

It is recognized that pupils in residential schools have social problems such as those discussed above, but it has often been assumed that children who live at home do not. In many cases their problems are just as great, and the parents and schools both need to work on these kinds of difficulties.

In an effort to help hearing impaired teen-agers in St. Louis County become better able to cope with our modern society, the Teenaiders organization was established in 1970. The group is made up of teen-agers with significant hearing losses who attend regular school classes. Adult advisors work with the club officers to plan and carry out activities. Development of leadership capabilities, exchanges of information at business meetings, and social events are included in the activities of the Teenaiders. (See page 226 for further discussion of Teenaiders.)

To Leave or Not To Leave — The Doubtful Children

Last we come to the children whom I have called "doubtful." These are the ones whom schools for the deaf hang on to for "another year or two" hoping that some "miracle" will happen and they will attain a level suitable for graduation or for public school entry. These "doubtful" children can be, and often are, spotted fairly early. They have common characteristics and may be separated into two main types.

The classic doubtful child. His IQ is low to average. His attitude may be good; he is a nice child who is cooperative and tries hard. His speech and speechreading skills are poor, regardless of a possible desire to improve. Both oral and written language skills need improvement, as does his work in academic subjects. His abilities to remember, to generalize, to work independently, and to obtain information from outside sources are all below average. The child makes little yearly progress in speech, language, or academics. When he finally leaves the school for the deaf, he is functioning at a very low academic level for his age and is held back by his poor speechreading, language, and speech skills. Socially he may or may not be immature.

If he is placed in a public school, difficulties arise immediately. Public school personnel are very reluctant to place a child too far below his age group, regardless of his academic level. Their reasons are related to the psychological and sociological aspects of the children involved. When this situation arises, the public school may compromise and place the child in a class above his academic level but below his age group — so he doesn't fit in anywhere. One example is a child in the sixth grade; he is 14 but is academically at a third grade level. The school would not place him lower than sixth grade, where he cannot do the work and is frustrated by the "silly" sixth graders. He realizes that he is out of place and is becoming a behavior problem.

There are several directions to go with a "classic doubtful child": 1) be resigned to the child's staying with special education all the way and attending a state school for the deaf for high school in order to have vocational training (in St. Louis County, the public vocational-technical high schools accept some deaf students); 2) decide early whether the child might be better served by another school and send him there; 3) keep him, do your best, and hope for some success in public school.

The Underachiever

His IQ is average or higher. His attitude is very poor, both toward school and society. His language is poor, but he shows the ability to do excellent work out of the classroom setting. For example, he may write stories or letters that show complicated language structures, advanced vocabulary, and great imagination. His speech skills are likely to be poor, with few attempts at improvement; but when he wants to communicate, he can. In academic areas, he may be low in some subjects and do excellent work in others, depending on what he is interested in. His ability to remember, to generalize, to work independently, and to get information from outside sources is likely to be very good.

When underachievers from schools for the deaf get out into public schools, they often flourish. They are challenged academically and they get a chance to work independently in areas of interest. Their speech and language usage may improve; the students may try harder because they know that they have to, while in the school for the deaf the teachers understood them even when they used poor speech. Because of their underlying ability they are likely to be placed in a class at their age level and thus be able to be with their peers. Social development and attitude may well show drastic improvement.

Basically these are the children who should have been sent to public school a year or two or three earlier—at a time when they were first able to move faster than the school for the deaf moved. So what if they don't know dictionary skills—their classmates probably don't either. So what if their speech is below par—it will improve. So what if they never do assignments—neither would you if you weren't challenged.

Conclusion

Many hearing impaired children from the schools for the deaf in St. Louis are successful in public school. Most of these children have some difficulties in academic areas, although their problems differ greatly in severity at different grade levels. Math, literature, and general vocabulary are the areas in which they are most deficient. Almost all hearing impaired children need to be taught to be more independent and to be made more aware of accepted social behavior and the happenings of the world around them. Good speech, speechreading, and study habits are necessities for success in public school. Children about whom there is a great deal of doubt should be evaluated carefully in order that the best educational possibilities for them can be utilized. The ultimate goal is for all students to be given the opportunity to progress to the maximum of their ability.

REFERENCES

Roberts, P. *The Roberts English series.* Chicago: Harcourt, Brace & World, Inc., 1966.
Sanders, R., & Rosato, G. *New directions in English.* New York: Harper & Row, 1969.
Yater, V. The St. Louis County Hearing Clinician Program. *The Volta Review,* 1972, **74,** 247-255.

Have You Thought Of . . .

. . . keeping a small spiral notebook at your fingertips throughout the day? As a child mispronounces a word, uses an incorrect ending, or indicates that he does not understand a concept, you can jot down the pupil's name and the word he needs help with. Then you will be prepared to help him as soon as the opportunity arises. — *Dorothy Hedgecock, Rochester, Minnesota.*

27

OSCAR P. COHEN

An Integrated Summer Recreation Program

The utilization of community resources is a valuable way to meet the social-emotional and recreational needs of hearing impaired children. Their participation in activities within their own neighborhoods will encourage a meaningful, on-going, and more natural interaction with hearing children. In planning a program, it is essential that teachers, recreation specialists, and others involved with hearing impaired children in an integrated setting consider such factors as: children's ages, social maturity, communication skills, ratio of hearing to hearing impaired participants, parental cooperation, orientation and training of staff, activity structure, and availability of special education resource specialists. After four years of experimentation, tne Lexington School has developed a model program utilizing the resources of community agencies to promote the social development ot nearing impaired children.

The Lexington School for the Deaf conducted its first summer community recreation program on the school's campus in July 1968. At that time, our immediate objectives were to provide both deaf and hearing children with an exciting summer recreation program and to expose them to new social experiences in an integrated environment. An important administrative purpose was to contribute to the development of Lexington School's role as a community center.

Participants: Thirty-eight hearing children and 13 deaf children ranging in age from 7 to 14 participated in the program. The hearing children, all from the immediate community, were contacted through neighborhood church and

Mr. Cohen is Director of the Division of Child Care at the Lexington School for the Deaf in Jackson Heights, Queens, New York.

school bulletins. Nine of the deaf children were students at Lexington School; four attended other schools for the deaf.

Facilities: The children used the school's gym, playrooms, and outdoor play areas. (The swimming pool and outdoor fields were still under construction during the greater part of the program.) A nearby industrial plant, in the spirit of community involvement, made available additional playing fields. Transportation to the program was provided by parents.

Activities: The program lasted from 9 a.m. to 12 noon, Monday through Friday. The morning was divided into four 45-minute periods for the various activities — quiet games, arts and crafts, athletics, treasure hunts, field days, and a weekly captioned movie. Special activities included trips to beaches, a Mets' baseball game, the New York Jets' football training camp, the Eastern Airlines Terminal at La Guardia Airport, and an all-camp cookout at a public park on Long Island to mark the end of the session. These activities were then summarized in a weekly camp newspaper.

Staff: The 12 staff members represented a variety of disciplines. One was a profoundly deaf doctoral student in psychology, another was a doctoral student in sociology, and four were undergraduate majors in speech pathology. Two counselors were trained teachers of the deaf and one was an art teacher. Completing the faculty were three students (one salaried and two volunteer) from the Lexington School.

Intensive orientation acquainted the group leaders with the aims of the program. In addition, they met each week for four hours to evaluate the degree of integration fostered in the previous week's activities and to plan the following week's program. They also discussed the behavioral differences between deaf and hearing children, including the ways in which the children communicated with each other and the role each child played in his group.

Observations on Program Effectiveness

Sociograms were made at the beginning and end of the program. They were constructed on the basis of answers to the following questions:
1. Whom would you like to sit next to?
2. With whom would you like to work on an art project?
3. Whom would you choose to be on your team?
4. Who is the quiet, shy person in the group?
The questions were communicated through speech, writing, and gestures, according to the needs of the children.

Since they were not prepared under carefully controlled conditions, the results of the sociograms are not statistically valid. However, they do suggest general changes that might have taken place in the acceptance of deaf children by their hearing peers, and vice versa. The later sociograms suggested significantly greater integration in four of the five groups. In answer to the first three questions the deaf children were chosen more times in the second sociogram.

While some deaf children were still named as the quiet members of the group, hearing children were also chosen.

The staff and its director made several empirical observations:

1. At the beginning of the program, the hearing children generally communicated with the deaf children through their counselors. By the end of July there was a more relaxed atmosphere, and the deaf and hearing children communicated more directly with each other, particularly in the younger age groups.

2. The deaf children also overcame a lack of spontaneity in verbal communication. Rather than communicating only when necessary, they initiated "small talk" with hearing children.

3. At first, the deaf children seemed less able to carry out the projects involved in the day's activities. It later appeared that the deaf children were merely more dependent on adult direction, not lacking in ability.

4. There was noticeably less interaction between deaf and hearing children in quiet activities, although this interaction increased toward the end of the month.

5. Because group rivalry united the deaf and hearing members of each group, competitive games resulted in the most successful integrated activities. The group leaders deliberately chose different captains each day; therefore, each deaf student became captain several times and was required to direct the others in the group.

6. The deaf girl in the Girls II group showed a significant degree of leadership. She was consistently chosen by the others as one of the most popular members of the group. The hearing girls in the group assumed her speech pattern when communicating with her and, with this adaption, they fully accepted her.

7. In the Boys II group (nine hearing and two deaf boys), three members were rejected. The three isolates, one deaf and two hearing, formed a subgroup and interacted successfully with each other, while the remaining eight boys (one deaf) also integrated well. In this case the subgroup was based on personality rather than physical differences. Generally, it seemed that if deaf children were rejected by the hearing, it was rarely because of their deafness, per se, but seemed instead to be a result of personality factors. At the same time we noted that the deaf child who was disliked but who was adept at verbal communication rated higher in the opinion of his group than a deaf child who lacked both an acceptable personality and verbal communication skills.

Problems and Challenges

The staff encountered certain problems which have been taken into consideration in planning subsequent programs:

1. Deaf children, and even the Lexington School student staff, tended to use a great deal of physical contact, such as pushing, pinching, wrestling, and pulling hair. This hyperactivity was not malicious, but it annoyed the others in the group. It seemed that this behavior was an attempt to maintain constant communication with other group members.

2. Deaf children did not seem to be as socially mature as their hearing peers,

possibly because of their limited experiences and inability to perceive many social nuances. In future programs, consideration should be given to the possibility of integrating younger hearing children with older deaf children, provided intellectual levels and physical skills are generally comparable.

3. Throughout the program, hearing children tended increasingly to accept deafness. An exception, however, was that the earlier acceptance of the deaf girl in the oldest group subsided toward the end of the program. The hearing girls became less sympathetic due to the constant repetition necessary to include the deaf girl in the group's activities. The group felt that this repetition held them back since communication flowed so quickly among the hearing girls. Even though they were interested in deafness and constantly asked questions about speech and hearing, they seemed to resent slowing their normal pace for the deaf person. (It was interesting that the group leader, a teacher of the deaf, felt the same impatience with the deaf girl.) Unlike the younger groups, this age group relied heavily on verbal communication. One possible conclusion is that the older the group, the greater the need for good oral skills on the part of the deaf member.

4. The staff felt that a one-to-one ratio of deaf to hearing children generally made it too easy for the deaf and the hearing to form parallel, segregated subgroups. Overloading the groups with deaf children resulted in a deaf subgroup and an isolated hearing group. Greatest success was found in an eight-to-two ratio with the hearing members in the majority. The deaf members had the security of deaf companionship, but did not form a subgroup. At the same time the hearing children were sympathetic and helpful to the deaf children. The group functioned as an integrated unit and not as a combination of subgroups.

Although we encountered many problems in implementing the original program, the immediate objectives were accomplished. The ease with which the deaf and hearing interacted after getting to know each other, the knowledge of deafness and hearing that each group acquired, and the many experiences gained by each participant made the program worthwhile.

Follow-up

We followed up our 1968 summer experience with summer programs and evaluations in 1969, 1970, and 1971, attempting to measure changes in social maturity, speechreading ability, language acquisition, and characteristics involving cooperation and competition between hearing and hearing impaired children in an integrated setting. We concluded that such a program based in a school for the deaf, while producing beneficial experiential effects for hearing impaired children, offers less than optimal opportunities for meaningful, long-lasting interactions and behavioral changes. In short, we were not fully satisfied with a four-week program in which hearing impaired children were bussed to a special education school from outside the immediate community to interact with local neighborhood children.

These conclusions prompted us to redesign our program and led us to what we consider to be a model-prototype conducted with optimal success during the summer of 1972. After evaluating the strengths and weaknesses of our former summer programs, Lexington School entered into formal affiliation with a Queens, New York, YM-YWHA*. The YM-YWHA, with a tradition of conducting eight-week summer day camp programs for all children within their general community, was chosen because of its social work orientation. In addition, the camp grounds, located about 20 miles from the city, represented a common turf for everyone. We selected hearing impaired children who lived within the catchment area of the 'Y' to join hearing children from their own neighborhood in a common experience. Changing the base of operations from Lexington School to the 'Y' Day Camp provided a more realistic and natural environment for integration to take place. The subgrouping which occurred in former programs as a result of hearing children coming from the immediate neighborhoods and hearing impaired children traveling from outside neighborhoods was almost nonexistent.

Two Lexington School resource specialists and an evaluator represented the school at the 'Y' camp. Their functions included conducting orientations for camp counselors and supervisors, training camp staff in dealing with hearing impaired children, troubleshooting problems which occurred at camp, participating in activity planning sessions with camp staff, acting as liaison between parents and camp staff, following up parents' concerns and problems, and, through observations and questionnaires, evaluating changes in attitudes and behaviors of hearing children, deaf children, camp counselors, and parents.

The nonsectarian program ran for eight weeks during July and August, twice the length of former summer programs. In addition, participation included a year's family membership in the 'Y' which enabled children, siblings, and parents to benefit from programs at the 'Y' during the year, a long term carry-over benefit which was not realized in former programs. Twenty-four of our children are presently enrolled in winter programs at the 'Y' as a result of this carry-over.

There is unanimous consensus of counselors, camp administration, parents, Lexington staff, and, most importantly, children that the camp was a successful experience for all. The essential features lacking in our former program — an eight-week experience, long term carry-over, utilization of a neighborhood community resource, a program based away from a special education facility, a 500 to 25 ratio of hearing to hearing impaired children, and the sensitizing of a community agency to the unmet needs of a population within their community — were realized in the 1972 integrated summer program. Plans are being made to conduct similar programs in coming summers, and future plans include opening up community agencies for hearing impaired children throughout New York City. We feel that we have essentially used our 1968 model of an integrated summer recreation program and expanded on it by changing its base of operations and extending its scope to include long-term benefits to and participation of children, parents, and community resources.

*Young Men's and Young Women's Hebrew Association.

28

CHARLES H. COSPER, JR.

Activities for Hearing Impaired Children

Suggestions of an Oral Deaf Adult

Integration should not be confined to the school classroom. It is an on-going process having relevance only if it is carried into the hearing impaired child's everyday experience. Exposing the child to a variety of extracurricular activities -- in the home and the community -- will help him develop the communicative and social skills that prepare him for the important years after graduation from high school. If begun at an early age, this social involvement will enrich the child's academic development, too. An oral deaf adult describes the types of activities he feels are particularly important for the integrated hearing impaired child.

Involving a hearing impaired child in social situations can and should begin quite easily and naturally when the child is very young — for instance, a toddler may accompany his mother to the store or neighborhood coffee party. As he grows older, more formal interaction through planned family activities and organized groups may serve to enlarge his social contacts. The focus should be on exposing the hearing impaired child to as many areas of social contribution as possible — through family experiences, hobbies, school and church activities — to help him develop a broad insight into his own personality and the things he enjoys and is able to do.

Your community is a good place to start. Scout troops and other organized groups are available in many neighborhoods for children as young as 7 or 8. Cub Scouts, Brownies, Boy Scouts, Girl Scouts, "Y" groups, and the 4-H Club are

Mr. Cosper, an oral deaf adult, is Resource Teacher for the Berrien County Day Program for Hearing Impaired Children, Berrien Springs, Michigan.

just a few of the national organizations for children in elementary and secondary grades. In addition, there are local church youth programs, community-sponsored recreational activities, baseball and softball leagues, tennis clubs, swimming programs, golf centers, and both formal and informal playground activities which provide good opportunities for social development. A week or two at a summer camp, where the hearing impaired child can participate with normally hearing children in an oral environment, may be particularly beneficial.

In any integrated social setting, it is recommended that there be just one hearing impaired child per group so that he is encouraged to interact with and become accepted by the hearing participants. Also, the counselor and other members will then have time to help the hearing impaired child and communicate with him on an individual basis, which would not be possible if there were four or five hearing impaired children in the group.

When looking for a social group that the hearing impaired child might be interested in joining, the parent should ask the leader, "Are you willing to work with my hearing impaired child?" If there is any hesitation, it is best not to enter the child in that group, but to wait to find a person who is willing to accept the challenge. It is probably best if the hearing impaired child attends the group meetings independently without his parents' supervision. This will avoid feelings of defensive partiality and give the child the opportunity to develop his individuality.

The Role of the Family

The hearing impaired child's social awareness can be increased by family visits to the parents' place of work, various community industries, educational facilities, theater, the city hall, the fire station, the police station, museums, places of historic interest, and state parks. Vacation trips to different parts of the country via bus, train, airplane, and car offer good educational opportunities.

A child who is well-informed and academically prepared will have increased opportunity for social and vocational development as he grows older. Parents should become aware of the child's academic strengths and weaknesses through conferences with his teachers, principal, and counselor. They should also be willing to work through a parent organization to encourage the school district to provide academic tutoring and speech help for the child in subjects where he is struggling. They may recommend to the teacher that the child be seated near the front of his classroom and that the assignments be written on the blackboard. At home, they can help by providing a good study center where the child can work and concentrate, or encourage him to use a quiet corner of the nearest library. He should be taught to observe regular study hours and to keep a small notebook listing daily assignments and activities.

Reading is an important part of a hearing impaired child's learning, and, therefore, it is to his advantage to be exposed to it at a very early age. Parents may stimulate a young child's interest by reading aloud to him in the evenings or before bedtime, buying at least one wholesome book or comic book appropriate for his age level every week, enrolling him in the library children's hour, or taking him to the library each week for an hour or so. As the child grows older, he might be invited to join a worthwhile book club or be given a subscription to a magazine he enjoys. An interest in reading will help him keep up-to-date on current events and give him security in group discussions and personal conversation.

Hobbies and Extracurricular Activities

Hobbies of all varieties should be encouraged — photography; working with microscopes and chemistry sets; collecting insects, flowers, rocks, stamps, coins; etc. Talent or interest in square dancing, sports, ballroom dancing, music, or artistic media of any kind can be fostered through lessons and individual help. Volunteer work such as that of Candy Stripers in hospitals or junior members of the Red Cross can also be valuable experience.

Earning money can be a social experience, too. Part-time jobs such as a newspaper delivery route, lawn and garden work, housecleaning assistance, and babysitting, provide numerous situations in which the child and the community can become acquainted with one another. We often hear the remark, "He'll work hard for his neighbor, but won't do a thing at home," and this applies to hearing impaired children, too. If the child can do a job at home for which someone else would normally be hired, he should be offered the task and paid accordingly. Hobbies are sometimes profitable also; children can make and sell leather crafts, plaster of Paris wall plaques, polished rock jewelry, wooden toys, carved animals, and many other gift items. Encourage them to use their imagination, and help by providing necessary tools or suggesting ways he can earn money to purchase them.

Youngsters should also be made aware of the many extracurricular activities available in elementary and secondary schools. Most schools offer a wide range of possibilities such as the photography, math, music, chess, or pep clubs, or vocationally oriented organizations such as Future Teachers of America. Students should be encouraged to try out for team sports or participate in intramural sports activities. Both group sports (softball, baseball, football, basketball) and individual sports (tennis, golf, swimming, wrestling, track) provide good learning experiences in social adjustment.

A hearing impaired child's participation in an organization or activity with normally hearing children is beneficial both to him and to the group. Young people need to develop a social awareness of individual differences through personal experience. Children who have friends who are deaf, retarded, crippled, or handicapped in other ways gain perspective and understanding. Efforts of parents and teachers to provide numerous and varied opportunities for the hearing impaired child to integrate with hearing children can be invaluable to the hearing impaired child and to those around him.

29

The Way It Looks to Me:
Views of an Integrated Student

A profoundly deaf high school graduate describes his experiences in integrated classes. Steven's speech training was begun when he was 2½, and at age 4 he entered his county's preschool program for the hearing impaired. Through elementary school he attended the special auditory classes located in the public schools and integrated into his first regular class — social studies — at age 9. He was fully integrated throughout senior high school and graduated in spring of 1973 among the top 10% of his class. Of the hard work involved, he writes, "It's all worth it! . . . As I am preparing to graduate I look back on my education and activities with a feeling of great indebtedness to my family and teachers for their commitment and positive attitude about me."

When I was a year old, my parents suspected that I might have a hearing loss. Their suspicion was confirmed at the Johns Hopkins Hospital and at age 2 I was fitted with a hearing aid. From that point on, my parents, my brother Barnett, relatives, and friends became involved in my education, problems, and welfare. My parents determined that they would do everything possible for me to reach my potential and be able to stand on my own two feet as an adult (whether it be as a milkman blue-collar worker or as a white-collar professional). Though they thought of the future, they planned one step at a time. Above all, they wanted me to be happy and a productive part of the community.

Mr. Rattner is a graduate of Montgomery Blair High School, Silver Spring, Maryland, and is beginning studies in mathematics and science at Montgomery College.

At the age of 2½, I took private speech lessons along with two other children with hearing problems. My attention span was very short, I was not very interested in learning, and words had little meaning to me. Then at the age of 4, I was accepted into the Montgomery County Public Schools' special diagnostic preschool program for children with language problems. I was the youngest child in the self-contained class. The teacher emphasized that her aim was to "make us little human beings" who could follow directions and be part of the class and the school student body. It was at that time that I became interested in learning. But I was still a rather stubborn child. (My teacher once sent a note home to this effect: "Steven insisted on a note because I gave one to someone else, and I was too tired to argue.")

Learning Independence

I remained in special auditory classes throughout elementary school. "Bussing" was not a controversial word in those days, and I was bussed to school from preschool through the ninth grade. (When my parents first learned that I would have to take two school buses, they got "cold feet"; but upon investigation they learned that the transfer took place on school property under supervision, and my worried father finally said, "It looks like we will have to give our 4-year-old his independence.")

It was in the early grades that I really began to want to learn and to do my best. I became interested in things around me, loved people, and wanted to know how things worked. I spent a lot of time building and fixing things. After school, I played with the kids in the neighborhood. For awhile, they all wanted to wear hearing aids. I really had two sets of friends — one group at school and another at home — and sometimes felt that I was living in two worlds. I was included in everything — class parties, neighborhood birthday parties, and family get-togethers — and was given many experiences. When I went to the store, my parents encouraged me to speak to the sales clerks and ask for my own purchases (though my speech was not always very understandable). I was very sociable and thought that everybody was my friend.

At the age of 6, I attended the special auditory classes held at Broadacres Elementary School with the hearing impaired students from all over the county. During these years, my feelings about being hearing impaired were perhaps quite unusual — I didn't mind it at all. Perhaps this was because I had always met people who really wanted to help me. The elementary school staff — supervisors, principal, teachers, teacher-aides, and secretaries — were interested in me. Everyone was friendly and spoke to me often, and my teachers earnestly continued to build my speech, language, and academic skills. I can still remember how much I hated to put on the headphones of the group auditory training unit which, in those days, were big, clumsy, and a pain in the neck! But the effort paid off as I learned to listen and to distinguish different sounds. This helped to improve my speech as well as my "hearing."

An itinerant music teacher visited the school twice a week and gave musical instrument lessons. I chose to play the clarinet and, after many lessons, played in the school band (June 1963). This was a good experience, and made me feel as if I were a real part of the school. I played the clarinet for about two years until, like any kid who gets tired of practicing, I told everybody, "I'm tired of blowing." (Even my parents had to admit that my face was unusually red when I was playing.) I recall how I enjoyed the sensation of the vibrations from the clarinet. I learned to recognize the different sounds of music, and especially loved the drums and the organ. Today's rock music is blaring enough for me to enjoy, too. Most times I miss the words from the records, but during live concerts I can often lipread the words; thus "my musical education" was certainly not wasted.

After school hours I took ice skating lessons and found it great exercise and a fun hobby. At the end of the season, there was a musical ice show, "Fantasy on Ice." I had to skate out at the right time with the other children in the "Peter Pan" scene and do a routine. Fortunately I followed the leader, or I might have ended up doing a solo on ice. I didn't have enough language to understand all the directions, but I had good eyes and good blades. It was a great experience to meet the challenge of performing with others (June 1962).

I was also enrolled in a recreational course in making model airplanes. There, I was on my own and had to make myself understood by kids who didn't know me. Though I did not go to the local school, I had a lot of neighborhood friends who were especially interested in me when I was building or making something. Soon we were building forts, club houses, and even a tree house; and together we built all the games for a neighborhood fund-raising carnival.

I went to Sunday School at age 9 and began religious training in a regular school for hearing children when I was 11. The religious studies were difficult for me because of my lack of understanding of higher level communication. There was much unfamiliar vocabulary, especially in the history class. (Once I remember underlining about 15 words per page that I did not know, and sometimes I wished there were a Hebrew school for hearing impaired children!) However, in one sense, I was at an advantage when we studied the Hebrew language because I had had so much help in phonics that I could learn some of the sounds rather quickly.

Beginning to Integrate in Academic Subjects

Up to that time, I was still in a self-contained class in school and received much help in speech, language, auditory training, reading, writing, and arithmetic. At 9, I began to integrate into my first regular class, social studies, for an hour daily. This meant that I had moved to a new world. While the self-contained class had consisted of about eight children, the social studies class had approximately 28. I began to understand better what life among the hearing was and that language and speech lessons would never end. My ability to learn began to improve as I worked on. On the last day of school, after six months in the social studies class, I stood up formally in class to say goodbye and to make a simple statement: "Thank you for trying to understand me. I liked being here." A student in the class quickly stood up and just as formally stated, "We have learned a great deal from you and we liked having you in the class. You're a great kid." This was very spontaneous. It was hard to say goodbye, for I had made some new friends.

The Auditory Program was transferred to Forest Grove Elementary School, a school closer to where I lived. I began to integrate into a math class. My language was only fair, but math concepts came easily. The written problems were complicated for me because of the way some of the questions were phrased (unfamiliar vocabulary and directions with new language constructions could throw me off). But we worked on this area, and to my amazement and my teacher's, I did very well on the first math test. This put me right in there with the other kids. That day, upon hearing the news, my special education teacher sent a note (which I still have) to my parents saying, "I'm on cloud nine today. Steven got the highest mark in the regular math class." This gives you an idea about the enthusiasm of the staff.

By the fifth grade, I was becoming quite involved in school activities — sports, plays, fund-raising, and special projects. The Audio Visual Committee was one of my real interests at this time and I was often called on to work the movie projector or to adjust it when it seemed to be out of order. This made me feel rather important. When the fifth and sixth grade classes went on a four-day overnight trip to Mar Lu Ridge, a science camp owned by the county, I was invited to go along and I had a great time. We took nature walks, studied, cooked out, square danced, and put on a play. Only when the lights were out was I cut off from the whispers of my cabin friends.

I graduated from elementary school feeling very excited about going to the secondary level, yet sad about leaving all of my special teachers, the other staff members, and my friends. But I was ready to move on, not worried about whether I could make it or not. I knew I had to.

Partial Integration in Junior High

The county's Auditory Program at the junior high level provided a resource room for the hearing impaired. Some students stayed in this class full-time, while others integrated in regular classes on an individual basis. I took reading, science, and English in the self-contained class where the teaching was based on my particular needs in speech and language. I also had speech and hearing therapy three times a week. I began to integrate in math, geography, art, and gym. (When I realized that I would not be able to wear my hearing aid during physical education, I felt lost. I had to rely on speechreading more than ever and had to pay careful attention to directions, especially during roll call. Sometimes, it meant speechreading 20 names until mine was called! My gym teacher also had a hearing loss, so he understood my physical handicap.) Occasionally, when I walked into one of my regular classes I would learn that a test was about to be given. Apparently, I had not heard the announcement the previous day. This was rather upsetting, so I made it a rule to keep "an eye out" for all announcements and to check with my notetaker.

Perhaps, at this point, I should discuss notetakers and notetaking. As I integrated in more subjects, I began to rely more and more on notes taken by classmates. Sometimes, the notetaker left out important facts. It took me a long time to explain to each one exactly how much I was depending upon full notes. Very few students were unwilling to cooperate. In fact, at the end of the semester, some of my notetakers told me that they had done better than usual because of the full notes they had taken on carbon for me.

At Sligo Junior High I continued to be very interested in math and science and entered a project in the Science Fair. I demonstrated my "light dimmer" and gave a prepared talk to the class. Though my written report had much technical vocabulary, I have to admit that in my talk I tried to use vocabulary that I was comfortable with. I did not want to worry about the pronunciation of too many difficult words. The Science Fair was a meaningful experience, for it taught me to "think on my feet." Other speaking opportunities came my way when classmates elected me to be the classroom representative to the student government. In all ways, junior high was a worthwhile preparation for high school.

Full-Time Integration in High School

Even now, I can remember the feeling I had when I first enrolled in Montgomery Blair High School. Before school reopened in the fall, my brother Barnett, who had graduated from Blair in 1968, showed me around and introduced some of his former teachers. I met my new counselor who had helped with my schedule, and during orientation I saw many of my neighborhood friends who were tenth graders like me. I was familiar with the school since it was the neighborhood high school; it was the first time that I had gone to a local school. I knew that my auditory teacher had previously been there to make special arrangements for my curriculum with the counselor and to speak to my teachers about having a hearing impaired student in the class. So I felt really comfortable about going to the new school and anticipated my new venture.

Looking back at these years at Blair, I cannot think of any major unpleasantness, discomfort, or discouragement. I only think of great things that happened and of meeting many dedicated teachers and new friends. Most of these teachers were very interesting and challenging. They went out of their way to help me understand the material. During the class sessions and after school they were available for extra help and discussions.

I took sociology and psychology in my junior year. The content of the courses, the classroom discussions, and the enthusiasm of the teachers brought about much interaction. Each person was required to write a real term paper (my first), and I chose as my topic "The Development of Language in a Deaf Child." I wanted to explore why I had so much difficulty with written language, and the paper gave me a good insight into this subject. I gave an oral report to the class accompanied by a demonstration using an overhead projector and two films which I ordered from the Clarke School for the Deaf. It really went over well. As a matter of fact, this project lasted two periods since the class was so interested in the subject. A student in that class even expressed an interest in becoming a teacher of the deaf!

In addition to sociology, I took chemistry, Algebra II, and English. Chemistry became one of my favorite subjects and my major interest. The teacher challenged me greatly. I was one of several students chosen to attend the Greater Washington Junior Science and Humanities Symposium held at Georgetown University (November 1971), and I was surprised and pleased to be accepted to the National Honor Society. My family and former teachers, who had worked so hard with me over the years, were all thrilled about this achievement, as were relatives, friends, and parents of younger children (Montgomery County Association for Language Handicapped Children*) who felt that this was an inspiration for them. I was glad that one of my "very special" elementary auditory teachers was invited to attend the ceremony.

In my senior year, I took calculus, English, art, and advanced chemistry. The chemistry course was designed to develop independent work habits in chemistry principles. I worked as a chemistry lab assistant in my free period. (Like all my other teachers, my chemistry instructor encouraged me to achieve all that I could.)

The Auditory Resource Teacher

For a hearing impaired student, the most important teacher in junior and senior high school is often the Auditory Resource Teacher. In my case, she is one of my best friends. I see her four times a week for one-hour sessions. Fortunately, she has made herself available in the evenings and Sundays and has made it clear to her students that she will help them with any additional problems at any time. She is a very inspiring teacher. These are some of the things that she has done to make me — and other students — more comfortable as we progress in school:

1. She regularly meets with all of my teachers and checks to see that I am on the track.

2. She is of particular help when we have a reading assignment because we can discuss the symbolism or theme of a story if I do not understand it. When I go into the regular class, I feel I know the material and am at a better advantage.

---

*My parents were the co-founders of this association, which was organized in 1959. Along with many other charter members, parents, professionals, and friends, they worked on behalf of hearing impaired and language handicapped children.

3. She helps me with vocabulary, speech, written language, and concept areas that I now know I shall have to work on all my life.
4. In the beginning of the year, she sends a personal note to each teacher. Then a special sheet of instructions is sent to the teachers of each hearing impaired student which explains our needs. Every six weeks an evaluation sheet is provided for the teacher's comments. (See examples at the conclusion of this chapter.)

In Montgomery Blair High, I have had the opportunity to have many experiences, both academically and socially. I was encouraged to participate in extracurricular activities as often as possible to use my speech in everyday situations and to become better acquainted with other students and the community. I participated on the tennis team during my sophomore year and enjoyed the team interaction. In my freshman year, I went out on my own and found a part-time job at the Sheraton Silver Spring Motel as a busboy. After 6 months, I was promoted to room service waiter. A year later, I found another job at a major chain of drugstores as a cashier and stock boy. In both jobs, when I've had to meet and communicate with the public, I have had only minor problems — most of them in speechreading (especially with a person with a beard or mustache).

Suggestions for Others

In adjusting to junior high and high school, the early training I'd received in self-contained classes was helpful — as it was designed to equip me with skills needed in integrating. I think that hearing impaired students have to work extra hard for what they learn and in doing so they develop good work habits. Every summer since the age of 4, I worked on speech and language development in the Montgomery County Public School Auditory Program, in other speech centers, and with a private tutor. Now I realize that this was essential. I've benefited from the experience in integrated classes and would offer this advice to other hearing impaired students going into regular classes:

1. Don't be nervous or shy.
2. Try to find a new friend in the class who can help you.
3. Explain your hearing and language problem to the teacher and friends.
4. Ask the teacher to help you find someone in the class who can take informative notes. Sometimes it is best not to ask the brightest student in the class because he might already know the information and would not feel the need to write it down. Try to find an average student who is available and conscientious about taking notes. Provide the notetaker with the NTID (National Technical Institute for the Deaf) carbon notebook.
5. Keep up with the daily work; don't fall behind, but don't get too far ahead. Rather, stay where the class is. Remember that it is your responsibility to get the material.

6. Don't feel embarrassed or upset if you are not sure of the home assignment. Just ask your classmates or stay a few minutes after class and ask the teacher.

7. If the teacher has a question to ask the whole class, try to participate in answering and don't feel embarrassed if the answer is wrong. Find out why it is wrong. If the teacher does not understand you, repeat your response in more understandable words. It is better to speak up in class than to hide. Then the class is given the opportunity to know you and to give you a chance. The more you speak, the better off you will be in social life.

8. Sit in the first row so that you can see the entire class during classroom discussions.

9. In oral tests, ask your teacher not to talk too fast. Also, make sure that you understand the questions. If not, ask your teacher for a question sheet. (Oral tests really throw me. While I am still writing the answer, the teacher is already dictating the next question. With my head and eyes down, I miss what is said.)

In conclusion, I feel that integration has a very important and unique meaning to the hearing impaired. It gives us an opportunity to get together with other people, especially hearing peers. Each successive year in an integrated program became easier for me. I have to rely on speechreading for what is said in class, use every possible cue, and work harder than most students to understand — but it's all worth it! I feel special because my parents have given me much confidence as well as encouragement and were very involved in my education. Parent involvement and good attitudes are the most influential factors in raising a child with a handicap. It is important for the parents to educate themselves to understand the problems of the children and to work with their children and the school staff. My family, teachers, and other school staff were in close touch with each other and this rapport has been very beneficial to me. To this day my teachers from the early years remain interested in my progress or problems.

As I am preparing to graduate, I look back on my education and activities with a feeling of great indebtedness to my family and teachers for their commitment and positive attitude about me. At this moment I am looking forward to September when I will be a first-year student at Montgomery College in Rockville, Maryland. Perhaps in four years I will be writing an article about integration in college. I hope that my experiences will indirectly help to make it possible for other hearing impaired students to achieve their goals.

(Please turn page for auditory resource materials.)

Sample Personal Note to Teachers from Auditory Specialist

Dear

I am delighted to join the staff here, and I look forward to meeting you personally as quickly as possible, after school gets underway.

The deaf and hard of hearing students are part of the regular program of this school. The basic educational premise here is that these students are to meet the standards set by the teacher for all the students.

For those who have not had the experience of having a deaf student in a class, I have noted some observations which I hope will be useful.

Please call on me for the special problems that may arise. I am here to help you as well as the students.

Sincerely yours,

Auditory Specialist

Subject

Student

Sample Sheet of Instructions to Teachers from Auditory Specialist

To the Instructor With a Deaf Student in his Class:

1. The deaf student depends upon vision to get the information that others pick up through sound. While he uses speech to give his ideas to others, he must "listen" through speechreading or lipreading. (A hearing aid does not provide normal hearing; it does reinforce certain speech sounds and gross sounds in the environment.)
2. Be sure the deaf student can see you easily. Try to put him in a front row seat. He can only speechread you when he can see your face. (If you turn your back, he loses you.)
3. It helps to emphasize a key word or new vocabulary word by writing it on the board.
4. A public address announcement needs to be repeated by the teacher or another student so the deaf student knows what has come over the PA.
5. It is not possible for the deaf student to follow a class discussion or to speechread another student unless he can see his face. Please assure the student that he has your permission to move his desk so he can watch the speaker.
6. The deaf student cannot take class notes or lecture notes; he must focus all his concentration for speechreading. It is therefore necessary for you to select one or two capable and cooperative students to take notes

for him. I will provide a notebook with specially treated paper which makes an automatic copy of the student's notes.

7. It has been my experience that often the average student makes a better notetaker than a superior one. He takes notes which are more detailed and copious and, therefore, of more value to the deaf student.

8. If you program a movie, record, tape, or any media requiring listening, please ask the notetaker to take notes. If there is written material available, it is often helpful for the deaf student to read it.

Sample Progress Evaluation Sheet

TO:

FROM:

DATE:

Dear   :

    I would very much appreciate your comments on the items below so that I may better evaluate the progress of the students with whom I am working. Just drop the completed form in my box. If it is more convenient for you to talk to me about a particular student, please let me know.

Student: Subject: Period:

Attendance:

Classwork:

Completion of assignments:

Tests and Quizzes:

Attitude:

Additional Comments:

Many thanks for all the cooperation you have always given me.

Sincerely yours,

Auditory Specialist

Part VI

The Secondary Years

30

HARRIET GREEN KOPP

Adolescence:
Adjustment or Rebellion?

The hearing impaired teen-ager can be assisted in his adjustment to adolescence by the understanding, realistic encouragement, and active involvement of the adults who are in contact with him. The parent-school-community team can play a critical part both in widening the opportunities for the hearing impaired youth and in stimulating him to accept these challenges and pursue his individual potential. The effectiveness of the parents and educators in this role depends on the substance and timing of their efforts.

As parents and educators who live and work with adolescent deaf and hard of hearing boys and girls, our basic goals are much the same as those voiced by parents and teachers of the hearing teen-ager. Our problems may be somewhat more complex, however. A hearing loss does not alter the premise that the teen years bring both a sense of rebellion against adult regulations and a desire for assuming responsibility for goals and actions and for self-determination. Nor does it modify the urgent need of the adolescent to identify with his peers, both those who can hear and those who can't.

It is unfortunate that this compulsion to conform in every detail may be strongest during the period when the young deaf adult is faced with increasing awareness of the problems posed by social adaptation and academic achievement. Such awareness may come earlier and less abruptly for those fortunate enough to have had frequent contact with hearing peers during the pre-teen years.

Dr. Kopp is Professor and Chairman of the Department of Speech Pathology, Audiology, and Education of the Deaf at San Diego State University, California.

Adjustment problems of the hard of hearing adolescent may seem to be minimal from the point of view of the adults in his world. The adult, especially the professional member of the team, tends to take the long view; he is encouraged by progress made toward long-term goals and can look ahead to later realization of his student's potential. For the teen-ager, himself, the goals are *now*; the problems are pressing, and the possible solutions may appear less probable than they do to his teachers and counselors. For the deaf adolescent, the intensity of his social and vocational problems may vary with the academic level which he has reached. Too often we do not provide adequate opportunity for the deaf student to continue his education. There may be lack of motivation for the student and for his family when his academic lag becomes evident. Hopefully, increased emphasis on curriculum in schools for the deaf and provision for a wider choice of secondary education, at the National Technical Institute for the Deaf, at Gallaudet College, at local junior colleges, or at other colleges or universities for the hearing, may combine to motivate the able deaf student to reach his academic potential.

Each community, school, and home imposes its standards on all its members. We have an obligation to interpret these standards realistically and to recognize that standards are modified continually by social and economic pressures. Occupational choices for the hearing handicapped are vastly different today than those of 10 or 15 years ago. For the intelligent, well-adjusted student with a high level of academic achievement, opportunities are limited only by adaptation to the physical aspects of his handicap. However, our complex society imposes increasingly stringent limitations on the variety of occupational choices open to those with lower levels of academic ability or with complicating social or emotional difficulties.

Helping the Adolescent Prepare for Adulthood

We cannot generalize about all teen-agers. Each adolescent reflects the sum total of the forces exerted on him by his home, his school, and the society in which he lives. The potential with which he starts may be more or less amenable to modification by these forces. Even his rate of development and maturation is particular to him as a function of his specific inheritance and environment. It is difficult, therefore, to explore the problems of teen-agers en masse.

It may be more sensible to investigate those areas of adjustment which the hearing adolescent finds most distressing and to determine the degree of complication imposed upon these areas by hearing loss. Perhaps we do not permit the teen-ager himself to assist us in understanding his evaluation of his needs and his concerns. Particularly in the case of the child with a language handicap, we tend to assume the active role in contrast to his more passive one in the determination of his goals.

Is there a more effective way in which we can involve the young hearing handicapped child in active exploration of his role in interpersonal relationships?

Can we assist him in sharpening his perceptions of his own reactions and of those of others? Can we help him to evaluate his assets and his liabilities objectively and thus to set realistic goals? Have we provided adequate opportunity for him to mature socially and emotionally? Have we provided meeting places and organizations in which he can interact socially with deaf and hearing peers from the community at large, so that he is not confined to school associates? Do we help the growing child to know and to use all available community resources so that he may take advantage of every possible avenue for self development? Has he been encouraged to accept responsibility for his acts and his decisions? Have we aided the child to understand the communication problems with which he must live, to accept them, and to compensate for them efficiently and effectively? Has he learned to cope with errors of judgment without catastrophic reaction patterns? Have we helped him to develop a variety of socially acceptable ways of expressing emotion, of releasing frustration, of responding to social and emotional pressures? Have we assisted him in formulating a functional code of ethics? Do we understand that these efforts must begin in the nursery and be continued systematically if they are to serve the adolescent and the young adult most effectively?

The Time Is Now

These are only a few of the questions which must be asked and answered by the parent-school-community team. If we wait for the panic period of adolescence to ask them, our answers will come too late. We have made enormous progress in many aspects of the teaching of communication skills and academic and vocational subjects to deaf children. It is high time that we focus a part of our attention on the development of the independent, responsible, mature deaf teen-ager. The transition from child to adult is not easy at best. Perhaps, by using all our resources wisely we can help our hearing handicapped adolescents to minimize the trauma with which they shed the cocoon of childhood.

Have You Thought Of . . .

. . . placing a hearing impaired child on the student council to facilitate integration in social situations? — *Barbara Todd, Louisville, Kentucky.*

Facilitating Integration at the Junior High Level

Observations of a Teacher-Tutor

The author writes from her experiences in the Rochester (Minn.) Public Schools, where the policy has been to integrate pupils with moderate to severe hearing losses, or those with profound losses which generally occurred after language was developed. She gives a realistic view of the problems associated with integration of hearing impaired pupils at the junior high level, explaining why adjustments become increasingly difficult at this stage of schooling. A major focus is on the role of the specialized teacher-tutor in helping each student adjust to junior high and in adapting the program to individual needs.

It would be presumptuous to claim that the problems involved in integrating hearing impaired pupils in a regular classroom at the junior high level can be completely overcome. Many cannot. But we are dedicated to doing the best possible job of compensating for these. I would like to discuss some of the problems which may be encountered and a few approaches that have proved helpful in dealing with them.

During the elementary years it is possible to control much of the school environment of a hearing impaired pupil. By working closely with the classroom teacher, the teacher-tutor can help the pupil function to the best of his ability in

Ms. Hedgecock is Coordinator of the Program for the Hearing Impaired in the Rochester (Minnesota) Public Schools Department of Special Education.

the school situation. The elementary pupil feels relatively comfortable in the familiar surroundings and with his long-time association with teachers, principal, and peers. Integration works fairly well at this level.

The difficulties related to integration multiply when the pupil enters junior high school. The child's physiological and psychological changes, added to the complexity of the school program and the exposure to an entirely new and broader group of associates, may account for the large number of pupils who have difficulty adjusting to regular public school and enter state schools for the deaf at this stage. Unfortunately, many of these pupils also have trouble adjusting at the state school. Often they are not accustomed to the discipline of institutional living. They may be placed in a classroom with youngsters of a different age group. Or, because they do not know sign language, they may be unable to communicate freely with their peers. Many prefer not to learn sign language. They may feel superior to more severely handicapped pupils in the school and find it difficult to develop relationships. Also, personnel at the state residential schools are not usually eager to receive pupils at this age. For these reasons, every effort should be made to keep the hearing impaired pupil integrated at the local level.

A New Environment

The hearing loss is a greater hindrance in junior high school because of the general noise level. Most elementary schools by comparison are fairly quiet. Children must talk softly in the halls and in the lunch room, and the hard of hearing pupil may find it easier to communicate in this quieter environment. In junior high school there is something akin to bedlam in the halls and lunchroom, and many schools even allow rock music in the cafeteria. The halls are crowded during changes of classes, and voices are raised. There may be pushing and jostling, which is particularly unpleasant to a pupil wearing a hearing aid.

Mixers are one of the chief forms of social activity at the junior high schools. The music is deafening, and the excited voices of the dancers cause confusion for hearing impaired pupils. Gym classes are large and loud. During swimming classes, without his hearing aid the hearing impaired pupil cannot hear the teacher's directions. There are many other times when a hearing impaired pupil is not able to hear well enough to respond appropriately. These are times of great embarrassment to pupils at this sensitive age.

Peer acceptance is all-important at junior high school. Pupils who have accepted their hearing aids eagerly in elementary school suddenly come to school without them. They are often afraid their classmates will know that they are hard of hearing. Some boys who wear body aids are embarrassed to undress in gym classes. Other pupils can be cruel at this age. They may laugh loudly when a hearing impaired pupil makes an inappropriate response. "In-groups" form and some of the hearing impaired pupils may be left out. It is interesting to note that pupils with moderate losses frequently do not want to associate with pupils with severe losses, who may appear to their hearing peers to be more handicapped.

It is helpful to keep in mind that this is usually the most difficult school period for the hearing impaired. By the time they reach senior high school many pupils are more secure and accept their losses more gracefully. Also, senior high is usually easier academically since the pupils have more choice over which subjects they take. New school policies often eliminate requirements for math, science, or foreign language in senior high school, and the students can take the subjects which are easier for them as their electives. It is helpful to have a student from senior high come to talk with the junior high pupils and give them encouragement and first-hand advice. One older pupil advised a group of junior high youngsters, "Wear your hearing aids and don't try to hide your hearing loss. Our friends know we are hard of hearing by the way we talk." Because the junior high pupils usually respect the older students, this type of advice is convincing. It can even lead them to laugh with each other over their embarrassing incidents.

The Role of the Teacher-Tutor

The importance of the teacher-tutor of a hearing impaired pupil at the junior high level cannot be overestimated. It is the tutor's job to interpret the academic subject matter to the pupil, to see that his teachers are aware of his difficulties, and to solicit their help in working as a team to help the pupil keep up with his normal-hearing peers. Many teacher-tutors also contribute to the pupil's social/psychological adjustment to his environment. For instance, the tutor may be available to discuss sex education with hearing impaired pupils who often don't acquire the information through casual conversation with friends.

Every minute of the child's tutoring session is precious. He doesn't have time to waste. In the tutor's eagerness to make the most of the hour, she may have the materials all laid out and expect to begin work the minute the pupil enters the room. However, the pupil may have something on his mind which he needs to talk over. It is thus a good idea to let the student take the lead for the first five minutes of the session.

In junior high school, teacher-tutors have a challenging assignment. They are working not with a single classroom teacher, as in the elementary school, but with as many as eight different instructors with varying attitudes and approaches. Many junior high teachers have as many as 125 pupils in their classes during the day, many of whom have problems. It is thus hard for the teachers to understand the seriousness of the language handicap of a hearing impaired pupil and the need to work with the tutor in explaining the assignments and expectations for the course.

The teacher-tutor is accepting of the pupil. In fact, she may be the only person with whom the pupil feels completely comfortable, evidenced by the disappointment the pupil often expresses when the tutor is absent. Any way in which the tutor can help the pupil gain self-confidence at this sensitive age is time well spent, for the pupil who has friends and a good self-image learns more easily. Teacher-tutors can encourage hobbies, arrange scholarships at the YMCA, transport the pupils to sports activities after school, and even help them find part-time jobs.

An important function of the teacher-tutor is to see that the pupil's hearing aid is working well. Most tutors immediately recognize the distinctive, anxious look on the face of a pupil whose hearing aid battery is low. It is frightening to the youngster to have the battery go dead in class, and he may anticipate that this will happen when he knows it is about time for the battery to wear out. This worry is eliminated when the pupil knows that the teacher has a battery on hand for him. Some service clubs are willing to provide batteries and earmolds for pupils whose parents find this a hardship. One service club, Sertoma, has a national project of helping the hearing impaired. A tutor can initiate this type of arrangement. Such a project usually brings satisfaction to the club members as well.

Earmolds may become too small as the pupil's ear grows, and the result is a squealing aid. In some cases the pupil may not hear the squeal and is inadvertently a disturbance to the class. Even if the other pupils don't react, it is distracting to the teacher. One junior high teacher has an inconspicuous signal to indicate to the pupil that the aid is squealing—he puts his hand over his chin, and the pupil turns off the aid. The availability of properly fitting earmolds paid for by Sertoma ensures that there won't be any squealing and that the pupil is getting the maximum benefit from the aid. The teacher-tutor may be able to work through various agencies to purchase new aids for students whose parents can't afford them.

Preparation and Certification for the Tutor

At the elementary level, a single tutor with an elementary teaching certificate is able to tutor a hearing impaired pupil. But at the secondary level, many schools require the teacher to have state certification in each subject he teaches. Even if this isn't required, the teacher who has specialized in language and auditory training usually hasn't prepared herself to teach modern math and science or power mechanics. Thus, a pupil may have a tutor twice a week to help him with math and science, a different tutor twice a week to help him with social studies and English, and a third tutor who helps him in the shop area where it is especially noisy and difficult to understand what is going on. (This area is important, since many of the pupils go on to vocational schools.)

However fortunate the pupil may be to have certified tutors in each area, they may come to him at the wrong time. One week he may have a big project to complete for social studies and need the social studies tutor every day, not needing the math and science tutor at all that week. Each tutor should try to assist in whichever area the pupil needs help on a given day, regardless of certification. Usually the tutor can be of some help, even though she doesn't have a thorough knowledge of the subject. Or she may arrange to trade times with the particular tutor who is needed at that time.

In addition to certification and a thorough understanding of the areas in which the tutor works, it is important for her to have an understanding of the language problems associated with a hearing loss. It is not easy to find a tutor with this combination of skills. Sometimes the orientation to deafness must be provided through inservice training if regular classroom teachers are used.

The Tutoring Room

Most schools are crowded and there is no convenient place to use for the tutoring room. The pupils want to be tutored in an inconspicuous place which their friends won't see them enter. In spite of the fact that they are dependent upon and usually devoted to the tutor, the pupils don't like to be different. Most of their peers don't have tutors. So they may ignore the teacher-tutor in the halls.

Once a nook is set aside for the tutoring room, the teacher-tutor can begin to make it attractive for the pupils. The pupils feel it is theirs when they are allowed to decorate it. Most of them love large posters, and many enjoy drawing cartoons. It gives them an outlet to be creative and to express themselves freely. The tutor can bring unusual items of interest to the room around which she can build language concepts. The room can be redecorated frequently to keep the pupils interested and alert. Friends are welcome in the tutoring room at almost any time and the children might work on joint projects. When the pupils begin to bring their friends along, the tutor knows that they are accepting the fact that they need her help. Pupils overcome much of their self-consciousness about being tutored when a friend says, "I wish I were hard of hearing and had someone to help me."

Meeting the Academic Problems

The language handicap of the hearing impaired pupil multiplies as the academic concepts become more abstract. At the junior high level it is not advisable to assume that the pupil is getting the same information from a class as are his peers with normal hearing. It is difficult to keep the pupil from feeling discouraged and frustrated when much of the work is beyond his understanding.

The trend in schools is to present subject matter by using multiple disciplines and a wide variety of teaching media. Several different texts, reference books, tapes, lectures, and films (whose sound tracks are often distorted) are included in the classes. Many of the new teaching techniques confuse youngsters who have difficulty in communication.

The most helpful thing in recent years has been the adoption of modular scheduling and "basic" classes in many schools. Modular scheduling enables the pupil to be scheduled into small-group "mods" exclusively. Obviously, the larger mods where a concept is explained to over 100 pupils at a time would be difficult for a hearing impaired pupil, but he can understand and participate in small mods with six to nine pupils.

The teacher-tutor can help the pupil individually in literature or social studies by aiding him in grasping the content of his reading selections. By briefly summarizing each chapter of the material and explaining the unfamiliar vocabulary and concepts before the pupil begins to read, the tutor assists him in comprehension. It is rewarding to the tutor when a pupil says, "Hey, you left out about . . ."

Sometimes it isn't possible to reduce concepts to meaningful ideas. For example, in science class, some concepts cannot be compared to anything within the pupil's experience or understanding. In these instances, the tutor can ask the classroom teacher to assign the pupil extra projects within his grasp, which can help bring up his grade for the effort he expends. When there is good rapport between the classroom teacher and the tutor, the teacher may allow the tutor to share in the grading.

Relationship of the Tutor to School Personnel

Even when qualified tutors are available, some school personnel may think them unnecessary. They may say, "The youngster should do the work on his own." Or the busy classroom teacher may be resentful of the tutor's intrusion on her time when she tries to explain the child's communication difficulty. The classroom teacher may feel defensive when the tutor makes suggestions for working with the pupil. The sensitive tutor is aware of this feeling and tries to take as little time as possible when explaining the implications of the handicap, requesting necessary materials and a general outline of the work to be covered, and asking for the dates when tests will be given and projects turned in.

The best ally of the teacher-tutor can be the pupil's counselor. Where all pupils have the service of counselors, a hearing impaired pupil will not feel exceptional if the counselor intervenes to modify his program. In most cases counselors are sympathetic, and the classroom teacher is usually accustomed to dealing through them.

Most school nurses are very interested in programs for the hearing impaired. If a classroom teacher is uncomfortable having a hearing impaired pupil in her room, the school nurse may help allay her concerns. Also, the teacher-tutor may work with the speech therapist in sharing the language materials she has prepared. Usually the speech therapist is willing to go over the material to reinforce the language patterns.

The success of the child's program rests in the cooperation and flexibility of the school personnel and their willingness to work with the tutor. By admitting to the classroom teachers that she knows it will be extra work for them to write out their lesson plans in advance and to prepare extra work-study sheets, etc., the tutor usually finds them willing to cooperate. Some teachers accept it as a challenge. The tutor should express her gratitude to them frequently. The word gets around when one teacher has found it interesting to have a hearing impaired pupil in her class. Having one or two successes in a school system paves the way for the next pupils.

It is essential for the teacher-tutor to be accepted in the school system. She can cooperate by volunteering to chaperone mixers, by relieving a teacher on hall duty, and by being friendly with teachers during the lunch hour. Depending upon his or her talents, the tutor may sponsor a group activity such as a camera club for the school or assist with a special course such as a gymnastics class.

As the need for continued frequent contacts with the classroom teacher arises, the tutor may find it preferable to leave notes in the teacher's box, rather than confronting her often with a conference. Another advantage of notes is that the teacher is reminded of the information when she has it on paper.

Keeping Informed

The tutor should try to make sure that her pupils are aware of what is going on in the school. The daily bulletin is usually presented over the intercom during their homeroom period, but the hearing impaired pupils are often unable to follow the language over the loudspeakers. The tutor can provide the students with a written copy to read. In addition, she might prepare a daily news sheet which doubles as a natural language exercise and a current events lesson. By being especially well-informed the pupils can initiate conversation. Also, by knowing what their friends might be talking about, they are able to read lips better.

The more flexible the school system, the greater the chance for satisfactory integration. Not all pupils with severe hearing losses experience all of the problems that have been mentioned, but it is a very difficult time for them, and the teacher-tutor may help facilitate their adjustment. The tutor must be flexible, imaginative, and, above all else, willing to put forth a great deal of effort to make integration successful for the hearing impaired pupils in junior high school classes.

(Note: See also pages 182-187 for discussion of integration in junior high and high school.)

ALICE SCHEELINE

Integration into Public High School: Optimistic Apprehension

Janet Scheeline made the transition from a school for the deaf to ninth grade in public school after attending a residential school for 11 years. Cooperation of her teachers — before and during her integration, the interest and support of her community, assistance of notetakers, help from a brother, and the continual encouragement from her parents all helped to make the adjustment possible. She is now a college graduate and is continuing her studies in a hearing environment.

Many school districts now provide a specialist within the system to help a hearing impaired child adjust to the regular classes; but such was not the case in our small town of Hollidaysburg, Pennsylvania, where facilities for teaching the deaf were almost nonexistent. After learning of our daughter Janet's profound hearing loss, we realized that we would need understanding and cooperation from our community. We tried to share our growing knowledge about deafness with the townspeople and found that we were warmly received.

Janet had attended Central Institute for the Deaf (CID) for 11 years and was ready to attend the regular neighborhood high school. She had always spent her vacations with hearing people, attended day camp for several summers, and participated on a swimming team with hearing children. Often, during Christmas and Easter vacations, she would visit in nursery school and, subsequently, elementary school as the proud guest of her younger brother. The spring of her

---

Mrs. Scheeline is a remedial reading teacher in Hollidaysburg (Pennsylvania) Area Schools and the parent of a hearing impaired daughter, Janet.

graduation year at CID, she spent a day in the junior high eighth grade with a friend who considered it an honor to introduce Jan to the teachers and students. When Jan transferred from residential school to ninth grade in public school, she knew the community and was accustomed to being part of a group where few dispensations were given for a hearing problem.

Preparing for the Transfer

It was a policy of Dr. Helen S. Lane, principal of CID at that time, to write an introductory letter to the principal of the school her graduates were planning to attend. She sent a transcript of the standardized test scores and made recommendations as to where Jan should be placed — neither in an accelerated section nor in a slow group. I imagine that she also gave the teachers a condensed course in the problems and joys of teaching the deaf.

Several months prior to the end of the school year, I spoke with the public school principal and guidance counselor. My attitude, as I look back, was one of optimistic apprehension. At the A. G. Bell Association Biennial Meeting in Philadelphia the year before, Mrs. Helen Page had described New York City's program for integrating deaf students into their huge school system and had provided printed sheets entitled "A Student with a Hearing Problem." We revised the sheet to fit the needs of our child and our school,* and the guidance counselor gave a copy to each teacher who would be working with Jan the following year.

The local school administration also gave me the opportunity to speak with the faculty. I showed them the film *Growing Up with Deafness* (courtesy of the Alexander Graham Bell Association for the Deaf), which gives a concise picture of the process of teaching speech and language. I then entertained questions, particularly on hearing aid use, which is often a subject of misunderstanding. We discussed communication in the classroom, and I urged the teachers to ask Jan to repeat if they didn't understand her. I stressed that grades should be based on actual achievement, not on padded points for the hearing handicap.

We felt that Jan should have some experience in a regular school before she entered the high school. Since our local school didn't offer any summer courses, we arranged for Jan to take typing at a nearby high school. Although it would have been more advantageous to attend classes in her own school, adjusting to a large class and speechreading a teacher who was not a trained teacher of the deaf nevertheless proved to be of value. At first, Jan was reluctant to talk to other students during the midmorning recess, but as the session progressed, she began to feel more comfortable and found communication much easier.

A Wide Range of Reactions

The teachers' reactions to Jan's hearing loss were diverse. Several encouraged Jan to see them before or after school, and she often took advantage of the offer. One teacher made up a seating plan for Jan so that she could easily learn

*See Appendix, page 274

the names of the students and look in the direction of the person reciting. Another teacher, expecting and fearing confusion, refused to call on her for many months. One teacher stated at the end of the year that she felt she had done a better job of teaching the class that Jan was in than she had her other classes because she had been especially careful with her preparation.

The driver education course was handled well. In the practical training sessions, when the instructor would talk to a student at the wheel, he turned to face Jan who was in the back seat of the car. By the time it was Jan's turn to drive, she had sufficient command of the terminology involved. After the allotted hours of driving she passed her state test, which included an oral examination.

Another teacher invited Jan to participate in the Junior Academy of Science. That entailed making a five-minute speech before a panel of judges and students from other schools. Jan not only presented a paper before the Academy all three years of high school, but also won a first place award in her junior year which entitled her to attend the state meeting. We have observed that when Jan is relaxed with people her speech is understood, but when she is ill at ease, as in a new situation, she has more difficulty speaking. For several weeks before the state meeting we worked with her on her oral presentation, concentrating on phrasing and articulation. When the judges asked questions concerning her scientific findings, Jan was able to answer in a spontaneous and acceptable manner and won a second place award.

At the end of each school year I wrote individual thank-you notes to each of Jan's teachers. We were very pleasantly surprised when a teacher wrote us a letter in return stating that he had found teaching our daughter one of the greatest experiences in his 13 years at the school.

The other students accepted Jan even more easily than the adults. To my knowledge, no one in the high school ever made fun of her speech. Jan made many friends and was active in a number of clubs. She served as vice president and later as president of the science club. Before each meeting we reviewed various points of order so that the sessions would go smoothly.

Special Provisions

Because there were no itinerant teachers of the deaf, we had to fill in the gaps in Jan's educational development. The greatest problem — then, as now — was that she would rarely recognize that she had missed something. Picking out main ideas rather than details in history and English was difficult for her, especially at first. When a math teacher would explain procedures while facing the blackboard, Jan would miss the "tricks" for problem solving. Our son was of invaluable aid with math. Although he was a year behind her, he was in an accelerated group and was taking the same course. He proved to be a fine teacher and made his "tutoring" sessions enjoyable for her.

Notetakers were a must in the high school classes. Before the first term began we arranged to have one notetaker for the homeroom period — when announcements were made over the public address system — and another for classes. We supplied them with carbon paper and notebook paper. Later, we read an article in *The Volta Review* describing the use of NCR pressure-sensitive pads at the National Technical Institute for the Deaf*, and Jan decided to try this system. Two notetakers were invited to use the pads, give Jan the original copy, and exchange with each other the second copy of their notes. The bonus of receiving an additional set of notes was an incentive for the notetakers. After the first two years of high school, Jan had no difficulty finding the notetakers herself.

Janet worked long hours, but the rewards of her labors justified the effort. Her goal had always been to attend a college for the hearing; we had reservations, and felt perhaps she should look into a technical school instead. Then we read a publication called *Deaf Students in Colleges and Universities*** which answered many of our concerns. Today Jan is a graduate of Monmouth College in Illinois with a B.A. degree in biology and is studying cytotechnology, again in a hearing situation. We feel that she has done what many deaf children could do if given the chance — integrate successfully into the hearing world.

---

*"NTID — After One Year," George W. Fellendorf. *The Volta Review*, May 1969, p. 303.

**Deaf Students in Colleges and Universities*, Stephen P. Quigley, William C. Jenne, and Sondra B. Phillips. Washington, D. C.: The Alexander Graham Bell Association for the Deaf, 1968.

Have You Thought Of . . .

. . . asking a hearing student to share homeroom announcements with his hearing impaired buddy via notes on an overhead projector? — *Fred Romney, Louisville, Kentucky.*

. . . using correspondence between children to enhance language skills? During the past year a student in our program moved out of the state. He was given a package of stamped envelopes as a parting gift. An interesting correspondence has developed and a "we care" attitude between class and pupil has been fostered. — *Elizabeth Bowman, Northport, New York.*

Learning To Be Self-Sufficient

Linda McArthur's auditory and speech training began when she was 3 years old and has continued ever since. For five years she attended an elementary school having special classes for the deaf and was then transferred to her neighborhood school. She has found friends among her hearing contemporaries whose interests are similar, i.e., sports. She has successfully competed in track events, having majored in physical education in college, and is now completing a master's degree in preparation to teach in a college for the hearing. Her goal through these years has been to be self-sufficient.

Only time and experience, I have found, will ease the transition into new life situations. My past experiences — participation in many different social groups and activities — eliminated many of the problems of social adjustment which often complicate the normally difficult move from high school into college.

The arduous process of learning to live successfully and self-sufficiently in the hearing world began when I was only 3 years old. My mother stressed the importance of language by having me sit down and talk to her. Then came three years at the John Tracy Clinic in Los Angeles where I received my first real auditory and speech training. For five years I attended a public elementary school with several special day classes for the deaf. In first through fourth grades I was placed in a hearing classroom for part of the day. As I began to feel a sense of "belonging" in those classrooms, I associated more and more with my hearing classmates and arranged to play with them after school.

Miss McArthur, who has a 90 dB hearing loss from birth, was a freshman at California State Polytechnic College, San Luis Obispo, when this was written.

At the age of 11, I was placed quite unexpectedly in the fifth grade of my own neighborhood school at the insistence of my teacher for the deaf. This was a dream come true for me. My brothers and sisters urged me on, for they were eager for me to attend school with them. Then, the desire to be able to attend regular school like everyone else gripped me. My handicap had to be overcome if I was to become a part of this hearing world. Only hard work did it for me, and still my work goes on!

My first major transition, then, was from classes for the deaf to a regular school. One possible problem — that of making new friends — had already been eliminated through association with an outside group. My friends from Campfire Girls, of which I was a member for several years, were more than willing to introduce me to *their* friends. As time went on, I came to realize the importance of certain factors in creating new friendships, and I continue to practice them now. First, I must make that important first move toward starting a conversation; unless I do, others might think I am not capable of speech. Improving my speech has helped immensely in raising my confidence about making that first approach. Second, I find it a tremendous advantage and means of gaining respect to excel in one field or another. And last, not least, I feel that it is important to develop an enthusiastic personality and a smile which will certainly help get you anywhere!

My most valuable experience outside school has centered around my participation in sports. Even now, I cannot say which sport is my favorite, but track takes up much of my free time. Again, I had a chance to get acquainted with an entirely new group of girls as a member of an A.A.U. track club. During my early experiences with this club, I developed confidence and independence as I traveled with the girls to various meets, including the A.A.U. Women's National Track Meet in Columbus, Ohio.

Learning To Benefit from Residual Hearing

I must stress the importance of my residual hearing as part of my work toward my goal of being self-sufficient. My hearing aid has become such an essential part of me that I wear it even in sports — tight against my body for greater comfort. For instance, without the aid I cannot hear the gun which starts a race. Once, however, I apparently did not hear a second shot go off (false start) and kept running around the track until someone stopped me. How embarrassing! The gun had been fired in an unusually rapid succession of shots, and I was not familiar enough with the sound of two shots to distinguish this from one. The two-shot sound became another sound to learn. This is the way I use my hearing — to learn through auditory training to distinguish different sounds, like the telephone and doorbell. Now, I have seriously begun to apply this method in speech. My hearing aid is largely responsible for my ability to use my residual hearing; even at its age (ten years) it was found to be better in quality and volume than many of the new models. With a properly fitted hearing aid, even music can become part of the auditory environment of the hearing impaired. Most of us love rhythm, and distinguishing the different musical instruments is good practice in auditory training and helps develop rhythm and intonation in speech.

Speech is the basis of success in my work, as it is the primary means of communication among the hearing. Unfortunately, I have little time aside from school for speech work, although some of my school friends have helped me with pronunciation. I realize that I am very fortunate to have had early experience in enunciation and voice with my mother, as my progress in the voice lessons I am now taking indicates an encouraging natural ability. Language development has been another important aspect of my work in speech. Skill in speechreading helps me to catch on to the colloquial language used in everyday conversation, although I occasionally have difficulty in following the highly individualized, almost foreign-sounding language of some groups.

Church remained a problem for a long while. My family did not attend very regularly, and it was difficult for me to understand the sermon and the Bible with their many abstract words. Now, as my brother and sisters are getting more involved in church affairs, I am beginning to read what I have missed in the past.

Maintaining a Positive Outlook

I feel that the greatest mistake the deaf can make is not to trust the good will of people. I would like to add that I have not once been rejected or refused an opportunity because of my deafness. It is the combination of other traits people have, such as a pleasing personality and attitude, an acceptable appearance, and a smile, that compensate for deafness. Thus, hard work must be put into developing these traits as well as solving the additional problems of social adjustment in order to achieve a satisfying self-sufficiency.

My parents should receive most of the credit for my achievements to date. Their secret was continuity. In fact, my mother recalls one incident after she spent a month-long vacation away from me in my early preschool years. She says, "All I could get out of you was a squeak!" And it took her three months to get my voice back.

Have You Thought Of . . .

. . . improving your "lipread-ability" by watching your face in a mirror while repeating a memorized portion of text without voice? You may see how modifications in your speaking habits may make it easier or more pleasant for a deaf person to read your lips. — *Mary Wood Whitehurst, Roanoke, Virginia.*

34

VERNA V. YATER

Teenaiders

Group Activities for the Hearing Impaired

The Teenaiders, a prototype of an established group for hearing impaired teen-agers, is described. The group is an ancillary but vital part of the support services provided for students who are totally integrated into regular public schools in St. Louis County, Missouri. It provides a framework for educational, personal, and social growth. The group utilizes the interest and help of parents, professionals, and others in the community.

An organized group for hearing impaired teen-agers can promote their involvement and self-confidence as they learn and grow in an integrated school program. In adolescence, a natural time of searching for identity, belonging to a group is one of life's necessities. The teen-ager wants and needs to be accepted by his peers. The need for a group exists universally; its purpose and make-up may vary in different communities.

The Teenaiders, a group of teen-agers with significant bilateral hearing losses in grades seven through twelve, was organized in 1970 in St. Louis County, Missouri, to provide a framework for educational and social growth. This group is viewed as an ancillary but vital part of support services provided for secondary level students. Currently there are 55 active members from throughout the St. Louis metropolitan area. Students are invited to join Teenaiders when they leave a school for the deaf or when they enter the Special District class for partial integration at the senior high level. Students from outlying areas who have heard of the group via word of mouth are also welcomed to the group.

Mrs. Yater is Supervisor of the Hearing Clinician Program in St. Louis County, Missouri.

226

Membership in the Teenaiders offers opportunities for the students to learn organizational and social skills in a small peer group and to apply those skills daily in their local schools. Although many participate in activities in their regular public or private secondary schools, they have felt the added need to develop interaction, communication, and leadership skills in a comfortable social situation. In addition to informal group activities, the students learn to conduct meetings, plan programs, and head and serve on committees and in offices.

Constitution

Members of the Teenaiders drafted a Constitution in which they listed as their major objectives the following: to enable hearing impaired teen-agers to get to know one another; to learn to be good leaders and to practice good speech and language; to have business meetings and service projects to help themselves and other people; and to plan social events to practice etiquette and to have fun. The Constitution provides that there be a minimum of one business meeting and one social or fund-raising event each month, and that each member participate in three business meetings and two fund-raising events to be eligible for the annual free trip or social event at the end of the year. The Constitution further states that the members must be courteous, helpful, trustworthy, and friendly, and that each must set a good example for younger hearing impaired children.

The Teenaiders are governed by an Executive Committee of seven student officers selected by the membership each spring. There are also a paid part-time professional advisor and three parent advisors who, together with the supervisor of the Hearing Clinician Program, all help to coordinate and guide the Teenaiders in their yearly activities. The Executive Committee and the advisors meet approximately every three weeks to plan both educational and social events.

Activities

During the last several years, topics for meetings have included drug use and abuse, alcoholism, human sexuality, self-defense, vocational opportunities, and water safety. Members have visited local businesses, industries, and hospitals in order to gain a broader perspective on work roles and opportunities. They have toured departments and organizations concerned with occupational therapy, physical therapy, recreational therapy, medical records, dietetics, merchandising, commercial art, banking services, photography, public relations, agricultural research, drafting, engineering, and several others. These educational excursions have been planned with the encouragement and participation of businessmen, hearing clinicians, and volunteers. During the past school year, members have sponsored a needy family's Christmas and visited elderly patients in a nursing home on a regular basis. Social activities included holiday parties and sports events. Summer activities have included informal recreational activities and, during the summer of 1972, a workshop on elections and mock political convention with speeches by candidates currently running for office.

Teenaiders help defray their operating expenses through membership dues. Support for the group is also supplied by the St. Louis County Special District in the form of mailings, meeting space at the Litzsinger School, transportation for educational excursions, and contributions of staff time. Three to four fund-raising projects are held each year to raise money for trips and activities of educational significance, and cash contributions have been received from local businessmen.

A two- or three-day visit to an out-of-state college or university is planned each academic year for the juniors and seniors. The officers and advisors select a different educational facility for each year, and in the future it is anticipated that the group may be split to visit several colleges in one year. In addition, a year-end one-day excursion is organized for all members to visit a place of general interest near St. Louis. In 1973 the group selected Silver Dollar City.

Information about forming a local group for hearing impaired students as well as recommendations and/or copies of the Teenaiders Constitution may be obtained by writing to the author at Litzsinger School, Section for the Auditorially Impaired, 10094 Litzsinger Road, St. Louis, Missouri 63124.

Have You Thought Of . . .

. . . having the hearing impaired child sit in the second row of the classroom (rather than always in the first row) where he can feel more a part of the class, can see students in the back more easily, and can speechread the teacher without straining his neck? In a week's time give him a chance to change his mind and try another placement. A teacher's judgment isn't always the best one. — *Linda McArthur, Arcadia, California.*

35

GEORGE W. FELLENDORF

On College Education
For the Hearing Impaired

Is there really any point in talking about higher education for hearing impaired youngsters in colleges and universities for the hearing? We believe so.

Surveys made by *The Volta Review* show that many hearing impaired high school graduates do go on and graduate from colleges for the hearing. A great number, however, are frightened away by the prospect of large lecture halls, impersonal faculties, and seemingly insurmountable barriers denying to them the educational opportunities available to those with normal hearing.

Before capitulating on higher education for capable hearing impaired students among the hearing, the evolving changes in college programs should be studied. In 1980 college enrollments are expected to be double what they were in 1965. To handle this fantastic growth, as well as to improve radically the education offered, exciting changes in colleges are underway.

Many century-old practices are in for modification, if not abandonment, and some of the changes seem to portend great things for the undergraduate with a severe hearing loss. Small seminars which were formerly reserved for juniors or seniors are now being offered to freshmen in many universities. "Stadium" type lectures in which the tardy student finds himself sitting up under the rafters are giving way to extended periods of independent study in which the student does most of his work in the library and through personal conferences with the instructor. Some institutions encourage the students themselves to determine the curriculum of their courses; many have eliminated a number of required courses.

Mr. Fellendorf is Executive Director of the Alexander Graham Bell Association for the Deaf, Washington, D.C.

Some colleges are even doing away with final exams. In many, students are able to take courses on a pass-fail basis rather than for a letter grade; the instructor's written evaluation may replace the traditional A, B, C, D, or F. Teaching machines, some fed by gigantic computers, are augmenting the faculty, and, in some schools, the classrooms are being brought right into the dormitories.

Also gaining in popularity is the year-round college; in many areas, the nine-month school year of the past is yielding to an all-year system enabling greater variety of courses during the year, continued study for the student who wants to accelerate, and perhaps greater flexibility for the student whose progress is slower and more irregular. Expansion of the junior college system has also increased opportunities for two-year programs leading to a job or, in some states, to entry into a four-year institution.

Whether these changes do represent better opportunities for hearing impaired students will, in large measure, depend upon the foresight of parents and educators of these children. It would seem that many of the innovations and trends would ideally suit the student who cannot hear and take notes in a lecture, but who can understand an instructor in a small group discussion. The hearing impaired student now has access to films that he can independently watch and run at his own speed, repeating if necessary. Programmed materials are already becoming available for the hearing college student — so why not for the hearing impaired?

Higher education for the hearing impaired among the hearing has exciting possibilities, as many students with hearing losses are finding. Let's hope that by the year 2000 many more hearing impaired youngsters will have taken advantage of them.

Have You Thought Of . . .

. . . asking honor students to volunteer support and encouragement to hearing impaired elementary grade students? — *Verna Yater, St. Louis, Missouri.*

. . . phrasing questions for the class in two or more different ways? Even when you are not speaking directly to the deaf student, this will help him follow the gist of the discussion and will benefit the other children as well. — *Mary Wood Whitehurst, Roanoke, Virginia.*

JANALEE REINEKE
WILLIAM LYTH

36

College – Changes, Challenges, and Rewards

A college student with a severe hearing loss describes how she and a hearing impaired friend have adjusted to the challenges of post-secondary education among hearing peers. They attended small liberal arts colleges where they were able to build positive personal relationships with both students and professors. Here they share their feelings about academics and social life and make some informal suggestions for other hearing impaired students who may be considering a college education in the future.

College years can be rewarding years for those who take full advantage of the academic, social, physical, and emotional experiences that they offer. These years are especially important to those of us who have hearing problems as we strive to be normal, accepted, and contributing members of society. Bill Lyth and I found that educational and social experiences during our childhood and adolescent years were the foundations for our entrance into the new world of college. We would like to share with others some of the challenges we have met.

Bill attends Nazareth College (Kalamazoo, Michigan) – a coed liberal arts school supported by the Sisters of St. Joseph of the Roman Catholic Church. It has a student body of a little over 400 and a professor-student ratio of one to nine. Bill lives at home and is a day student. I attended Manchester College (North Manchester, Indiana), also a small liberal arts college, supported by the Church of the Brethren. It has a student body of about 1400 and a professor-

Miss Reineke attended Manchester College, Indiana, for two years before entering Indiana University Medical Center, Indianapolis, to study occupational therapy. Mr. Lyth is majoring in education of the emotionally disturbed and mentally retarded at Nazareth College in Kalamazoo, Michigan.

student ratio of one to 17. Most of the classes at Manchester College accommodate 20 or more students, with its science classes having over 100 for lectures. At Nazareth College many of the classes contain from two to 20 students, with many opportunities for tutorials and independent studies. A great advantage of small classes with a good professor-student relationship is that the course subject can be presented in an interesting, understandable, and informative way. At both of these colleges, as in many other small schools, a friendly atmosphere prevails. This is partly a result of available assistance and a desire on the part of the college community to help the individual attain his goals.

Communication with Professors

Academically, a hearing impaired person has to work harder than ever to obtain from a course what he wants of it. Frustrating situations may be experienced when class lectures and discussions cannot be absorbed due to the student's inability to speechread all the words of professors and classmates. For this reason, a hearing impaired student should feel at ease to discuss any academic difficulties with the professors. The longer he waits to solve a problem faced in class, the more difficult the problem becomes. Consequently, it sometimes can be embarrassing to talk to the professor about a problematic situation that is long "overdue."

For example, Bill had a professor (with a beard and mustache) whom he simply could not understand in class. When speaking to the professor personally, there was no problem; but in the classroom situation — even when Bill sat in the front row — he had difficulties. I had a professor who was very hard to speechread because he seemed to "talk inside his mouth," giving the impression of poor enunciation. Although these dilemmas had no easy solutions, the sooner we could talk about the difficulties, the better it was. Speaking to our professors aided us by making them more aware of our problems. Hence, in Bill's case, the conversation with the professor led to further conferences in which Bill was able to discuss lecture topics on a one-to-one basis, which proved to be profitable personally and academically. In my case, the problem was alleviated to some extent by the professor's willingness to loan me his lecture notes after realizing that I found it difficult to understand him. Many valuable hours in class would have been wasted if we had not spoken candidly to the professors. The values of knowing our professors have been evident in many facets of our college experiences. The professors — some of whom had never talked to a deaf person before — seemed to be at ease in communicating with us. We came to know them as special personal friends, shared our happy and baffling times with them, and felt free to consult them for advice.

Bill finds seminars are invaluable learning experiences because it is easy to see everyone's face for speechreading. But I often find group sessions a great challenge because of the difficulty in following the trend of a discussion. Background noises can drastically interfere with my total understanding. Solutions to problems which arise in class sessions having emphasis on discussion groups will vary with the subject and type of group involved. It has been Bill's experience that he perceives sounds behind him first (his hearing aid is a behind-the-ear model), so in order to reduce the possible amplification of extraneous sounds, he usually sits with his back to the quieter area. I have found it very helpful to suggest that the group move to a more secluded area.

Newly developed audio-visual media is responsible for another type of predicament. Although in a small college video presentations are not as common a means of instruction as in larger universities, situations may occur where they are used. In a zoology class that I took, over half the class time was spent in the labs which were equipped with tape recorders. Only when the professor supplied his rough draft of the tape manuscript was I able to participate fully in the laboratory sessions. Whenever possible, therefore, I try to obtain a copy of the text or narrative accompanying a film, tape recording, or other presentation.

Notetaking can be an ever-present problem. Bill and I try to remedy this by asking several classmates to take notes using a special type of carbon paper or by looking over the notes of our friends after a lecture or discussion. Sometimes we receive the permission of the classmates whom we are sitting beside in a lecture to copy their notes as they are writing them. We find it is best to review the notes of more than one person to be sure to obtain the maximum amount of information gathered from the lectures. At times even this method is not satisfactory, particularly when a comparison of the several sets of notes show discrepancies ranging from inaccurate facts to incorrect interpretations of the professor's ideas and of the major point of the lecture. Discussions outside of class, commonly referred to as "rap sessions," are helpful to us in obtaining feedback from other students to correct false information and to ascertain the exact emphasis of the lecture.

Organizing our Time

It is imperative that we plan carefully our use of time, not only to get studies completed, but also to learn more vocabulary in order to comprehend the vast amounts of reading. We try to do individual research on the subjects being studied in classes to broaden our understanding. The more we know about a topic, the more we can understand and participate in class sessions. For example, if a professor mentions an unfamiliar person or event, we jot down the name and investigate further. This usually makes the subject more relevant *and* more interesting.

Because of our difficulty in grasping fully the facts of current affairs through radio and television presentation, it is also important for us to set aside time to read newspapers, bulletins, and periodicals. Our hearing friends listen to the news in the morning as they get ready for classes, and during the day their conversations often reflect their feelings about what is happening outside the campus — such as issues involving national politics or local community events. If we are behind on local or world affairs, it is sometimes hard for us to understand the feelings of our friends and professors.

With the vast amounts of speechreading and independent reading required in college we occasionally experience some physical discomforts, such as headaches and eyestrain. To alleviate these problems I often take short naps during the day and thus gain the physical stamina needed to endure the long hours of studying. Being different from other people in that we wear hearing aids, we *do* have one advantage in studying: we can easily eliminate background or bothersome noises by simply turning off our aids. This can create a world of envy among others, especially in the noisy dormitory situation.

Social Challenges

To find fulfillment socially, we have to learn how to put people at ease about our hearing impairment. First of all, we realize that people are not usually well acquainted with the implications of a hearing loss. Therefore, if we do not know people very well, we make an effort to talk with them on several different occasions and then casually mention the hearing impairment. We do not publicize our deafness, but we do feel that, in developing friendship, it is easier for others to find out about our hearing loss from *us* rather than "via the grapevine." By this time, we have gotten to know a little bit about the other person and he or she is usually not at all uncomfortable about our hearing handicap. As Bill quoted in one of his college papers, "I try to go out of my way to be friendly to people; they are a wonderful part of life. In conversing with others, I try to take an interest in what they really think and feel. Meeting people is a never-ending source of stimulating experiences."

In the beginning of Bill's freshman year of college, he felt the need for people to accept him as a "normal" person rather than as a *hearing impaired* person. So he tried to keep his hearing loss confidential. He found this unsuccessful because there was always the possibility that he would not hear or might misunderstand what a person was saying to him. For instance, this was particularly evident when Bill would miss social greetings coming from behind him in hallways or in classes. With no response from Bill, the greeters usually assumed that he was purposely ignoring them or was acting "snobbish." When he became aware of the problem, Bill told his friends that he was a *speechreader*. Then people made sure they had his attention first, and they were understanding if he missed or misunderstood what they said. Many friendships have developed as a result of an awareness and understanding of the hearing impairment.

In college, social life can be as much of a learning experience as academics. When Bill is not preoccupied with classes or studies, he is with friends in the student lounge, library, dorms, or cafeteria. Participation in several college clubs and organizations rounds out his active social agenda. Specifically, serving as a member of the Student Financial Committee, chairman of the Emergency Student Loan Fund, and secretary of the Student Education Association has developed leadership capabilities and furthered Bill's skills in communicating and transmitting ideas. I have been a member of the Manchester College Symphonic Band — playing in the first clarinet section. It was hard for bandmates and friends to realize that I was deaf, especially since I played both the piano and clarinet. The girls who live in my dorm also have trouble realizing the full impact of my hearing impairment. For instance, one night there was a rather humorous incident when we had a fire drill in the middle of the night and I had to be dragged out of bed because I had not heard the alarm. Another incident clearly illustrated to me that my closest friends had accepted me as a normal person: at a college dance, with loud rock music blaring in the background, my roommate Carol came up to me and my date and started to whisper in my ear! She suddenly remembered that she could not communicate with me that way.

Daily Life

Living in the dorm can be as valuable and rewarding for the hearing impaired as it is for normal students. There are many opportunities to grow in independence and gain self-assurance. One thing which I have found vital in dorm living is the use of a special alarm clock (vibrating attachment to regular electric alarm). On mornings when I have to arise before my roommate or on weekends when she is away, I can be totally self-sufficient. Bill finds that the use of the alarm gives him independence from his family's schedule. Some hearing impaired students prefer an alarm which is attached to a flashing light and a buzzer system.

Both Bill and I strongly urge hearing impaired college students who use hearing aids to have a spare aid if at all possible. And it is vital to make sure the aids are in good repair at all times. There is no substitute for a properly functioning hearing aid during busy college days.

Speechreading and auditory discrimination are lifelong learning experiences and require constant effort. In our opinion it must definitely be continued throughout college. Speechreading proficiency is facilitated when auditory perception is acute. The daily use of the telephone helped me develop auditory skills. Also, in the dorm it is a necessity to be able to communicate over a phone since it is the only means of contact in some emergency situations. With the installation of an amplifier, I can do this. The telephone in Bill's home has a special set of chimes mounted above his bed (but attached to the regular phone). This he can hear without his hearing aids. Again, flashing lights may be attached to the phone.

Maintaining good speech and enunciation is a constant challenge for the hearing impaired. People have told Bill and me that our speech improved greatly since we have been college students. Perhaps, this is because we realize fully the need for adequate and understandable speech to produce the results we desire. The motivation to speak distinctly is ever-present. The daily "rewards" are being understood and/or seeing people express their surprise that we are hearing impaired.

New slang expressions and the phrases, quips, and jokes heard in everyday conversation are difficult for us to pick up. Our communication and conversations with close friends and relatives helps us in this — as does reading popular publications in which colloquial expressions are used. I well remember when I missed 10 points on an exam because I did not know the meaning of the expression, "scapegoat." The book, **A Dictionary of Idioms For the Deaf,*** is a vital companion.

Like other college students, we often find ourselves facing changes and frustrations; yet we understand that although our disability is a challenging and grave one, it can be conquered. A vast amount of encouragement from family, teachers, and friends helps us continue toward fulfilling our goals. The resulting rewards are immensely greater than the frustrations, and the sense of achievement helps us gain personal satisfaction in what we are and what we shall be.

**A Dictionary of Idioms for the Deaf,* compiled and edited by Maxine Tull Boatner and John Edward Gates. West Hartford, Connecticut: American School for the Deaf, 1966.

Have You Thought Of . . .

. . . collecting idioms and current slang from the hearing children to teach to the hearing impaired? It helps the former to understand the language; the latter, to "belong." — *Lois Germain, Lexington, Kentucky.*

. . . keeping your eyes smiling when the deaf student responds slowly or asks for repetition? Small signs of annoyance or irritability may discourage him from "bothering" you with questions and lead him to "bluff" when he doesn't understand. — *Mary Wood Whitehurst, Roanoke, Virginia.*

Part VII

Parent-Teacher Interaction

37

BRUCE D. SHEPHERD

Parent Potential

The father of two deaf children outlines the reactions of parents from the time a suspicion of abnormality occurs with suggestions as to how these may be dealt with and utilized. The problems of lack of communication between parents, clinicians, and teachers are discussed, and practical aspects of parent guidance are described. Some of the experience gained from the organization and administration of a preschool center for deaf children in an integrated environment is recorded.

As a parent of two profoundly deaf children, I have always been saddened by the communication gap which seems to exist between parents and educators. Perhaps this illustrates a constant feature of education of the handicapped; that is, the tendency for us to align ourselves into camps: parents in one camp, educators in another.

It appears to be a fact of life that once an alliance such as this exists, a state of suspicion arises between the two groups which one hesitates to label as a paranoia, although certain features of paranoia may be present. As far as I can see, this is a perfectly normal state of affairs; the state of affairs which exists between nations, between doctors and patients, etc. The important thing, I believe, is that we recognize this for what it is and that we overcome it. It appears that great educators, as well as great doctors, either consciously or subconsciously cross this gap and establish an empathy with the other group — an empathy which is one of the major factors in bringing their work to fruition.

Dr. Shepherd, an orthopedic surgeon in Sydney, Australia, is the co-founder of the Shepherd Centre for Deaf Children and Their Parents at the University of Sydney.

In my own medical profession this "paranoia" was almost part of the curriculum. I can always remember being taught by so many of my masters that when treating a child we must get rid of the parent. It took a number of years to realize the folly of this. Sometimes we must get rid of the parent; sometimes the parent is our greatest ally.

When our children first started school, my wife sought their curriculum from their teachers in advance in order that she could go over the lessons with them. Initially, the teachers could not understand this attitude and, I feel, suspected that their work was being checked on. They became concerned and over-reacted; immediately my wife over-reacted. However, there was one very wise and rather wonderful lady, a teacher of the deaf, who recognized the situation for what it was. She intervened and placated both sides. The initially suspicious teachers became close friends of my wife, and parent guidance in that school took another step forward. I am not saying for one moment that suspicious and resentful parents do not exist and that malignant trouble-makers do not have to be summarily dealt with; but I believe that it is a wise educator, indeed, who is able to turn the energies of the concerned, involved parent in the right direction in order to help his or her own work as well as to help the handicapped child.

What Do We Want for Our Children?

The wishes and the needs of parents are identical with those of educators, that is, the welfare of our children. Perhaps I can express to educators at least some of the wishes and aspirations that we as parents have for our handicapped children. Undoubtedly all of us, at the time the handicap is diagnosed, wish to eliminate it completely. There is a period that may be months, years, or an eternity in duration which the parent needs in order to become reconciled to his child's disability. It is important, however, that this reconciliation is not so complete that it becomes a passive acceptance; for our handicapped child requires harnessed discontent in order to help him to overcome or, at least, to reduce his disability. Undoubtedly, each of us wants our child to be able to lead a happy life and, undoubtedly, the hardest thing of all is to know how best we can achieve this. It is in this area that the tremendous responsibility of educators lies, for overeducation can be as disastrous as undereducation.

Having tritely said that I wish my children to be happy, not only as adults but also as children, perhaps in a general way and rather hesitantly I can suggest some of the things I, as a parent, believe are important.

First, I would wish my children to be able to achieve as great a level of independence as is possible. Even the most gifted normal person is dependent on others, so it is unrealistic to entertain the aim of total independence for the handicapped; nor will their handicap enable them to become as independent as a normal person. Frequently, however, strength in one area will help to overcome weakness in another. Thus, education and training need to be directed toward a specific handicap, *keeping in mind the environment for which that child or person is being prepared* and further bearing in mind that it is the responsibility of educators to continue to make contact with that environment and, if necessary, to bring their influence to bear to alter it when necessary. This, I believe, is one of the important advantages of training and education in an integrated situation.

The second ingredient for our children's ultimate happiness is an involvement and an interest in others both more and less fortunate than themselves. This must surely be one of the ways of enabling them to tolerate their own disability. Obviously each educator is very involved with his fellow man and derives satisfaction from this involvement. The handicapped also need it.

Third, I would hope that throughout their lives, circumstances will enable them to feel a sense of achievement no matter how low that achievement may seem by ordinary standards. Incidentally, we as parents are ever fearful that our excessive ambition for our children may threaten this.

Fostering Realistic Expectations

Perhaps I may illustrate instances, although not in the handicapped world, where I believe early training in education has destroyed this sense of achievement. There is little doubt in my mind that the 100,000 engineers in India who were out of work in 1972 have had the sense of achievement they experienced on graduation severely dented. In our own country those aspects of tertiary education which lead to a depth of knowledge in the humanities and, undoubtedly, a greater appreciation of the environment often have an undesirable by-product. There is a tendency to believe that a university education in itself is sufficient to guarantee a safe and lucrative livelihood. Very often the frustration which occurs when such is found to be false can more than eradicate this heightened appreciation of environment. A beautiful painting or a magnificent symphony may not appear as impressive to a person with an empty belly.

In the area of the handicapped, nothing could be more frustrating for a child than to find that he may be trained and, indeed, well-trained in a pursuit only to find that the world has not been prepared for him and that his hard-earned skill must remain frustrated. Surely the responsibility of the educator to maintain perpetual vigilance in order that his aims for those in his charge are realistic is paramount.

A very reasonable criticism of my views so far is that it may appear that I believe "the role of a parent" is to tell educators their role. Possibly there is a little truth in that. I certainly cannot claim to have experienced the whole scene, as my children are still quite young, but I would like to describe a scheme my wife and I inaugurated as the result of having borne two profoundly deaf children. It may help to illustrate what we believe to be the role of the parent.

One of the first things that struck us as parents was how difficult it was to convince anybody that we believed we had a handicapped child. It appears remarkable to me that, not only in this country, it is frequently left to an untrained person, i.e., a parent, to first recognize that all is not well with his child. In this regard, members of my own profession are most remiss. I suppose nobody wishes to be the bearer of bad news, but sadly this reluctance leads to numerous occasions where ill-founded reassurance has been given — reassurance which the parents are only too happy to accept but, unfortunately, reassurance which leads to irretrievable delays in attacking the problem. Perhaps clinicians and educators *underestimate the toughness of parents.* It is hard to convince those who are in authority that it is far better that a parent be told of a suspicion of a handicap which may later prove to be ill-founded than to reassure him and later have a handicap proven. Having experienced this, I now take a great deal of notice of parents in my own field when they tell me they think there is something wrong with their child. Thus, one of the first things we have done is to encourage an awareness in my profession of these facts so that all suspicions of parents are seriously considered and a real endeavor is made to prove or disprove the suspicion.

The Need for Direction

Once a diagnosis has been made, parents are often left floundering without any direction as to how to handle the problem. Fortunately, there are more and more wonderful schemes where total care and responsibility is taken from the time of diagnosis. It is our aim at the Shepherd Centre to foster this. We must regard parents in a completely ambivalent fashion. First, we parents have intelligence to know that something is wrong. We are generally dedicated and anxious to help our children (often excessively so), and even the simplest of us can make profoundly worthwhile suggestions. On the other hand, we are capable of the most unintelligent behavior and in need of direction in initiating and carrying out the simplest activities.

In our scheme we do our utmost to help the parents to help the child. In this respect we do not believe that a teacher giving a lesson to the child in front of the parent is a great deal of use. We believe that this is like teaching a person to drive a car by sitting him in the passenger seat. Thus, our parents of both sexes are obliged to attend the center regularly and to prepare material for and give lessons to their children and to other parents.

When the diagnosis is made and the child comes into our care, one of our teachers visits his home. From the beginning, the mother is shown how to stimulate and direct the child with a minimal disturbance of her everyday activities. Until the child is 3 years old, regular visits are maintained, but parents must come to the center for lectures to give them understanding of their child's handicap and how to deal with it. And most important, they come into contact with other parents with the same problem. In fact, I believe that one of the major roles of parents is to give confidence and reassurance to other parents.

Integration for Preschool Children

So far as integration is concerned, at the age of 3 years our deaf children are enrolled at a kindergarten as near as possible to their own homes. A preschool teacher who is trained in instruction of the deaf attends at that kindergarten where, for certain hours of the day, the deaf child receives specialized teaching. The mother attends once or twice a week and also receives instruction. For much of the time, the child plays with hearing children and is involved in the normal everyday activities of the preschool kindergarten. With this program we hope to achieve the following:

(1) By maintaining contact with hearing children, our own specialized teachers are relieved to some extent in the extremely arduous task of training a preschool deaf child.

(2) Our teachers do not lose sight of the achievements of normal children due to the lack of exposure which may occur in a segregated school.

(3) Other children are less likely to feel the embarrassment or negative reaction which may occur if they are confronted with a handicapped child and are not used to the experience.

(4) The handicapped children tend to develop more of the normal mannerisms and behavior patterns which promote social acceptance and help prevent their isolation in adult life.

Our own two children now attend normal hearing schools which have never before had a deaf child. We have been told by many educators that as time goes on they will find social contact with hearing children more and more difficult. It is well known that friendships between hearing and deaf children are not common and we accept the fact that such may well be the case with our children. If, as is usually the case, our children seek to segregate themselves with other profoundly deaf persons in adult life, we are quite prepared to accept this. However, we feel that, as far as possible, we have made the choice theirs, rather than forcing a fait accompli upon them.

Finally, I believe that the role of a parent, each according to his ability, is to do just a little more for the handicapped community than to help his own child, and I believe part of the role of the educator is to show the parent how he can best do this.

LINDA PETERSON

Telling It Like It Is

During a hearing impaired child's first year in an integrated setting, every day presents new challenges. His family may experience encouragement and disappointment in equal amounts as innumerable and unexpected variables affect the child's daily adjustment. Yet, through persistence, understanding, and cooperation, the integration experience can be a worthwhile one for the child and his family as well as the school.

We are the parents of an 8-year-old profoundly deaf son, Pete, who is now attending regular classes in our local school district. Pete originally attended special classes for the deaf; however, we became concerned about the long hours spent on the bus and the fact that Pete could not be with normal-hearing children. Also, because an increasing number of children are now being recommended for partial or full-time integration, the self-contained class was too small to allow for homogeneous grouping. We therefore decided to move Pete to his home school.

Our decision was not at all well received by the special education advisors for the hearing impaired. It is their philosophy to integrate only those children who "perform as hard of hearing" even if the hearing loss is clinically regarded as severe or profound. Our son did not fall into this category. Also his speech was very poor — another serious factor against his integration. Yet we decided to bypass the traditional system of referral. Pete's language and speechreading abilities were well above many of his classmates', and we had the enthusiastic support of the Director of Special Education, administrators, and teachers to

---

Mrs. Peterson, of Wayzata, Minnesota, is the mother of three children, one of whom is profoundly deaf.

"give it a real good try." What more can parents ask, especially when the district secured the services of a speech clinician and a teacher of the deaf to provide individual tutoring for Pete during the regular school day?

The following graph gives an indication of the "agony and the ecstasy" which ensued the first year. It was a difficult time for us, but worth every minute of it. There were many days when we were frustrated and discouraged to the point of tears (after Pete was in bed) but, I may add, never defeat. We did and still do have a determined belief that many more profoundly deaf children must be given the *chance* to sink or swim in a hearing environment.

Given the needed support, many will eventually catch up to their hearing classmates and compete on a par with them. This will not make them hearing individuals, but it certainly will give them an equal chance to adjust at an early age to a big world of hearing people. It is time we stopped asking, "What can't he do?" and began asking, "What *can* he do?" right from the beginning.

We had four guidelines which served as criteria for our decision:
1. Pete has to make an adjustment to a world of hearing people sooner or later.
2. No one, hearing or nonhearing, has an easy time making adjustments.
3. The sooner Pete's peers, teachers, and adults in general are exposed to the problems of deafness, the better it will be for everyone.
4. A "coordinator" (someone who understands the needs of hearing impaired children and can act as a liaison between the child, his parents, and teachers) is essential in order to make the program work, especially in the first year.

Initially, Pete's tutor assumed this last role. Now, we are extremely fortunate that our district is served by a special Title III, ESEA Interdistrict Project for the Hearing Impaired. This means a team of speech and hearing specialists has the sole function of providing inservice training to regular classroom teachers and to other school personnel who have had little or no previous contact with a hearing impaired child. It has proved to be the biggest help we have had to date, since it removes the parent from the active role of advisor to the school.

Once the above criteria were established, we took a long and realistic look at what our child's special needs were in terms of additional personnel. Pete has been helped by each of the following at one time or another during the past three years: 1) a tutor, knowledgeable about the educational needs of deaf and hard of hearing children; 2) a coordinator, as mentioned above; 3) a speech clinician to work on voice and speech production; and 4) a volunteer aide or helper from the community or the high school to give help in the classroom on a one-to-one basis. (While many schools have such a program, it is, for us, the least necessary of the four factors mentioned.)

We have found that there must be an "esprit de corps" that includes trust and cooperation among parents, teachers, and principals. There must be willingness on the part of parents to give the time or assistance required of us whenever it is necessary, plus a willingness on the part of the regular classroom teacher to coordinate her efforts with parents, tutor, and speech clinician.

Pete has been completely accepted socially (and the sociograms prove it). He is making genuine academic headway. One factor we hadn't anticipated is the effect he has had on classmates and teachers along the way. We feel they have become more tolerant, receptive persons because of their exposure to him. And, most certainly, our son has benefited *equally.*

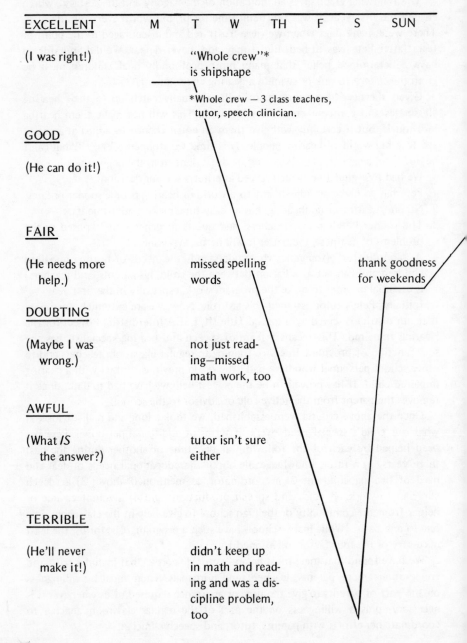

EXCELLENT   M   T   W   TH   F   S   SUN

(I was right!)   "Whole crew"*
                              is shipshape

                              *Whole crew — 3 class teachers,
                                tutor, speech clinician.

GOOD

(He can do it!)

FAIR

(He needs more   missed spelling   thank goodness
   help.)   words   for weekends

DOUBTING

(Maybe I was   not just read-
   wrong.)   ing—missed
                      math work, too

AWFUL

(What *IS*   tutor isn't sure
   the answer?)   either

TERRIBLE

(He'll never   didn't keep up
   make it!)   in math and read-
                      ing and was a dis-
                      cipline problem,
                      too

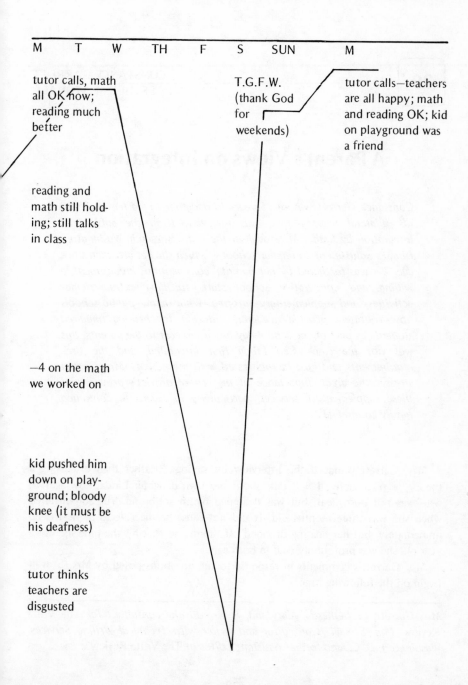

M   T   W   TH   F   S   SUN   M

tutor calls, math
all OK now;
reading much
better

T.G.F.W.
(thank God
for
weekends)

tutor calls—teachers
are all happy; math
and reading OK; kid
on playground was
a friend

reading and
math still hold-
ing; still talks
in class

—4 on the math
we worked on

kid pushed him
down on play-
ground; bloody
knee (it must be
his deafness)

tutor thinks
teachers are
disgusted

39

CONSTANCE GARRETT
ESTHER M. STOVALL

A Parent's Views on Integration

Constance Garrett, whose 15-year-old daughter Linda has an 85-90 dB bilateral hearing loss, was interviewed on the subject of integration by Esther M. Stovall at the Volta Bureau in Washington. Linda's adjustment to regular school — which she has attended since age 7 — was furthered by her parents' conscientious involvement, a willing and cooperative school staff, fulfilling extracurricular activities, and supplementary tutoring. While many public schools now routinely provide academic tutoring for hearing impaired students as part of the school day and at no cost to the parents, this was not the case when Linda first integrated, and the time requirements and cost factors rested with the parents. Mrs. Garrett stresses the great importance of the school district's provision of these supplementary services, particularly in regard to continued family counseling.

Mrs. Garrett prefaced the interview by saying: "Rather than discussing a theory or philosophy, I will talk about my own daughter Linda, now age 15, who was not born deaf, but was deafened by an antibiotic drug administered when she was three months old. It did not cause her hearing to be destroyed immediately, but her hearing dropped off rapidly so that by the time she was a year old she was profoundly deaf in both ears."

Mrs. Garrett's comments in response to the questions posed by Mrs. Stovall begin on the following page.

Mrs. Garrett, of Bethesda, Maryland, is an editorial consultant for The Volta Review. *Mrs. Stovall is an editor and writer with Technical Writing Services, Washington, D. C., and former Assistant Editor of* The Volta Review.

At what point in Linda's development did you make the decision to put her in an integrated educational program?

When Linda was 7. She had been in a day school program for deaf children for two years, and I found that her speech and language did not seem to be progressing as I thought they could and should. I visited her classroom and saw how little opportunity there was for good oral speech to come about. So, we looked for a school for normal-hearing students that would consider her. We were fortunate in finding a private school near our home that was willing to take her on a trial basis if we would provide a tutor to work with her in speech, speechreading, vocabulary development, language comprehension, and auditory training. She has been in this school for eight years now.

In what ways have the tutors worked with her?

Originally we had the school bus drop her off at the tutor's house at the end of the day, but this was not successful because, by that time, she was a pretty exhausted kid and was unable to really benefit from the tutoring. In the classroom Linda had to constantly have her eyes on the teacher, or whoever was speaking, in order to know what was going on, and this required a lot of energy. So we worked out an arrangement for the tutor to go to the school and, during the course of the day, take Linda out of class for an hour or so at a time when her classmates were involved in some activity that she could not benefit from too much, such as group reading. We didn't want to make the tutoring a punishment for her by having her miss out on things she enjoys like recess, art, or sports.

Throughout the years the tutors have put the greatest emphasis on reading comprehension, which is the key to learning for Linda. She has to learn the meaning of the written word and try to excel in all reading skills because this is her greatest source of information. Linda has to try very hard to learn the vocabulary for each special subject; the vocabulary for science is unique, and some of the terms in social studies are rather abstract. So she's had to work very hard—and not always so willingly—in that area. As she's grown older, however, her natural interest in math and science has motivated her to have more patience and to apply herself more diligently, and her father — who is a bio-engineer and mathematician — has become one of her favorite tutors.

In addition to tutors, what other special help was particularly beneficial? Perhaps there was something that you as parents did.

The important thing was to get Linda to be more and more responsible for her own education. I recall hearing a talk by an oral deaf adult, when Linda was very young, who pointed out the value of not only learning history, but of learning history as it is occurring. So I have tried to encourage her to watch the daily news on TV and to read the newspapers as much as possible, although the language in the newspapers creates difficulties.

We also try to encourage supplementary reading, although I recognize that it is a chore for her because every other word is an obstacle to her understanding. She does enjoy the sports page of the daily newspaper, and there's enough motivation for her to overcome the impediment of a tricky vocabulary. Since *World Traveler** started publication, we have noticed that she will pick it up and read it from cover to cover because she has the assurance that there is not going to be language in it that is too difficult. She does enjoy biographies, and is finally beginning to read for pleasure.

What did you do to help Linda adapt to the integrated setup at the school?

We met with the entire staff of the school and Linda's tutor for an orientation session during which we tried to point out Linda's special needs, the nature of her hearing loss, and the necessity for her to see the person who is speaking. We also pointed out that, if at all possible, verbal instructions should be reinforced in written form, which is beneficial to the other children in the class, too. We mentioned the importance of having her seated in a position where there is no glare, because it is impossible for her to speechread if she's facing a bright window. We asked the teachers to make sure they were on the right level for her to have the full benefit of seeing their faces. This is particularly important for a young deaf child. We stressed the importance of speaking as normally as possible and avoiding exaggerated speech. We made it clear that the tutor would act as liaison between us and the school staff and that she would be available to them for advice and counsel, and would check with them from time to time to see if there were any problems that she could help out with on a one-to-one basis with Linda.

What has been the attitude of the teachers toward having a hearing impaired pupil in the class?

There has been a very healthy, positive attitude in the school from the beginning. They accepted Linda. The teachers saw that the whole class—the whole school, as a matter of fact—benefited from the experience of working and interacting with a child who has a deficit, but still has some strengths and can make a contribution. Naturally, some teachers lent themselves to the situation better than others. From the first day the art teacher had no problem in communicating with Linda. She had that certain sense of knowing how to communicate her ideas—and Linda has always enjoyed art. Some of the teachers had the mistaken notion that as long as Linda was next to them she would be able to hear with those earphones on her head. We have had to point out more

---

*Published by the A. G. Bell Association, with the cooperation of the National Geographic Society. For information, write *World Traveler*, P.O. Box 479, La Salle, Illinois 61301.

than once that she has to see the teacher's face. We did try to encourage the teachers to see that some student would, in a discussion situation, point to the person who was speaking so that Linda would have the benefit of knowing who was talking. She has begun to use more of her auditory ability and is now aware that someone is speaking even though she's not looking at him.

Do you think that being in the integrated situation has increased her desire to use her speech and hearing more?

Absolutely, from the very first. Two weeks after she had been in the oral environment her spontaneous language shot up, and her desire to communicate grew by leaps and bounds. She would come home from school and comment on what she had done, and she had the language and the desire to learn. This was a very heartening experience for me. Bring immersed in a hearing environment has helped her develop language in a natural way—what Mildred Groht calls natural language.* She uses contractions rather than the stilted *can not,* etc. She uses a lot of idiomatic expressions and understands them. She is very unselfconscious in social situations and is not reluctant to talk.

Shortly after she started going to the new school she visited her former deaf classmates at the old school. Later I found out from the teacher that Linda had not spoken once during the whole day. I could only conclude that she realized that these were deaf kids and that she didn't need to use her voice to communicate with them.

Have you and the tutors specifically worked on developing Linda's use of residual hearing?

Not as much as I would like. I am convinced more and more that auditory training is the key to success even for a profoundly deaf person. From time to time one or another of her tutors has done some concentrated auditory training, with tremendous results. We've just begun an intensive program utilizing a cassette recorder, working with her on discrimination of individual speech sounds, words that sound alike, and simple sentences. Her father plays an important role here because she can "hear" the lower pitch of his voice more easily and clearly than mine. She works at least once — sometimes twice — a week on listening and auditory discrimination.

I am sure that even though this experience has been successful and everything has worked out well for Linda, there have been problems along the way. Would you like to mention some?

There have been many problems, believe me. One that comes to mind immediately is the fact that we have had a total of six tutors in eight years—they

---

*Natural Language for Deaf Children, Mildred A. Groht. Washington, D.C.: The Alexander Graham Bell Association for the Deaf, 1958.

have moved away or started raising a family. It has been traumatic for me because they didn't always leave at a convenient time of the school year, and I have found myself suddenly confronted with the job of locating a new tutor.

Another problem is the lack of companionship because she is not going to a neighborhood school. We're fortunate in having lots of kids in the neighborhood, but most of those her age are boys. That's fine for Linda at the moment because she enjoys playing football or softball, or whatever sport is in season. But she has in the past lacked the companionship of girls, and this is one of my concerns.

Lately she has been invited to overnight sleeping parties at other girls' homes, but it has always been a frustrating experience for her. When the other girls giggle and talk after the lights are out, she can't know what is going on and can't get in on the jokes. On occasion I have spoken with the girl who invited her or her mother to explain the situation, and they have tried to help. For instance, one mother left the light on in the hall so that there was enough light in the room for Linda to speechread with a certain amount of effort, but it still wasn't very successful.

Over the years, what were some of the things most helpful to you as parents?

One of the most important was to continue to visit other programs for the deaf to learn what curriculum offerings are available and what kinds of activities deaf children are experiencing. Also, we have constantly gone out of our way to meet with oral deaf adults to gain some insight into their backgrounds and what they thought was instrumental in their success. These experiences have given me encouragement at times when I was feeling somewhat discouraged. I think that the most instrumental thing in launching Linda and me into oralism was our association with the John Tracy Clinic. The audiologist who diagnosed Linda's deafness advised us to reconcile ourselves to the fact that no surgical procedure would correct her nerve deafness and to get in touch immediately with the John Tracy Clinic for their correspondence course and with the Alexander Graham Bell Association for their literature.

Reading articles in *The Volta Review* on a monthly basis has been a big help to us. Although they didn't always address themselves to parents, I got a lot from those written by teachers and other professionals. I borrowed books from the Volta Bureau Lending Library and purchased others through the A. G. Bell Association. I would say reading and visiting other programs are both very important.

We have made it a point to schedule a conference every spring with the school director, the tutor, and Linda's classroom teacher to evaluate her academic achievement and social development. We take this opportunity to point out to the school that although Linda is not at the top of her class, she has certainly progressed further than she would if she'd been limited to a deaf environment. As long as we see progress we have to be content—not satisfied, but content for the moment.

What types of outside or extracurricular activities have been particularly helpful to Linda in her adjustment with other children, both in school and in social situations?

One important thing is that sports are an integral part of the curriculum in her school, so she's been exposed to soccer, softball, hardball, and various activities like these where she can excel and gain confidence. Another thing—they do learn a lot of card and board games, like monopoly, at school. She knows the rules and is ready and willing—and able—to engage in a game; so there is an opportunity for her to interact with a friend, and this is good experience for her.

Two years ago we sent her to an eight-week summer camp where there were only one or two other deaf children in the whole camp. She had the opportunity to take part in swimming, tennis, water skiing, and softball. Being such a good athlete, however, she did experience some rivalry. Several of the other girls were jealous of her expertise and did not understand that while this was one area where she could excel, there were other activities where she was at a disadvantage. It was a growing experience for her, even though it was frustrating at times.

What about the impact of a deaf child on a family?

I think it can be devastating—devastating to a family to have a child with any handicap. I remember one time when our older daughter said at the dinner table, "I wish I were deaf. Maybe then you'd care more and be more concerned about me." I think all parents who have a child with special problems desperately need counseling from the time they are first aware of the problem.

Does the expense sometimes prevent parents from seeking counseling?

Yes, I think this is so, even though many clinics arrange for payment on a sliding scale. But we must accept the fact that counseling is a necessity, not a luxury. School systems are going to have to provide this service. The child's education is the responsibility of both the parents and the school, and they must work together as a team. Counseling is part and parcel of the whole package. The Bill Wilkerson Center in Nashville, Tennessee, and St. Joseph Institute in St. Louis do provide this service. The John Tracy Clinic in Los Angeles was conceived with the philosophy that parents must be given information and assistance in working with their deaf children, and will not even consider a child for the four-year preschool program unless both parents agree to participate in evening seminars where psychological and emotional problems are dealt with.

On the basis of your own experience, would you recommend integration for all deaf children?

Absolutely and immediately, if not sooner, so long as their deafness is not connected with a related disorder that precludes attendance at regular school. I think that every deaf baby, just as soon as it is old enough, should be enrolled in a nursery program for regular children. This immersion in an oral environment is absolutely essential, and reinforces the idea that lip movement has meaning. Being treated as a child who happens to be deaf rather than as a "deaf child" is very important. Every child is unique and has many areas of strength which should be emphasized. Our key to success, which may help other parents, is early identification, early diagnosis, early amplification, early education, and early parent counseling.

Would you do it all over again?

That's a tough question. It's been a rough road. It's not a very secure thing because you never know from year to year whether things are going to continue to work out. It's been fraught with frustrations and problems—sacrifices, financial and otherwise; but when we see Linda today we know it was well worth it. Our ultimate goal for Linda is for her to have the broadest possible options as an adult—both academically as well as vocationally and socially. We feel that the best way this can be achieved is for her to be comfortable with her hearing peers and within the hearing world.

Have You Thought Of . . .

. . . asking a deaf child to share his handicap with the class and discuss listening, lipreading, and personal use of hearing aids when his class studies the five senses? He can help others better understand his deafness and lower the barriers between them. — *Linda McArthur, Arcadia, California.*

. . . encouraging class members to speak one at a time? Babbling voices are difficult for any student to follow, especially the hearing aid user. — *Mary Wood Whitehurst, Roanoke, Virginia.*

40

NELL COLE

Hear the Wind Blow

A parent describes the difficulties and rewards encountered in seeking the best possible educational opportunities for a severely hearing impaired child who is also black and has had additional health problems. Her son Paul's early training began at home, with the help of a desk auditory trainer and numerous family activities to stimulate speech. His "formal" schooling in an integrated setting started at the kindergarten level and was continued through the elementary and secondary years despite continual pressure on his parents to transfer him to a residential school for the deaf. Paul is now studying electrical engineering at a small college for the normally hearing.

Excited, rosy-cheeked, face alight with wonder, Paul ran in and grabbed me and exclaimed, "Mommy, did you know that the wind sounds like a train when it blows?" It was fall. The leaves were falling and, as the wind blew, they made a rustling sound. Why all the excitement? Paul is severely hard of hearing. He had just received new hearing aids that were powerful enough for him to "hear the wind blow."

I am not sure just when I suspected a hearing impairment. I remember no abnormal behavior in Paul's infancy. He was acutely allergic and my preoccupation with his general physical condition completely engrossed me. It is hard to describe the vague misgivings I had about his speech development. Possibly, in his struggle for survival, I missed the signs of unusual development. I do know, however, that when he was 18 months of age I called to him from a

---

Mrs. Cole is a speech therapist at Branford Public School in Branford, Connecticut.

distance and was chilled by his complete lack of response. I never ceased trying to be sure about his hearing after that day.

I soon noticed other "peculiar" behavior. When Paul wanted an object, he never used words; he gestured or tugged at my skirt. Quite frequently he ended up stretched out on the floor in the throes of a temper tantrum with me standing over him in tears. I became more and more sensitive to his behavior and more adept at making excuses for him with friends and relatives.

Finally, I summoned the courage to make appointments with first the pediatrician and then the ear specialist. Because of Paul's medical history, both were annoyed with me. They felt that I was expecting too much from a child whose body was so frail. I listened to lectures from both and went home unconvinced. Deep inside I knew that there was something wrong with my child. I thought at first that he was possibly brain damaged and that they didn't want to tell me. I withdrew puzzles, games, anything that would challenge his intelligence and reveal the thing I feared. I couldn't read to him — his attention span was too short. I protected him from strangers, made excuses to friends.

Shortly before Paul's third birthday, I became ill. It was necessary for my mother to care for Paul and his older brother for several weeks in her home. She knew nothing about my apprehensions about Paul's development and treated him just as she had his older brother at a similar age. When he returned home after this prolonged visit, he was very different. To my amazement he could complete very complex puzzles at first exposure. He had developed a very intricate set of gestures that my mother understood. Temper tantrums were infrequent, although his speech development was practically unchanged. I went back to the doctors and demanded hearing tests.

Diagnosis

After a series of tests, the audiologist diagnosed Paul as severely hard of hearing. He described the loss as sensorineural, cause unknown. Then he explained that the loss was irreversible. At about the same time, Paul had minor throat surgery and we learned that he had a congenital deformity of the nasal passages and of the Eustachian tubes. This, along with the audiological diagnosis, made further medical help unlikely.

My state of depression was deep but short-lived. I knew that somehow, somewhere, there had to be help for this child. We had not kept him alive against all kinds of odds to let him just exist. I had two remarkable persons for inspiration. My own father was severely deaf and had been since childhood. Yet he had worked his way through college and dental school and was enjoying a very full life as a practicing dentist. Helen Keller was from my home town and I knew of her struggle and her victory. I was determined that we would share the victory. Had I known the barriers or dreamed of the difficulties, I am sure that my optimism would not have been so high. Deafness is not visible. It does not provoke much sympathy. Rather, so few understand what it means to be in the world but not of it that it is like living in a foreign land and not knowing the language. I did not want to stand as interpreter for Paul. I wanted him to learn the language.

Early Training

I learned of a residential school in a not too distant town and immediately rejected it. Paul was much too frail to risk poor care in return for the inadequate training we felt he would receive there. Somehow his early training would have to be accomplished within the home environment. During this crucial period an article appeared in the local paper telling of a new preschool day program right in our home town. The audiologist made an appointment for me to tour the facility and to enroll Paul.

I should have known — but when you are desperate, somehow you forget. The special program was located in an elementary school in a white neighborhood. We are black. The director was polite but firm: my child could not be enrolled. This was Birmingham, Alabama, 1956, and laws were laws.

Some asked why we didn't fight to force admission. This was our child and we loved him. We wanted no harm to come to him, either physical or emotional. The odds were already nearly insurmountable. We decided that this was not the time to challenge laws, no matter how unjust.

The audiologist who had tested Paul then offered to work with him. We purchased a desk auditory trainer unit and under the direction of this very kind man set out to teach Paul. I was permitted to participate in the lessons and taught to use the follow-up materials. At home we talked to Paul constantly, played games — anything to stimulate and reinforce speech. I used lotto games and word bingo to teach sounds and then words. Sometimes his brothers joined in and made it more play than work. Whenever possible we made field trips to reinforce the lessons.

Paul was an early speechreader. He would never talk with anyone unless he could see his face. He would frequently begin a conversation and then, as the other person unconsciously turned away, Paul would walk around to peer into his face. His frequent plea was, "Look at me — you know you can't hear me with your back." He associated sound with the eyes and thought that others heard as he did.

Discipline a Problem

It was always difficult to discipline Paul. It was not that he was a difficult child, but rather that I could not always know when he understood. As he became older, he used the hearing loss to keep from obeying. He would frequently ask us to repeat so that he had enough time to think either of an answer or of a way to evade. We knew that Paul had to exert much more effort than the normally hearing child if he were to achieve, and therefore he would have to be well disciplined. There were times when I had to prod him even when it hurt us both.

Teachers — Sensitive and Insensitive

For kindergarten, Paul was enrolled in a nearby parochial school. There were no supportive services available, so we continued the daily therapy lessons. The teacher was cooperative and Paul developed some independence and made friends with many children his own age. The next year he had a teacher in the same school who resented the extra effort demanded of her. He somehow sensed her resentment and became sullen and withdrawn. He cried each morning and had to be forced into the classroom. He showed his resentment by actually "turning her off." Once in the classroom, he would remove the batteries from his hearing aid and put them in his pocket.

His day was too long and exhausting. In addition to the school and therapy, we began what was to become our way of life. He needed tutoring and I had to serve as tutor. He was overtaught and I was usually overtired. We were both frequently irritated with each other, but he made progress. At the end of the year the teacher "regretfully" informed me that her superior thought it best for Paul that he not return and suggested that the kindest thing we could do would be to place him in a school with "his own kind."

These two years were repeated over and over again throughout Paul's elementary years. There were teachers who were willing to help him and those who did not want that "deaf and dumb" child in their classroom. There was a superintendent who offered to do what he could to start a class if I could find the children. This, in a town without a screening program. Then there was the teacher who tutored Paul in her home after school just because she recognized a small boy who needed help and because she could not give it to him during the day along with the other 45 children in her class.

In 1962 we moved to New Haven, Connecticut, with the hope that better educational opportunities would be available to our children and that people would be more enlightened and cooperative. We might have been in Birmingham for all the difference we found. The official school audiologist would not give permission for Paul to attend the regular public school, but insisted that he be sent to a residential school for the deaf. We knew that he could remain at home and refused to accept the decision. One teacher gave him passing grades because he was quiet, but would not promote him. Another treated him just as she did the other youngsters in her class and he thrived. I continued to tutor him evenings.

Junior High School

When it was time for junior high school a concerned teacher suggested that we seek a private school. She feared that Paul might be assigned to a remedial division in public school and never be challenged. After searching, writing, interviewing, and being rejected even before Paul was seen, we finally found a school willing to accept and give him as much attention as seemed necessary. We had learned that private schools, like many public schools, frequently want only the gifted exceptional child. We were convinced that Paul's best chance to develop depended on his being kept within the hearing world with children able to communicate normally. We knew that this placed additional burdens on him and on his teachers and his family, but we were willing to continue to try.

The school we chose — indeed, the only one that accepted him — has a strong individualistic program. There were usually eight youngsters in a class and Paul was provided tutorial help as needed. His seventh grade master, recognizing Paul's timidity and insecurity, carried trinkets in his pockets and gave them to him as bonuses. During all that first year, Paul still needed and expected me to work with him evenings. The need was much more psychological than academic. Even when he did not need assistance, he wanted me to sit with him while he worked. His reading was slow and labored. All assignments required twice as much time as they should have. A reading specialist was made available to Paul; progress was slow but steady.

At all times we had the support of the administration. This is important. Frequently Paul was assigned to a teacher who did not understand his hearing problem. This is one of the hardest parts of being hard of hearing, rather than deaf. Many people cannot understand how you hear and respond to some sounds and not to others. It is urgent that teachers, as well as others, have some understanding of the problem. Our audiologist, who had worked with Paul for more than three years, helped when needed to explain this. I have, with his help, provided teachers with as much written material as possible and, most recently, with a record that is scientifically filtered so that you can hear much as does a person with a sensorineural hearing impairment. This record was made available by the administration to each of Paul's teachers.

Senior High School

In fall of 1970 Paul began his senior year of high school. He enrolled in a college preparatory program, although it was frustrating for him to earn "C's" while in competition with hearing youngsters. A summer in a tutoring camp, however, helped him develop a great deal of self-confidence. His grades improved and he became a bit more sure of himself.

Throughout high school, Paul was encouraged to pursue the college directed program. His interest in electrical engineering developed early. We felt that he was fortunate in having a real talent in an area that did not require perfect hearing. Many times he spent the night before an important exam tinkering with a device he had envisioned instead of studying. This interest and talent has led to a college program in electrical engineering. At the present time Paul is a second year student at a small, highly regarded engineering college for the normally hearing.

College, like all other new situations, presented challenges. We visited many schools and were interviewed by many admissions officers. Paul's high school record was impressive, as were his mathematics and science college board scores. He was accepted at every school of engineering to which he applied. We also investigated programs designed specifically to assist the hearing impaired. We were advised to let him make the decision and he decided to try a school for the normally hearing since he functions as a hearing person.

Meeting the Challenges

The problems that first year were almost unbelievable. For a time I thought that we had come to the unhappy end of a long struggle. Paul contracted infectious mononucleosis just three weeks before school opened. Although his doctor said he could begin school, he was quite weak and had a difficult time just staying awake. His advisor was very young and had never known a hearing impaired person. Paul refused to accept notetaking assistance. I had purchased several special note pads from the bookstore at R.I.T. (these are now stored in our basement) which he refused to use. His professors were told that he had a hearing problem, but few really believed that it was severe. Disaster seemed imminent. His grades were quite unsatisfactory but Paul refused to give up. Somehow, he developed a determination to succeed that had never before been so strong. I tried to appear calm and encouraged whenever he was home. Telephone conversations were never satisfactory as Paul cannot hear sufficiently well to get a message.

His roommate appeared to be the most positive factor at this trying time. He is a very quiet, very kind, and very bright young man. He and Paul now say that they knew that they would be friends from the first few minutes together. Somehow each supplemented the needs of the other. Paul, who is quite social, made friends and always included Ed in the relationship; Ed had excellent study skills and insisted that Paul not give up but try harder. Somehow, Paul made it through the year.

The summer between the first and second year found me again actively trying to teach a school how to best serve a hearing impaired student. Many letters and telephone calls were exchanged. I sent literature for the advisor, the dean, and any instructors Paul might have. Along with this information I sent the record "How They Hear." I think that this record did more to convince the advisor of Paul's needs than anything else.

Paul is enrolled in the Independent Planned Instruction program designed for the more mature student. He is given a study guide and a book and does not attend lectures but reports to his professor whenever he has a problem he cannot solve or when he feels prepared to be examined on an area. His time schedule is the same as that of all the others in this program. It has been a most successful year, and he has earned the respect of both his peers and his professors. More importantly, he has proven to himself that he is capable of mastering a very difficult program of instruction. I have never seen him more assured.

Paul has many friends, and fortunately, he has never really had hard-core prejudices. He very proudly announced that he and four friends, including his present roommate, will share an apartment unit in the dormitory for next year. The interesting part is that they decided to break with the all black concept and two of the friends are white. When challenged, he explained the decision by simply stating that "they are our friends."

Paul leads a very full, normal life. He worked one summer as a supervisor/ evaluator in an inner city program of the Office of Economic Opportunity. He is currently a part-time employee of the United Parcel Service in Worcester. While we do not really approve of his working during the school year, his academic work has remained acceptable and so we say nothing.

Few parents of children without handicaps can experience the joy of seeing their child accomplish what seems to be impossible in spite of overwhelming obstacles. We take so much for granted. The everyday achievements are just that — everyday achievements. With Paul I have learned to savor these, for I know how much has gone into them.

In Retrospect

I am sure that some years ago I must have asked, "Why my child?" I tried to protect him from people and things as I did not want him hurt and did not know his capacities. It is a delicate task of balance: helping a child experience the satisfaction and security that all children need, yet at the same time facing squarely the reality of the handicap. There have been many situations for which we sought answers, although sometimes it seemed as though there were none.

Paul would tire of the ever-present therapy and rebel. He could not understand the fear we had of leaving him alone because he couldn't hear the doorbell or the telephone. We tried to allow him the same privileges as any other teenager although this was not always easy, for the tendency is to overprotect.

Our Paul is fortunate in that he possesses the factors required for successful adjustment. He is intelligent, has sufficient hearing to manage with supportive services, and has a sense of humor that permits him to laugh at himself. And it is important to him that his parents have faith in him as a person. Paul does "hear the wind" and he knows that it makes a beautiful sound.

Have You Thought Of . . .

. . . encouraging a mother to leave a familiar sweater or scarf in class during the first few days of nursery school to reassure a worried hearing impaired toddler that mother will soon be back? — *Winifred Northcott, Minneapolis, Minnesota.*

41

WALLACE BRUCE

The Parent's Role
From an Educator's Point of View

The term "integration" is used to describe a wide variety of educational programs for the hearing impaired. It is essential that parents be cognizant of the long-term objectives of an educational program and of what methods are being utilized to measure the degree of attainment. Parents can be a positive support to the hearing impaired child as well as a stimulating complement to the school.

Oralism — the promotion of speech, speechreading, and maximum use of aided residual hearing — is a philosophy of education which had its roots in the private residential school, which, by virtue of the physical setting, was usually in complete control of the environment of its hearing impaired students. The students' eventual placement in classes with hearing peers was a long-term objective, usually not scheduled for attainment until junior or senior high school.

With the rapid urbanization of the country and an acceptance of program responsibility by local school districts, day schools and classes have gradually assumed a more dominant position in the education of the deaf. In many communities and states, integration with hearing peers has become a "now" reality rather than an eventual objective.

Some integrated programs are the result of considerable parent/educator planning and cooperation; others were created by administrative fiat; and no small number were born of efforts to placate parents. The current state of turmoil in education of the hearing impaired is evidence that not all programs

Dr. Bruce is Director of Tucker-Maxon Oral School, Portland, Oregon, and President-Elect of the American Organization for the Education of the Hearing Impaired.

have successfully achieved the educational, communicative, and social objectives for which they were established.

Integration — When and Why?

Integrated educational settings for the hearing impaired range from those that offer mere physical proximity with hearing students to those in which the hearing impaired children are completely independent of supportive personnel. A child may be integrated as early as 0-3 years of age or as late as high school age. The effective implementation of integration is dependent on the quality of personnel, equipment, transportation, and curriculum.

Current literature abounds in subjective and theoretical expositions on the merits as well as the hazards and limitations of integration. Yet there is a paucity of objective research identifying the characteristics of a "successful" integrated student.

Some educators maintain that children can be prepared for eventual integration only through actual participation in an integrated setting. Others question whether "integration" in the social sense is achieved at all and caution against viewing "passive indifference" on the part of hearing peers as "general acceptance" of the hearing impaired students. A few educators contend that preschool integration may be of less value to the young deaf child than to his parents and teachers, for whom it provides baselines for language processing, vocabulary development, and other areas of special interest. In short, there is little agreement on the actual amount of group interaction occurring among young integrated children.

Only in recent years have specialists been relatively successful in identifying and weighting component parts of an effective integrated educational program and in describing the attributes of hearing impaired students who are likely to succeed in merging into the mainstream of education. Rudy and Nace (1973), for instance, have developed a "transitional quotient" for deaf students being considered for integration. The objective is to estimate the probability of success and to identify possible problem areas prior to actual placement in classes with normally hearing students. A study sponsored by the American Organization for the Education of the Hearing Impaired (1971) identified a number of factors considered essential to adequate educational programming for the deaf; several relate directly to their integration into regular classrooms.

Caught between their aspirations for their hearing impaired child and the realization of the academic and social implications of a hearing loss, parents are often confronted with educational decisions as challenging as the traditional one on modes of communication. They should thus become acquainted with projects and evaluative instruments such as those mentioned above. *Each* child and *each* educational program should be studied in order to reduce the possibility of failure. If parents are sufficiently oriented to the basic characteristics of an adequate integrated program, they can contribute much to ensure that eventual success for their child will be a probability — not merely a possibility.

Pupil Evaluation in an Integrated Setting

Philosophies and methods used in reporting academic progress vary so widely among schools that parents must become somewhat sophisticated in ferreting out the exact academic status of a hearing impaired student in an integrated program. Is the deaf student being graded without special dispensation for any language and/or vocabulary limitations? Are the class members compared on the traditional "curve"? Is there a differentiation between effort expended and knowledges and skills attained? Are students advanced for social reasons, academic merit, or a combination of both? Do staff members tend to be somewhat lenient because of the hearing handicap?

Parents should be knowledgeable about their child's reading ability and the tests used to measure it. They should expect the school to describe the degree of speech intelligibility in terms of its usefulness in daily contacts with a wide cross-section of the community. Speechreading skills should be stated in terms of degree of usefulness in class lectures, social discussions, and on-the-job training experiences.

It is not the purpose of this paper to espouse any particular evaluation or reporting system; however, it behooves parents to become familiar with current practices of the local school district. The academic and vocational aspirations which are gradually formed by parents and by the deaf student himself should be tempered by an understanding of how the professionals are measuring his progress. Realistic appraisals may seem harsh and unfeeling, but altruistic anticipations or encouragements steeped in misapplied sympathy can only result in disillusioned parents and embittered young adults.

Parent/School Interaction

Parents are expected to be supportive of the educational staff and the general academic objectives of the integrated program. However, they should also be alert to uncommitted and/or incompetent professionals who, by nature of their limitations, are unable to assist the hearing impaired student in achieving his potential. In this sense, mothers and fathers ofttimes must balance the roles of grateful recipient and uncompromising critic. To the dedicated educator falls a similarly challenging assignment of assisting families to grasp fully the implications of having a child with a handicap rather than "a handicapped child."

The outpouring of love and acceptance by parents in the home must be unconditional — never rationed out nor dependent upon the child's performance as a student. The home must serve as a bastion from which the child learns to go forth, coping with the vagaries of his peers, the demands of his teachers, and the occasional rebuffs from an unthinking society. Mothers and fathers should be forever encouraging, never berating, and increasingly able to demonstrate true empathy (not to be confused with sympathy) with their hearing impaired child.

Daily experiences within an integrated educational setting often accentuate the academic and communicative differences between hearing and deaf students. Hours of painstaking effort by teachers, parents, and the hearing impaired child may be quickly surpassed by seemingly half-hearted efforts on the part of normally hearing peers. The commercialized cliche, "When you're number two, you have to try harder," was perhaps never more applicable than to the deaf student and his family. The effective and supportive home is one which never wavers in encouragement and love, but maintains high expectations in academic, communicative, and social experiences.

Self-Reliance

Without intentionally doing so, parents may become overprotective toward a hearing impaired child. They may press for an hour's ride in a special school bus or purchase a second car rather than teach the child how to use the public transportation system. Running errands, shopping alone, paying family bills, exchanging merchandise, or attending appointments with the doctor or dentist should be scheduled into the child's independent activities. Rather than being concerned about what might happen, parents would do well to ensure that the child knows what to do *if* something does happen. Paper routes, part-time jobs, and volunteer activities bring the deaf child into the community as an active participant rather than a mere apprehensive onlooker.

Vocabulary Expansion

From the time the hearing impaired child discovers that the world of language consists of "who" and "what" and supportive terms to describe condition and action, parents should continue to stimulate vocabulary expansion. The linen closet, work bench, kitchen cabinets, and book shelves are just a few sources of basic terminology. The home itself can offer a wealth of information to the young child if his parents take advantage of its potential.

The expressions of daily living are best used in context and should not be relegated to the teacher's domain. As the deaf child enters the mainstream of education and community living, his basic vocabulary requirements rapidly accelerate. His ability to take an active role within this milieu is dependent in part upon his receptive and expressive vocabulary. Parental responsibility here is not transferrable.

Independent Reading

Successful integration can seldom become a reality without extensive independent reading. For the hearing impaired child, this can provide some of the information input which hearing peers receive through mere passive listening. Parents can serve as models by demonstrating a wide range of reading interests and by scheduling substantial amounts of "prime time" for reading and discussion of the daily newspaper, current magazines, paperbacks, and library selections. The child should be encouraged to share with the family a short synopsis of what he finds particularly interesting. Family trips to the library or book store foster a conviction that reading is a vibrant part of the "good life."

Feelings of Self-Worth

Much has been written about the psychological implications of deafness. However, the hearing loss in and of itself isn't responsible for the personal problems affecting some hearing impaired children. Dr. Richard Thompson, a clinical psychologist who happens also to be deaf, once observed: "Frankly, I question very much whether there is such a thing as a psychology of deafness, which seems to imply that deafness makes a person develop a unique personality with different kinds of problems than those of persons who are not deaf."

Parents should be concerned about how hearing impaired children feel about themselves and how others (teachers, hearing peers, the community in general, and the family) react to them. One of the primary objectives of both home and school is to ensure that the young deaf child will develop as a mature individual, confident in his abilities and possessing a strong conviction in his worth as a person. That parents are able to rejoice in their supportive role in this joint venture is compensation enough.

REFERENCES

American Organization for the Education of the Hearing Impaired. *Guidelines for oral programs for hearing impaired children.* (Mimeographed booklet). Washington, D.C.: The Alexander Graham Bell Association for the Deaf, 1971.

Ginott, H. G. *Between Parent and Child.* New York: Macmillan Co., 1965.

Nace, J. G., & Rudy, J. P. *A Transitional integrative program for hearing impaired students,* Newark, Delaware: Sterck School for the Hearing Impaired, 1973.

Patterson, G. *Families.* Champaign, Ill.: Research Press, 1971.

Skousen, W. C. *So You Want to Raise A Boy.* Garden City, N.Y.: Doubleday and Company, 1962.

Thompson, R. Address to Massachusetts Parents Association for Deaf and Hard of Hearing, January 25, 1966.

Appendix

Forms for Observation, Evaluation, and
Assistance of A Hearing Impaired Child in an
Integrated Setting

Glossary of Terms

Contributing Authors

Bibliography of References

Index

Appendix

Table 1

Criteria for Admission of a 3-Year-Old Hearing Impaired Child
To a Regular Nursery School Program

(As One Component of a Comprehensive Special Education Program)

1. A chronological age of about 36 months
2. Adequate diagnosis of hearing loss
3. Medical and audiological evaluations
4. Full-time use of recommended hearing aid(s)
5. Enrollment of parents and hearing impaired child in an individually prescriptive special education program for the child in the Minneapolis Public Schools
6. An appropriate nursery school which includes:
   A. Facilities licensed by the State Department of Welfare
   B. Direct educational service to child by a teacher holding appropriate certification from the State Department of Education (nursery-kindergarten-primary levels)
   C. A curricular model providing opportunity for:
      a. Peer group interaction
      b. An environment that encourages cognitive growth through appropriate materials and play-learning experiences
      c. Rich listening and speaking experience through adult and peer group stimulation
   D. Willingness of nursery staff to participate in statewide workshops and conferences with parents and special education personnel
   E. On-going dialogue to support parents through telephone conversation, conferences, written notes, and encouragement of parent visitation
7. Availability of a suitable nursery school for an individual child based upon:
   A. Geographical proximity
   B. Payment of nursery school tuition by local school district of residence
   C. Pre-visit to nursery school (if this is first-time placement of a hearing impaired child) for determination of suitability
      a. Teacher-pupil ratio (15 children maximum to one teacher and one aide)
      b. First-hand observation of a sample day (variety and substance)
      c. Knowledge of the general daily schedule
      d. Personality of staff
8. Characteristics of the hearing impaired child or his family
   A. The audiogram is not the determinant. However, the degree of hearing loss must be considered in the educational expectations following placement.
   B. Inability of parents to provide an adequately stimulating oral home environment for one or more of these reasons:
      a. Deaf parents
      b. Motor and intellectual skills sufficient to participate in group activities (teacher observation, case conference)
      c. No hearing siblings or neighborhood peers

Tables 1, 2, and 3 were prepared by the Minnesota State Department of Education, UNISTAPS Model Demonstration Project for Hearing-Impaired Children, 0–6, and Their Parents (P.L. 91-230, Title VI, Part C, Sec. 623).

Table 2
Criteria for Continuance of a Hearing Impaired Child
In a Regular Nursery School Program:
Six Months Review

1. Demonstrated growth in receptive and expressive language, determined by means of:
   A. Speech and language sample
      a. Audio tape
      b. Video tape
   B. Observation of special education teacher (program for the hearing impaired) upon site visitation to nursery school
      — Completion of checklist: Teacher—Child Relationship
   C. Reported observations of nursery teacher in case conference
   D. Observations and report of parents
      —Completion of checklist: *Structured Observation of a Child in School:* Communication
   E. Developmental log kept by teacher
      —Weekly Progress Report
   F. Differential Language Scale
   G. Boone Infant Speech and Language Scale
2. Demonstrated social and emotional growth
   A. Vineland Social Maturity Scale
   B. Improved peer group interaction
   C. Ability to impose control upon himself
   D. Ability to set and accept limitations
   E. Completion of checklist by parent and special education teacher
      a. Classroom Behavior: Social Interaction
      b. *Structured Observation of a Child in School:* Social and emotional behavior; Relationship with adults
3. Continued supplemental program of individual teaching (Infant Program, Whittier School) with emphasis upon:
   A. Sequential activities in the training of residual hearing
   B. Introduction of sentence cards and experience charts for reading readiness and ideo-receptive reading
4. Continued parent support: individual and group therapy; "Fathers Only" meetings.
   A. Individual and group therapy
   B. "Fathers Only" meetings
   C. Group mothers' meetings
   D. Parent education program
   E. PIPS—support of parents new to program, by selected parents of older children (4—6)
5. Nursery school staff participation in special education inservice meetings

---

Table 3
Criteria for Nonrecommendation of Entrance of a Hearing Impaired Child
Into a Regular Nursery School Program

1. Late identification of hearing loss requiring an immediate and intensive special education program
2. A severely multiply handicapped child
3. Extreme social and emotional immaturity
4. Irregular hearing aid usage.

Table 4
Classroom Observation Checklist
For Teachers of Hearing Impaired Children

Check the items in each category that best fit the classroom you are observing.

Physical Aspects:

1. Room size:
   a. large———
   b. medium———
   c. small———

2. Capacity:
   a. crowded———
   b. not crowded———

3. Type of seating used:
   a. desks———
   b. tables———
   c. chairs with writing arms———
   d. combination of tables and chairs———
   e. other (indicate what)———

4. Lighting:
   a. fluorescent— No.rows of lights———
   b. shaded bulbs— No. bulbs———
   c. unshaded bulbs— No. bulbs———

5. Windows:
   a. complete wall———
   b. individual windows——— No.———

6. Floor surface:
   a. rubber tile———
   b. hardwood———
   c. carpeting———

7. Wall surface:
   a. wood———
   b. brick———
   c. acoustic tile———
   d. other (indicate what)———

8. Blackboards:
   a. on 2 sides of room———
   b. on 3 sides of room———
   c. on 1 side of room———

Environmental Aspects:

1. Room location:
   a. next to gym———
   b. next to principal's office———
   c. next to bathroom———
   d. next to playground———
   e. next to outside door entrance———
   f. facing highway———

2. General room noise level:
   a. high———
   b. medium———
   c. low———

3. Specific room noises:
   a. squeaking chair———
   b. creaking radiator———
   c. banging pipes———
   d. dripping faucets———
   e. scraping chairs———
   f. squeaking doors———
   g. rustling Venetian blinds———
   h. flapping window shades———
   i. whirring fan———
   j. other (indicate what)———

Teacher-Child Aspects:

1. Teacher's speech and voice:
   a. loud———
   b. soft———
   c. well modulated———
   d. good articulation———
   e. poor articulation———
   f. good voice quality———
   g. poor voice quality———
   h. readability of lips———

2. Teacher mobility:
   a. faces children when speaking———
   b. moves while speaking———
   c. uses large hand gestures while speaking———
   d. other (indicate what)———

3. Teacher-Child interactions:
   a. free discussion———
   b. questions asked by teacher———
   c. student questions———
   d. other (indicate what)———

4. Child's attention:
   a. always attends to speaker_____
   b. rarely attends to speaker_____
   c. usually attends to speaker_____
   d. speechreading skills
      are utilized _____
   e. speechreading skills
      are not utilized _____

5. Child's speech in the classroom:
   a. very intelligible_____
   b. intelligible most of the time_____
   c. unintelligible_____

6. Child participation in class:
   a. volunteers information_____
   b. answers questions when they
      are directed to him _____
   c. does not participate
      in class discussion _____

Table 4 provided courtesy of Mrs. Verna Yater, St. Louis County Special School District, Missouri; and Minneapolis Public Schools Special Education Division, Title III Interdistrict Project for Hearing-Impaired Children.

Table 5

Administrator Questionnaire

For Placement of Hearing Impaired Pupils in the School

MINNEAPOLIS PUBLIC SCHOOLS   TITLE III Interdistrict Project
Special Education Division   For Hearing-Impaired Children

ADMINISTRATOR QUESTIONNAIRE

NAME_____

PROFESSIONAL TITLE_____

SCHOOL ADDRESS_____

_____

_____

1. How many hearing-impaired children are in your building?

2. How many students per teacher in your building (average)?

3. Would you accept hearing-impaired students in your building next year? (please check one or more)

_____a. Yes

_____b. Only if tutorial and speech services were available.

_____c. Only if class size were limited to less than ____ 25 ____ 30.

_____d. Only if staff received inservice and supportive help.

_____e. No.

Please write any additional qualifications or comments:

Please give to your consultant, _____, or mail to:
Anne Seltz, Project Administrator, Shingle Creek Elementary School, 5034 Oliver Avenue North, Minneapolis, Minnesota 55430

Table 6

Teacher Questionnaire
For Placement of Hearing Impaired Pupils in the Classroom

MINNEAPOLIS PUBLIC SCHOOLS   Title III Interdistrict Project
Special Education Division   For Hearing-Impaired Children

TEACHER QUESTIONNAIRE

NAME_____GRADE_____PROF. TITLE_____

SCHOOL AND DISTRICT_____SUBJECT (Secondary)_____

1. Do you have a hearing impaired student(s) in your room?_____

2. How many?   _____

3. Total number of students in your room; or average per instructional class hour. _____

4. How well is the hearing impaired student(s) doing academically? _____

Above average for class	Average for class	Below average for class

5. How well is the hearing impaired student(s) accepted by peers?

Above average for class	Average for class	Below average for class

6. Would you accept a hearing impaired child in your class next year?
   Please check one or more.

_____a.   Yes

_____b.   Only if he were receiving tutorial and/or speech services.

_____c.   Only if class size were limited to less than_____25_____ 30.

_____d.   Only if I received inservice and supportive help.

_____e.   No.

Please write any additional qualifications.

Return to your consultant, _____or mail to:
Anne Seltz, Project Administrator, Shingle Creek Elementary School, 5034 Oliver Avenue
North, Minneapolis, Minnesota 55430

Table 7
Information Checklist for School Personnel:
Future Discussion Topics

MINNEAPOLIS PUBLIC SCHOOLS   TITLE III Interdistrict Project
Special Education Division   For Hearing-Impaired Children

FUTURE DISCUSSION TOPICS

Please check if interested in knowing more.
Give to your itinerant consultant.

___ 1. Anatomy and physiology of the hearing mechanism
___ 2. School hearing screening
___ 3. Audiological evaluation
___ 4. Audiological terminology
___ 5. Hearing aids: Their use and care
___ 6. Hearing aids: Different types
___ 7. Hearing aids: How do I know they are working?
___ 8. Speech and language of the hard of hearing
___ 9. Role of the parent in the education of the hard of hearing
___ 10. Speech and language evaluation
___ 11. Speech and language therapy
___ 12. Establishing realistic educational goals and objectives for you and your student
___ 13. Discussion of materials and resources
___ 14. How to work better with physicians
___ 15. How to work better with audiologists
___ 16. Discussion of medical treatment of ear infections
___ 17. Discussion of state law relating to hearing impaired children
___ 18. Demonstration of teaching skills
___ 19. Psychological evaluation of hearing impaired children
___ 20. How to measure progress of hearing impaired children
___ 21. Active vs. passive listening
___ 22. Signal/noise ratio
___ 23. Language development
___ 24. Acoustic characteristics of speech sounds
___ 25. The buddy system
___ 26. Quick methods of assessing a child's understanding of directions
___ 27. Vocational alternatives for the secondary hearing impaired

Other

___ 28. _____
___ 29. _____
___ 30. _____
___ 31. _____
___ 32. _____

Name _____

School District _____

Professional Title _____

Mailing Address _____

_____

_____

Table 8

Suggestion For Classroom Teachers
Of Hearing Impaired Pupils

The Acoustically Handicapped Pupil Gains Information Through Speechreading

1. Assign the hearing handicapped pupil to a favorable seat, usually toward the front of the classroom.

2. Face the child when you speak so that the child can read your lips. As you speak the light should be shining in your face, not in the child's eyes.

3. Speak in a careful yet natural manner. Avoid exaggerated lip movements.

4. When the child does not understand you it is better to rephrase a sentence than to repeat it constantly. "Did you do the assignment?" can be changed to "Did you do your homework?"

The Acoustically Handicapped Child Gains Information by Reading

5. A simple outline of the lesson on the blackboard provides clues which aid in speechreading.

6. Placing words or phrases on the blackboard as the lesson progresses helps the hearing handicapped pupil follow the lesson more readily

7. It is helpful for the deaf or hard of hearing pupil to have the assistance of a "buddy," a classmate who is willing and able to give information and explanations when necessary. The "buddy" should be one who takes good legible notes and is generous about sharing them.

8. Whenever possible indicate the location of related passages in texts or workbooks so that the child may find material he has missed in class.

9. Written versions of oral tests should be given to these students whenever possible.

10. Assignments should be made in writing.

Table 8 provided courtesy of Mrs. Isaiah Scheeline of Hollidaysburg, Pennsylvania. Mrs. Scheeline's description of her daughter's first year in an integrated high school may be found on pages 219-222 of this book.

Table 9
Checklist for Teacher-Clinician Communication

TO_____

SUBJECT_____

In order to keep an up-to-date account of how the children with whom I am working individually are doing academically and socially, I would like your comments and observations regarding _____'s performance in your class.

	Excellent	Good	Fair	Inadequate
Attention				
Participation				
Assignments				
Test Scores				
General Classroom Behavior				

Areas of Strength_____

Areas of Difficulty_____

Working up to Ability_____ Yes_____ No

Additional Comments: _____

_____

_____

_____

Thank you

Hearing Clinician

Table 9 provided courtesy of the Special School District of St. Louis County, Missouri.

Table 10

Teacher-Tutor-Clinician Communication Form

This form, prepared by Pat Etten, Minneapolis tutor of hearing impaired children, is used to obtain a weekly program of studies from the classroom teacher. It is placed in the teacher's box on Friday and returned to the clinician on Monday.

Name of Child_____ Week Beginning _____

1. Reading:

    Pages:

    Workbook:

    New Vocabulary:

    Special skills:

2. Math

3. Social studies and/or science units

4. Comments-observations-special needs-etc.

Table 10 provided courtesy of the Minneapolis Public Schools Special Education Division, Title III Interdistrict Project for Hearing-Impaired Children.

Glossary of Terms

Academic Tutor: A resource specialist who provides individual or small group supplementary instruction for hearing impaired children integrated on a part- or full-time basis in regular classes. (This teacher may not require certification as a teacher of the hearing impaired, particularly at the secondary level.) (See **Itinerant Teacher.**)

Acoustic Feedback: An undesirable high-pitched squeal produced by the leakage of sound from the hearing aid receiver, which is picked up by the microphone and re-amplified.

Adventitious Hearing Loss: A hearing loss occurring after birth as a result of disease or accident. The time of onset of hearing loss may affect language and speech patterns.

Ambient Noise: Background noise exclusive of intentional signals.

Amplification: A magnification or increase in intensity of sound. Also referred to as **gain.**

Aphasia: A breakdown or lack of power to use language resulting from congenital or adventitious brain damage.

Audiologist: A professional specialist in hearing, including the normal aspects as well as the study and prevention of hearing impairments and associated disorders, the evaluation and habilitation of hearing impaired persons, and the selection and monitoring of hearing aids.

Audiology: An area of knowledge that involves the science of hearing, including anatomy and function of the ear, impairment of hearing, prevention of hearing loss, and education or re-education of the person with the hearing loss.

Audiogram: A chart of the thresholds of sensitivity of hearing to pure tones measured at several different (usually discrete) frequencies and recorded in decibels (sound intensity).

Audiometrist: A technician trained and qualified to administer audiometric tests who usually works under the supervision of an audiologist or otologist.

Audiometry: The technique of measuring the sense of hearing by means of an audiometer and a variety of tests designed for this purpose.

Auditory Discrimination: Ability to distinguish one sound (or series of sounds) from another.

Auditory Memory: The perception, storage, and recall of verbal and nonverbal auditory events, such as speech, music, or environmental noises. Three types of auditory memory have been defined: precategorical or immediate memory, short-term memory, and long-term memory. Usually the immediate memory fades quickly, whereas about seven items can be stored in the short-term memory, and the capacity of long-term memory — which has to be reached through the other two memory processes — is enormously large and long-lasting.

Auditory Sensitivity: Ability to detect auditory signals. Auditory sensitivity for tones of different frequencies is shown by the points plotted on an audiogram.

Auditory Training: Specific training in the use of impaired hearing which aims to teach auditory discrimination skills, recognition and identification of speech and nonverbal sounds, and the development of auditory memory.

Auralism: (See **Oralism**.)

Bilateral: Pertaining to the right and left sides, as in bilateral hearing loss.

Binaural Hearing: Hearing or listening with both ears.

Binaural Hearing Aids: Two complete aids — amplifiers, microphones, and receivers — one set for each ear.

Bone Conduction: Transmission of vibrations (of frequencies within the range of hearing) through the bones of the skull to the neural pathways of the inner ear.

Conductive Hearing Loss: Impairment of hearing due to damage or obstruction of the ear canal, drum membrane, or ossicular chain in the middle ear; a failure of air vibrations to be adequately conducted to the cochlea. This type of deafness is often responsive to medical or surgical treatment.

Congenital Hearing Loss: A hearing loss which exists at the time of birth. The term does not refer to the cause of the hearing problem — only to the time of onset.

Deaf: The term used to describe persons in whom the sense of hearing is nonfunctional for ordinary use in communication, with or without a hearing aid. (See **Hearing Impairment**.)

Decibel (dB): A unit for measuring the relative intensity of sound; the tenth part of a Bel. Expresses logarithmic ratios of intensity, power, pressure, etc. Its reference base must always be given, i.e., **SPL** (sound pressure level), **SL** (sensation level), **ISO** (International Standards Organization), **HL** (Hearing Level), etc.

Earmold: A plastic piece designed to couple a hearing aid with the ear canal and to provide an acoustic seal against feedback.

Electroacoustic: Pertaining to the branch of electronics that deals with the conversion of electricity into acoustical (sound) energy, and vice versa.

Feedback: (See **Acoustic Feedback**.)

Fingerspelling: Standardized finger configurations, each representing one letter of the alphabet. Also called **Dactylology** or **Manual Alphabet**.

Frequency: Number of double vibrations or cycles per second of a sound wave, referred to as Hertz (Hz). The frequency range of human speech is approximately 100-8000 Hz for male speakers and 200-8000 for females and children. **Pitch** is the psychologic correlate of frequency. **High frequency** generally refers to any frequency above 1000 Hz. **Low frequency** generally refers to any frequency of 1000 Hz and below.

Hard of Hearing: A term used to describe persons with enough residual hearing to use hearing (usually with a hearing aid) as a primary modality for the acquisition of language and in communication with others. (See **Hearing Impairment**.)

Hearing Aid: An electroacoustic amplifying device which brings sound more effectively to the individual with a hearing loss.

Hearing Aid Gain/Volume Control: A switch or dial which makes possible an increase or decrease in the amount of amplification of sounds reaching the listener's ear.

Hearing Clinician: A specialist with a background in audiology, speech and language pathology, and/or education of the deaf who assists with individual placement and programming for hearing impaired children integrated into regular schools and provides orientation for the staff and other support specialists.

Hearing Impairment: A generic term indicating a continuum of hearing loss from mild to profound as indicated on an audiogram. It includes the subclassifications **deaf** and **hard of hearing** and is often broken down into five categories: **mild** (27-40 dB ISO), **moderate** (40-55 dB ISO), **moderate-severe** (56-70 dB ISO), **severe** (71-90 dB ISO), and **profound** (91 dB ISO and greater).

Hearing Threshold: Minimum effective sound pressure of the signal that is capable of evoking an auditory sensation in a specified fraction of the trials.

Hertz (Hz): A synonym for cycles per second (cps), named in honor of the German physicist Heinrich Hertz.

Integration: The placement of a hearing impaired pupil in regular classes for those with normal hearing, on a part-time or full-time basis.

Intensity: A measure of the quantity of sound energy, generally expressed in decibels. **Loudness** is the psychologic correlate of intensity.

ISO Calibration: The audiometric standard promulgated by the International Standards Organization and adopted for use in the U.S. in 1964 to replace the former American Standards Association calibration standards. Same as American National Standards Institute standard. There is approximately 10 dB difference in sound pressure level across test frequencies; thus, a measured loss of 50 dB on ASA standards will appear as a 60 dB loss in ISO standards.

Itinerant Teacher: A general or special educator who functions as an academic tutor, providing individual or small group instruction to hearing impaired children integrated in regular classes who may be located in more than one school within a district or region.

Mainstream Educator: A preschool, elementary, or secondary school classroom teacher of children with normal hearing who holds general certification at the appropriate grade level.

Mixed Hearing Loss: A combined conductive and sensorineural hearing impairment. The conductive component may be amenable to medical treatment. The sensorineural component can be partially compensated for through special education and use of a hearing aid.

Monaural: Pertaining to use of one ear, or to reception of sound through one source.

Oralism: The philosophy and practice of educating hearing impaired children through development of speech communication skills — which include the use of residual hearing, speechreading, and speech but exclude signs and fingerspelling. **Auralism** is a development within oralism — beginning after the advent of hearing aids — in which *hearing*, although impaired, is treated as the primary and most important sense modality. Oral education in which the use of residual hearing is stressed is sometimes referred to as *auditory/oral* or *oral/aural*.

Otologist: Medical doctor specializing in diseases and surgery of the ear.

Otology: The medical and surgical study, diagnosis, and treatment of the ear.

Pure Tone: A tone or note which has only one frequency with no harmonics or overtones.

Residual Hearing: Term usually used in cases of severe and profound hearing loss to refer to remaining hearing.

Resource Room Teacher: A special educator holding certification as a teacher of the hearing impaired who provides instruction to hearing impaired children in a self-contained setting — usually within a regular school — for a portion of the school day.

Rubella: A disease which if incurred in the first months of pregnancy may cause severe hearing loss and other impairments in the unborn child. Also called **German Measles.**

Sensorineural Loss: A general term to indicate that the locus of the hearing loss is either in the inner ear (cochlea) or along the VIIIth cranial (auditory) nerve. Also called **Nerve Deafness** or **Perceptive Deafness.**

Sign Language: An orderly system of manual gestures and symbols for communication of thoughts and ideas.

Speech Awareness Threshold: The level in decibels at which awareness of the presence of speech sound (not understanding) occurs in a specified number of trials.(Sometimes referred to as **Speech Detection Threshold.**)

Speech Pathologist/Speech Clinician: A professional in the field of speech and hearing who specializes in speech, hearing, and language defects and disorders and methods of correcting them.

Speech Reception Threshold: The minimum level in decibels at which 50% of spondaic test words (words of two syllables having equal stress) are discriminated and reported correctly.

Speechreading: The art of comprehending what is being said without hearing by observing the movements of the speaker's lips and facial expressions. Also referred to as **Lipreading.**

Threshold: (See **Hearing Threshold.**)

Special acknowledgment is given to the following consultants who assisted in the preparation of this glossary: *Dr. Richard H. Israel,* Director of Professional Programs and Services, Alexander Graham Bell Association for the Deaf, Washington, D.C.; *Dr. Daniel Ling,* Professor and Director, School of Human Communication Disorders, McGill University, Montreal, Quebec, Canada; *Robert McLaughlin,* American Speech and Hearing Association, Washington, D.C.; and *Dr. Howard M. Quigley,* Convention of American Instructors of the Deaf, Washington, D.C. In addition, the following sources were valuable references: "A Complete Dictionary of Audiology," James H. Delk, *National Hearing Aid Journal,* 1970, 24(2) — 1973, 26(4); "Glossary of Terms Relating to Children with Hearing Problems," Georgina Rushford, *The Volta Review,* 1964, 66, 750-53: and the "Glossary of Terms" prepared by the Southern California Hearing Council.

Contributing Authors

The Editor of this book, Winifred H. Northcott, Ph.D., is Director, UNISTAPS Model Demonstration Project for Hearing-Impaired Children, 0-6 (P.L. 91-230, Handicapped Children's Early Education Program), Minnesota Department of Education, and consultant in private practice, education of the hearing impaired. A member of Phi Beta Kappa and Pi Lambda Theta, she received her Ph.D. from the University of Minnesota. She has taught in the field of deaf education at preschool through college levels, and has served as Hearing Consultant, Minnesota Department of Education; Coordinator, Hearing-Impaired Program, 0-21, Minneapolis Public Schools; school board member for 15 years; and as a trustee of Connecticut College. Dr. Northcott is a member of the National Advisory Committee on Education of the Deaf; the Executive Board of the Council on Education of the Deaf; the Board of Directors of the Alexander Graham Bell Association for the Deaf; and the U.S. National Committee for Early Childhood Education (OMEP). Her published articles, book chapters, and international presentations relate to parent-oriented preschool programs and a systems approach to integration.

Lee F. Auble, Superintendent of the Berrien Springs (Mich.) Public Schools since 1952, has been instrumental in both the establishment and development of the nationally recognized school program there for hearing impaired children. A graduate of Western Michigan University, Mr. Auble holds an M.A. from Michigan State University. He is a member of the Michigan Association of School Administrators and the American Association of School Administrators and has served as an officer at the local and state levels in both organizations.

Mrs. Susan Bilek is a classroom teacher at Level IV at Iona Avenue School in Montreal, Quebec, Canada — a regular public school into which hearing impaired children from Montreal Oral School for the Deaf are integrated. She received her B.Ed. from McGill University.

Grant B. Bitter, Ed.D., is Assistant Professor of Special Education at the University of Utah, Salt Lake City, where he directs Project NEED — a program for facilitating the integration of the hearing impaired into regular school classes — and supervises the teacher education program in the area of the deaf. Father of a profoundly deaf daughter, he is intimately involved in national activities concerned with integrating exceptional children into all aspects of society. He spearheaded and supervised the religious educational programs for

282

exceptional children with the Church of the Latterday Saints and currently serves as an educational consultant for the Alexander Graham Bell Association for the Deaf. He completed his doctorate in Special Education at Wayne State University, Detroit.

Carole Blumberg, the mother of an integrated deaf child, is Liaison to Outside Programs at the Lexington School for the Deaf. As a member of Lexington's Integration Department, her professional activities include parental guidance and provision of orientation and consultation to staff members of regular programs. Previously, as a tutor of 3-year-olds, Mrs. Blumberg initiated and administered a speech and hearing program in a Long Island (N.Y.) public school system. A graduate of Adelphi University, she is presently doing graduate work at Teachers College, Columbia University.

Elizabeth W. Bowman, Ph.D., has been on the staff of BOCES #3 (Board of Cooperative Educational Services), in Suffolk County, New York, for 14 years and presently supervises the resource room program for hearing impaired students. A graduate of the University of Toronto, Teachers College (Columbia University), and the Teacher Training program of the Lexington School for the Deaf, Dr. Bowman has had a lifetime involvement in the education of the deaf. She has taught at the Rhode Island School for the Deaf, the Rochester (N.Y.) School for the Deaf, and P.S. 47, New York City; has contributed articles to *The Volta Review;* and has addressed local, national, and international conferences.

Wallace Bruce, Ed.D., is Director of the Tucker-Maxon Oral School in Portland, Oregon, and a member of the faculty of Pacific University, Forest Grove. Previously he was affiliated with the Utah School for the Deaf, the University of Utah, and the Clarke School for the Deaf. He is currently President-Elect of the American Organization for the Education of the Hearing Impaired and has served on the Board of Directors of the Alexander Graham Bell Association for the Deaf.

Donald R. Calvert, Ph.D., is Director of Central Institute for the Deaf, St. Louis, and Associate Professor of Speech and Hearing at Washington University. He served as Executive Director of the San Francisco Hearing and Speech Center for 10 years and holds a Ph.D. from Stanford University, an M.S. from Washington University, and a B.A. from the University of California. Previously an official with the Bureau of Education for the Handicapped, HEW, he was involved with the development of the Early Education for the Handicapped Act and the Project for Deaf-Blind Children's Centers and Services.

Peggie Chambers is Coordinator of the K-12 Programs for the Hearing Impaired and Visually Impaired in the Denver, Colorado, Public Schools. Previously a teacher of the hearing impaired for the Denver Public Schools and the Archdiocese of Chicago, Miss Chambers received a B.S. degree from Loretto Heights College, a master's in speech pathology from Denver University, and a master's in education from Loyola. In 1964 she was awarded the citation for "Professional Woman of the Year" by Loretto Heights College.

Oscar P. Cohen is Director, Division of Child Care, at the Lexington School for the Deaf. He has taught hearing children in the New York City public schools as well as elementary and secondary school deaf children. At Lexington School, Mr. Cohen has initiated integrated community center and summer day camp programs, a group home for resident children, and various community-oriented living environments for adolescent residential students. He recently studied residential schools in Great Britain and is presently involved in the utilization of community resources to meet the needs of hearing impaired children and in the formulation of training programs for residential child care staff.

Sarah Nell Cole, Speech, Hearing, and Language Clinician for Branford (Conn.) Public Schools, is the mother of two normal-hearing children and a 19-year-old hearing impaired son. As a past president of the New Haven Area Hearing League she was actively involved in the passage of legislation for the education of hearing impaired preschool children. She serves as the Connecticut Speech and Hearing Association's representative to the ASHA Congressional Action Network and recently lectured at workshops for parents of hearing impaired children. A graduate of Fisk University, she received her M.S. in speech pathology from Southern Connecticut State College.

Charles H. Cosper, Jr., is a teacher/counselor and head of the resource room component at the Berrien County Day Program for Hearing Impaired Children, Berrien Springs, Michigan. He holds an M.S. in deaf education from the University of Kansas and taught for eight years at the Jane Brooks School for the Deaf, Chickasha, Oklahoma. An educational consultant for the Alexander Graham Bell Association for the Deaf and a member of its Oral Deaf Adults Section, Mr. Cosper has served on various committees for the Association's national and regional conventions. He is also a member of the Board of Directors of the Michigan Association for Better Hearing and Speech. His articles on activities for deaf children have appeared in *The Volta Review.*

Marian Marienau Ernst is Educational Audiologist at Porter Memorial Hospital in Denver, Colorado. She received her M.A. in educational psychology from the University of Nebraska and holds the Certificate of Clinical Competence in speech and audiology from ASHA. Mrs. Ernst was the founding teacher of the Omaha (Neb.) Hearing School, served as clinical supervisor at the University of Denver, and has taught in a variety of public and private school settings, including both regular and special classes for the hearing impaired and classes involving multiply handicapped children.

George W. Fellendorf has been Executive Director of the Alexander Graham Bell Association for the Deaf and Editor of its monthly journal *The Volta Review* since 1962. He is the father of three daughters, one of whom is profoundly hearing impaired and attended integrated classes from fifth grade to the college level. Mr. Fellendorf, who holds degrees in electrical engineering (B.S., Union College, Schenectady) and management engineering (M.S., Rensselaer Polytechnic Institute), is currently working toward a doctorate in education at Teachers College, Columbia University. He is a member of the Council for Exceptional Children and the Maryland Speech and Hearing Association and is Editor of the *Bibliography on Deafness* published by the Bell Association in 1967 and 1973.

Elizabeth A. Frick is Coordinating Teacher in the Advanced Department and an Instructor in the Professional Training Program at Central Institute for the Deaf, St. Louis, Missouri. Formerly a hearing clinician for the Special School District of St. Louis County, Mrs. Frick was responsible for all professional activities related to integration of hearing impaired students into public schools, grades K-12. She received her master's degree from Washington University, St. Louis, and was the Goldstein scholar of the CID professional training class. A member of a number of professional organizations, Mrs. Frick was a participant in the International Conference on Education of the Deaf in 1970.

Andrew R. Gantenbein is Head Teacher at the Berrien County Day Program for Hearing Impaired Children, Berrien Springs, Michigan. A graduate of St. Mary's University in San Antonio, Texas, he received an M.Ed. from Southern Methodist University in Dallas, Texas. Prior to heading the program at Berrien Springs, Mr. Gantenbein taught hearing impaired children in the classroom for 10 years in Grand Rapids, Michigan, Eau Claire, Wisconsin, and at the Wisconsin State School for the Deaf. He has developed a strong integration program at Berrien Springs and in 1972 organized a mini-conference on "Normal Youth with Hearing Losses," in Benton Harbor, Michigan. He was a featured speaker at the Alexander Graham Bell Association's Conference on the Auditory Approach in May 1973.

Constance Garrett, Parent Editorial Consultant to *The Volta Review,* will see her hearing impaired daughter Linda attend her neighborhood junior high school in the fall of 1973. Mother of four daughters, Mrs. Garrett is a graduate in elementary education from Antioch College. She is presently pursuing a master's degree in special education at the University of

Maryland and teaching in special education for Montgomery County, Maryland, public schools. A parent member of the Council for Exceptional Children since 1965, she served as assistant to the legislative chairman for the state chapter in 1971-72 and represented the chapter in the delegate assembly at the 50th Anniversary International Convention.

Lois Bell Germain is Head Teacher for the Program for the Hearing Impaired in the public schools of Lexington, Kentucky. Previously she developed a preschool program at the Indiana University Speech and Hearing Center, taught language and reading at the high school level at Lexington School for the Deaf, and tutored in reading at the Alexander Graham Bell Elementary School, Chicago, Illinois. A member of the Alexander Graham Bell Association for the Deaf and contributor to *The Volta Review*, Mrs. Germain received her B.A. from the University of Texas and her M.A. from Columbia University.

Phyllis Gildston, Ph.D., is Associate Professor of Communications Disorders at Brooklyn College, Brooklyn, New York. She holds a B.A. from Cornell University, a master's degree from Queens College, and a doctorate from Columbia University. Dr. Gildston has previously served as assistant professor of speech pathology and audiology at Brooklyn College, as consultant in speech pathology and audiology to the Indus Home for the Blind, and as administrator of speech and hearing services for Garden City (New York) Public Schools.

Dorothy Hedgecock is Coordinator of the Program for Hearing Impaired Pupils of the Rochester, Minnesota, Public Schools, which integrates pupils with moderate to severe hearing losses. Active in the Southeastern Minnesota Association for the Hearing Impaired, Mrs. Hedgecock volunteers her time to teach speechreading to senior citizens. Previously she taught in the state schools for the deaf in Oklahoma, Texas, and New Jersey. Mrs. Hedgecock is a graduate of Oklahoma College of Liberal Arts and received training in deaf education at Eastern Michigan State University.

E. W. Johnson, Ph.D., is Director of Clinical Audiology for the Otologic Medical Group and Consultant in Otorhinolaryngology for the School of Medicine, University of Southern California. Born and raised in Minneapolis, he was Director of Admissions at Gustavus Adolphus College for 12 years. Following the birth in 1948 of his youngest daughter Linda, who was diagnosed as profoundly deaf, the family moved to California. There Linda was enrolled in the John Tracy Clinic and Dr. Johnson began his Ph.D. program at the University of Southern California. He has authored more than 25 articles for professional publications.

Kay A. Johnston is Coordinator for Project NEED (Normal Educational Environment for the Deaf), based at the University of Utah (Salt Lake City) Department of Special Education. Formerly she was a teacher of the deaf at Pennsylvania School for the Deaf (Philadelphia) and in Broward County, Florida; and she has done internship work with multiply handicapped children at the Mailman Center for Child Development in Miami. Miss Johnston received a B.S. in deaf education from the University of Wisconsin (Milwaukee) and a master's in education from Florida Atlantic University. In addition, she has done post-master's work in educational psychology at the University of Utah and in education of the deaf at the University of Miami.

Barbara L. Jones, Ph.D., is an Assistant Professor in the Special Education Teacher Training Program at the University of North Florida, Jacksonville. Formerly a clinical audiologist at the San Diego Hearing and Speech Center, Dr. Jones received training in the education of the hearing impaired at California State University, earned an M.A. in audiology at Case Western Reserve University, and received her Ph.D. in education from the University of Washington. A member of various professional associations, Dr. Jones won first place in the 1973 student Literary Competition sponsored by the Division for Children with Communicative Disorders, Council for Exceptional Children, for her paper, "The Audiologist in the Educational Environment."

Harriet Green Kopp, Ph.D., is Professor of Speech Pathology and Audiology at California State University, San Diego, and Chairman of the Department of Speech Pathology, Audiology, and Deaf Education. Dr. Kopp, a fellow of the American Speech and Hearing Association, served as Chairman of the National Advisory Committee on Education of the Deaf in 1970-72. She is the author of a number of textbooks and publications in the areas of cognitive processing, the teaching of speech to the deaf, and experimental and physiological phonetics. Dr. Kopp has served on the Board of Directors of the Alexander Graham Bell Association for the Deaf (1962-1970) and as Chairman of the Editorial Policies Committee.

Doris Leckie is Principal of the Montreal Oral School for the Deaf in Montreal, Quebec. Born in Canada, she was educated at Sir George Williams University and the National Teachers College in London. Mrs. Leckie is primarily recognized for her work in integration of hearing impaired children into regular schools and is currently working on a research project on the relationship between psycholinguistics and the problems of the hearing impaired at McGill University. She was recently elected as Provincial Representative to a Consortium to Study Services for the Hearing Impaired in Canada.

William Lyth is majoring in education of the emotionally disturbed and mentally retarded at Nazareth College, Kalamazoo, Michigan. Hearing impaired since birth, he has a 65 dB loss in the better ear and wears binaural hearing aids. Bill attended both special and regular classes in the elementary years and has been fully integrated since the fifth grade. His interests include camping, sports, antiques, and volunteer service activities.

Linda Gray McArthur is a graduate teaching fellow in physical education at Eastern Washington State College, Cheney, Washington, and a member of the Oral Deaf Adults Section of the Alexander Graham Bell Association for the Deaf. Born in Los Angeles, she received her B.S. in physical education from California State Polytechnic College, San Luis Obispo. She has been a graduate teaching assistant at New Mexico Highlands University, Las Vegas, and is now completing her master's degree at Cheney. Her professional contributions have included an article in *The Volta Review* and guest lectures.

Lynnita Mattock (See **Lynnita Mattock Seitenstich**)

John G. Nace, Ed.D., served as Coordinator of Special Projects at the Sterck School for the Hearing Impaired after his retirement as Headmaster of the Pennsylvania School for the Deaf in 1969. Prior to his appointment as Headmaster he had been teacher, principal, and assistant headmaster there. Dr. Nace was a member of the National Advisory Committee on Education of the Deaf (1967-1971) and has served on many other committees relating to the hearing impaired.

John Nuernberger is a Psychological Examiner with the Special School District of St. Louis County, Missouri. He received a B.A. and an M.A. in psychology from the University of Tulsa, Oklahoma, and is a member of the Missouri Psychological Association, the National Association of School Psychologists, and the Council for Exceptional Children. He also serves as psychological consultant for United Cerebral Palsy Association of St. Louis and St. Louis County. Prior to his work in St. Louis, Mr. Nuernberger was a clinical psychologist at Children's Medical Center in Tulsa.

Shirley G. Parker has been a teacher of normal hearing classes, nursery through third grade, for nine years, and a teacher of hearing impaired children, nursery and kindergarten, for 14 years. She presently teaches an all-day nursery in the UNISTAPS project, Minneapolis public schools, in which hearing impaired children are joined by hearing peers in the afternoons for a totally integrated social and educational experience. A graduate of Miss Wood's Kindergarten-Primary Training School now affiliated with Macalester College, St. Paul, she has been an active member of professional organizations and served on the UNISTAPS writing team for *Curriculum Guide: Hearing Impaired Children, Birth to Three Years, and Their Parents.*

Linda Peterson is the mother of an 8-year-old hearing impaired child and two younger children. A graduate medical technologist, she is an active member of the Minneapolis Association for the Hearing Impaired, where she served on the Board of Directors and is currently editor of the newsletter. Her interests include classical ballet, and she would like to teach ballet to hearing impaired students.

Doreen Pollack, is Director of the Speech and Hearing Services of Porter Memorial Hospital, Denver. A native of England, she graduated from the University of London and taught there before coming to the United States in 1948. She began to formulate her approach to the early education of hearing impaired children, now known as acoupedics, while working at Columbia Presbyterian Medical Center in New York City. Author of *Educational Audiology for the Limited Hearing Infant* and other publications, she is a member of professional associations and a charter member of the Listen Foundation, formed by parents to promote the acoupedic approach and assist needy children attending Porter Hospital.

Steven Lee Rattner, an 18-year-old graduate of Montgomery Blair High School, Silver Spring, Maryland (Class of 1973), has a severe to profound bilateral sensorineural hearing loss. He was educated orally in the Montgomery County Public Schools where his early years were spent in self-contained classes; at the secondary level he was integrated in all subjects. At graduation he ranked 60 in a class of 633 with a grade point average of 3.5. A member of the National Honor Society and the Washington Junior Academy of Science, he is active in community groups. He hopes to pursue a career in chemistry and is currently attending Montgomery College, Rockville, Maryland.

Janalee Reineke is an occupational therapy major at Indiana University Medical Center, Indianapolis. Hearing impaired since birth, she has an 85 dB loss and wears one aid. She attended oral preschool classes for the deaf from age 2½ to 6 and has been in integrated classes in public schools since kindergarten. During her first two years of college she studied pre-medicine at Manchester College, Indiana. She enjoys varied interests — music, traveling, and sports, is a member of Pi Theta Epsilon, and serves on the executive board of the Occupational Therapy Club.

Mark Ross, Ph.D., is Director of the Willie Ross School for the Deaf, Longmeadow, Massachusetts. Formerly Professor of Speech Pathology and Audiology at the University of Connecticut, he is still associated there as an adjunct professor. Dr. Ross is organizing a number of alternative programs at the Willie Ross School, including integrated nursery and kindergarten and full integration programs in local schools. A fellow of the American Speech and Hearing Association and member of the Academy of Rehabilitative Audiology and other professional groups, Dr. Ross is a frequent contributor to professional journals and publications.

J. Paul Rudy founded the Sterck School for the Hearing Impaired in Newark, Delaware, in 1966 and served as its Director and Principal until 1973. Previously he was a teacher of the deaf, audiologist, and speech pathologist in Delaware. He now resides in Canaan Valley, West Virginia, where he is president of a resort realty firm.

Genevieve Russell, Academy of Certified Social Workers, is a School Social Worker in a Regional Facility for the Deaf in Portland, Oregon. Formerly Child Welfare Supervisor with the Salem (Ore.) Department of Public Welfare, she also established the school social work program in the Salem public schools. Miss Russell participates in parent-teacher programs and orientation programs for parents of young hearing impaired children at the Oregon State School for the Deaf. An art major from Marylhurst College, Miss Russell did graduate studies in medical social work at St. Louis University and received her master's degree from the University of Washington. She also holds degrees in special education, speech correction, and school counseling.

Alice R. Scheeline is Program Coordinator and Teacher in a Title I Remedial Reading Program in Hollidaysburg, Pennsylvania. A graduate of Wheelock College, Boston, she received a B.S. in education from the University of Cincinnati and an M.A. in remedial reading from Columbia University. Mrs. Scheeline is Past President of the Family and Children's Service of Blair County and helped to recruit and obtain a grant for training a teacher for the Blair County public school class for hard of hearing children. She is a life member of the Alexander Graham Bell Association for the Deaf and author of three articles in *The Volta Review*.

Lynnita Mattock Seitenstich, who holds a B.S. in psychology from Colorado State University, Fort Collins, was a teacher for three years at Berrien Springs Elementary School in Berrien Springs, Michigan. During her first year she taught a class of hearing impaired children (of the Berrien County Day Program for Hearing Impaired Children), the next year an integrated group in a regular classroom, and the third year a class of regular students. She has since married and now lives in Three Oaks, Michigan.

Anne Seltz is project director of the Title III Interdistrict Project for Hearing Impaired Children, Minneapolis Public Schools, which works with mainstream staff to facilitate the integration of hearing impaired students into their neighborhood schools. Born in China, Ms. Seltz received her M.A. from the University of Minnesota with a major in audiology and minors in psychology and child development. Her experience includes public school speech pathology, hospital clinical audiology, and appointments with the University of Minnesota. Also, she has coordinated an experimental language-oriented nursery school for economically deprived children. Active in professional associations, she has presented a number of papers at national conventions.

Bruce D. Shepherd, M.B., B.S., B.D.S. (Sydney, Australia), had devoted his career to the profession of dentistry and orthopedic surgery until the birth of his first child. This daughter, now 11 years old, was born profoundly deaf, and a second profoundly deaf child, a son, was born 18 months later. Dr. Shepherd's subsequent involvement with handicapped children resulted in his becoming the co-founder of the Council for Integrated Deaf Education, which administers the Shepherd Centre at the University of Sydney. This training center for preschool teachers controls a group of integrated programs at neighborhood kindergartens. Dr. Shepherd also holds F.R.C.S. degrees from England and Edinburgh.

Raymond A. Stassen is Chief Supervisor of Clinical Audiology, at the Speech and Hearing Center of Teachers College, Columbia University. After receiving an M.A. in speech pathology from the University of Minnesota, he was appointed assistant director of the Audiology Clinic and instructor in the department of otolaryngology at the University's Health Sciences Center. There his major interest was in monitoring the development of preschool and school-age children with hearing impairments. His articles in the area of habilitative and rehabilitative audiology have appeared in the *Journal of Speech and Hearing Disorders* and *Clinical Otology: An International Symposium*.

Virginia W. Stern of Westport, Connecticut, is the mother of four children, one of whom is deaf. She holds a master's degree in deaf education from Gallaudet College (Washington, D.C.) and is presently the Editor of *Ideas for Families*, a pamphlet for parents published by the Lexington School for the Deaf in New York City. Mrs. Stern has been an active member of the International Parents' Organization of the Alexander Graham Bell Association for the Deaf and has served on the Association's Editorial Policies Committee.

Esther M. Stovall, formerly Assistant Editor of *The Volta Review*, is a free-lance editor and writer specializing in health- and education-related topics. While with the Alexander Graham

Bell Association she edited and prepared for publication a number of books, including *Speech for the Deaf Child, Knowledge and Use.* Recently she assisted with the publication of *Curriculum Guide: Hearing Impaired Children (0-3) and Their Parents* (Northcott), and *Structured Language for Children with Special Language Learning Problems* (Monsees). A graduate of the Medill School of Journalism, Northwestern University, Mrs. Stovall is a member of the American Newspaper Women's Club and Women in Communications, Inc.

Thomas J. Watson, Ph.D., is Reader in Audiology and Education of the Deaf at the University of Manchester, England. In 1956-58 he was chairman of the National College of Teachers of the Deaf, England, and in 1960-61 was visiting professor at the University of Minnesota. He has lectured in a number of centers in the United States and in Europe and has acted as a consultant for several state departments. He is the author of *The Education of Hearing Handicapped Children,* a monograph on *The Use of Residual Hearing in the Education of Deaf Children,* chapters in several books, and numerous articles in professional journals.

Verna V. Yater is Supervisor of Integrated Programs at the Special District of St. Louis County, Missouri. For the past nine years, as supervisor of the Hearing Clinician Program, she has coordinated professional services for hearing impaired children (K-12) in integrated settings. She has served as a consultant to federal projects on integration, conducted symposiums and workshops, and addressed national conventions. After receiving her M.A. from the University of Minnesota, Mrs. Yater worked with children and adults with various communication difficulties and served on teams studying cleft palate and the effects of adult aphasia. Active in professional associations, Mrs. Yater has written articles on integration and language assessment and development.

Compiled by
GRANT B. BITTER
KAY A. JOHNSTON

Bibliography of References on Integration

Published Articles

Berg, F.A. A model for a facilitative program for hearing impaired college students. *The Volta Review*, 1972, **74**, 370-375.

Bitter, G.B., & Mears, E.G. Facilitating the integration of hearing impaired children into regular public school classes. *The Volta Review*, 1973, **75**, 13-22.

Bothwell, H. What the classroom teacher can do for the child with impaired hearing. *The NEA Journal*, 1967, **56**, 44-46.

Bowling, W.C. Day classes for the deaf — Covina Plan. *The Volta Review*, 1967, **69**, 54-57.

Breunig, H.L. Analysis of a group of deaf students in colleges with the hearing. *The Volta Review*, 1965, **67**, 17-27.

Bruce, W. Social integration and the effectiveness of speech. *The Volta Review*, 1960, **62**, 368-372.

Carruth, K.J., Kryeger, A.H., Lesar, D.I., & Redding, A.J. Possible effects of integration of the deaf within a typical vocational school setting. *Journal of Rehabilitation of the Deaf*, 1971, **4**, 30-41.

Carver, R.L. A parent speaks out on integration in the schools. *The Volta Review*, 1966, **68**, 580-583.

Cohen, O.P. An integrated summer recreation program. *The Volta Review*, 1969, **71**, 233-237.

Cole, N. Hear the wind blow. *The Volta Review*, 1971, **73**, 36-41.

Community college of Denver provides integrated programs. *The Volta Review*, 1971, **73**, 190.

Dr. Bitter is Project Director of Project NEED at the Department of Special Education, University of Utah, Salt Lake City. Ms. Johnston is Project Coordinator.

Connor, L.E. Early intervention. *The Volta Review,* 1971, **73,** 270-271.

Connor, L.E. Integration. *The Volta Review,* 1972, **74,** 207-209.

Deaf graduates of schools for the hearing. *The Volta Review,* 1971, **73,** 282-319.

Desa, N. (Stephen High School for Deaf and Aphasic, Bombay, India). An integrated approach to the rehabilitation of deaf individuals. *Silent World,* 1971, **6,** 28-32.

Dixon, C.C. Integrating . . . a positive note. *Hearing and Speech News,* 1968, **36,** 16, 18.

Elser, R.P. The social position of hearing handicapped children in the regular grades. *Exceptional Children,* 1959, **25,** 305-309.

Flegel, E. Services for the hearing handicapped in a special school district. *The Volta Review,* 1964, **66,** 253-257.

Frick, E. Adjusting to integration: Some difficulties hearing impaired children have in public schools. *The Volta Review,* 1973, **75,** 36-46.

Garrett, C., & Stovall, E.M. A parent's views on integration. *The Volta Review,* 1972, **74,** 338-344.

Gildston, P. Hard of hearing child in the classroom: A guide for the classroom teacher. The Volta Review, 1962, **74,** 239-245.

Harper, P.M. Problems of a small day class program. *The Volta Review,* 1966, **68,** 660-664.

The International Parents' Organization. The value of integration. *The Volta Review,* 1968, **70,** 258.

Johnson, E.W. Let's look at the child not the audiogram. *The Volta Review,* 1967, **69,** 306-311.

Keaster, J. How shall the deaf child be educated? *The Volta Review,* 1954, **56,** 293-297.

Kowalsky, M.H. Integration of a severely hard of hearing child in a normal first grade program: A case study. *Journal of Speech and Hearing Disorders,* 1962, **27,** 349-358.

Leckie, D.J. Creating a receptive climate in the mainstream program. *The Volta Review,* 1973, **75,** 23-27.

Leigh, D. The deaf child enrolled in a hearing school. *The Volta Review,* 1963, **65,** 312.

Lewis, D.N. Lipreading skills of hearing impaired children in regular schools. *The Volta Review,* 1972, **74,** 303-311.

Lexington School for the Deaf. Giving deaf children needed experience with the hearing world. *Audiovisual Instruction,* 1969, **14,** 98-99.

Lloyd, L.L. Have you a pupil with a hearing handicap? *Instructor,* 1962, **72,** 62, 136.

McArthur, L. Learning to be self-sufficient. *The Volta Review,* 1967, **69,** 259-261.

McGee, D.I. The benefits of educating deaf children with hearing children. *Teaching Exceptional Children,* 1970, **2,** 133-137.

Mecham, S.R., & VanDyke, R.C. Pushing back the walls between hearing and hearing impaired children. *The Volta Review,* 1971, **73,** 359-64.

Miller, A.S. Academic preparation to insure adjustment into classes with hearing students. *The Volta Review*, 1964, **66**, 414-425.

Monaghan, A. Educational placement for the multiply handicapped hearing impaired child. *The Volta Review*, 1964, **66**, 383-387.

Niemann, S.L. Listen! An acoupedic program. *The Volta Review*, 1972, **74**, 85-89.

Northcott, W.H. Candidate for integration: A hearing impaired child in a regular nursery school. *Young Children*, 1970, **25**, 367-380.

Northcott, W.H. An experimental summer school: Impetus for successful integration. *The Volta Review*, 1970, **72**, 498-507.

Northcott, W.H. Integration of young deaf children into ordinary education programs. *Exceptional Children*, 1971, **38**, 29-32.

Northcott, W.H. A hearing impaired pupil in the classroom. *The Volta Review*, 1972, **74**, 105-108.

Northcott, W.H. Tutoring a hearing impaired student in the elementary grades. *The Volta Review*, 1972, **74**, 432-435.

Northcott, W.H. The hearing impaired child: Programming for the under three's. *Exceptional Children*, 1973, **39** (6), 455-463.

Northcott, W.H. The hearing impaired child: A speech clinician as interdisciplinary team member. *Journal of Language, Speech, and Hearing Services in Schools* (ASHA), 1972, **3**, 7-19.

O'Connor, C.D. The integration of the deaf in schools for the normally hearing. *American Annals of the Deaf*, 1961, **106**, 239-245.

O'Connor, C.D., & Connor, L.E. Study of the integration of deaf children in regular classrooms. *Exceptional Children*, 1961, 27, 483-486.

Owrid, H.L. Education and communication. *The Volta Review*, 1972, **74**, 225.

Owsley, P.J. Can a residential school program integrate students into public schools? *The Volta Review*, 1973, **75**, 28-31.

Paul, R.L. Resource room for hard of hearing children in the public schools. *The Volta Review*, 1963, **65**, 200-202.

Pollock, M.B., & Pollock, K.C. Letter to the teacher of a hard of hearing child. *Childhood Education*, 1971, **47**, 206-209.

Reynolds, L.G. The school adjustment of children with minimal hearing loss. *Journal of Speech and Hearing Disorders*, 1955, **20**, 380-384.

Roberts, W. Regular school teachers' views on integration. *Voice* (Montreal Oral School), 1968, **11**, 13-17.

Rooney, A.G. A public school program for multiply handicapped deaf children. *The Volta Review*, 1970, **72**, 552-559.

Rosenthal, C. Social adjustment of hearing handicapped children. *The Volta Review*, 1966, **68**, 293-297.

Salem, J.M. Deaf students in a "hearing" college. *The Volta Review*, 1967, **69**, 36-41.

Salem, J.M. Deaf students in a "hearing" college — a follow up. *The Volta Review*, 1969, **71**, 435-436.

Salem, J.M. Partial integration at the high school level. *The Volta Review*, 1971, **73**, 42-46.

Scheeline, A. Integrating deaf children into public schools. *The Volta Review*, 1971, **73**, 370-373.

Schwartz, M.G. Deaf child in my hearing class. *The Volta Review*, 1964, **66**, 627-630.

Silverman, S.R. The hard of hearing child: How the classroom teacher can recognize and help him. *N.E.A. Journal*, 1950, **39**, 136-137.

Skinner, M. Some pros and cons for integrating deaf children into hearing schools. *Rehabilitation in Australia*, 1971, 3-7.

Stern, V.W. Fingerpaint on the hearing aid. *The Volta Review*, 1969, **71**, 149-154.

Sugrue, T.J. New York City's high school program for the deaf. *The Volta Review*, 1967, **69**, 247-252.

Sullivan, C.D. Deafness is not insurmountable. *The Volta Review*, 1967, **69**, 262-263.

Sykes, G. Tips on notetaking. *The Volta Review*, 1965, **67**, 307.

Teel, P.L. Tacoma's program for intermediate hearing impaired children. *The Volta Review*, 1971, **73**, 557-564.

Warnke, E.F., Integration of hearing impaired with normal hearing students. *Hörgeschädigte Kinder*, 1972, **9**, 57-59.

Watson, F.J. Use of hearing aids by hearing impaired pupils in ordinary schools. *The Volta Review*, 1964, **66**, 741-744.

Weinstein, G.W. Nursery school with a difference — deaf and normal children at New York. *Parent's Magazine*, 1968, **43**, 66-69.

Weis, J.T. Integrating the hearing handicapped. *Instructor*, 1968, **78**, 102.

Whitehurst, M.W., & Kennedy, M. Suggestions for friends and relatives of the hard of hearing. *The Volta Review*, 1969, **71**, 81-88.

Whorton, G.P. The hard of hearing child: A challenge to educators. *The Volta Review*, 1966, **68**, 351-353.

Whorton, G.P. Integrating the hearing impaired. *Instructor*, 1968, **78**, 102.

Witcher, B. Teacher, I love you. *The Volta Review*, 1971, **73**, 480c-480d.

Witheford. Hearing children's attitudes to deaf children in a well-established unit. *New Zealand Journal for Teachers of the Deaf*, 1972, **4**, 38-42.

Worthington, A.M. Psychological implications of integration of deaf children with hearing children. *American Annals of the Deaf*, 1958, **103**, 467-472.

Yater, V. St. Louis County hearing clinician program. *The Volta Review*, 1972, **74**, 247-255.

Books and Pamphlets

ABC's in ways the regular classroom teacher can aid the hard of hearing child. Salem, Oregon: State Department of Education, Division of Special Education, 1967.

Bitter, G.B., Johnston, K.A., & Sorenson, R.G. *Integration of the hearing impaired: Educational issues.* Washington, D.C.: U.S. Office of Education, Bureau of Education for the Handicapped, 1973.

Dale, D.M.C. *Deaf children at home and school.* London: University of London Press, 1967.

Fiedler, M.F. *Deaf children in a hearing world: Their education and adjustment.* New York: Ronald Press, 1952.

Herbel, D.W. *Integration of pre-school hearing impaired in regular academic setting nursery school level.* Topeka, Kansas: Division of Special Education.

Johnson, E.M. *A report on a survey of deaf children who have been transferred from special schools or units to ordinary schools, carried out between 1st February and 12th April, 1962.* London: Her Majesty's Stationery Office, 1963.

Johnson, J.C. *Educating hearing impaired children in ordinary schools.* Washington, D.C.: Volta Bureau, 1962.

Justman, J., Muskowitz, S., Nass, M.L., & Alpert, L. *The integration of deaf children in a hearing class.* Studies of children with physical handicaps, Number 4. New York: Bureau of Educational Research, Board of Education of the City of New York, 1956.

Loughlin, J.J. *Mandatory special education plan for the administration and implementation of public school programs for hearing impaired.* Indiana: State Division of Special Education, Lafayette, Indiana, 1970.

Northcott, Winifred H. (Ed.) *The hearing impaired child in a regular classroom: Preschool, elementary, and secondary years.* Washington, D.C.: The Alexander Graham Bell Association for the Deaf, 1973.

Regular classroom teacher's manual for aurally handicapped children. Garden Grove, California: Stanford Elementary School, 1969.

Rudy, J.P., & Nace, J.G. *A transitional integrative program for hearing impaired students.* Newark, Delaware: Sterck School for the Hearing Impaired, 1973.

Stuckless, E.R. *A notetaking procedure for deaf students in regular classes.* Rochester, New York: National Technical Institute for the Deaf, 1969.

Vaughn, G.R. *Education of deaf and hard of hearing adults in established facilities for the normally hearing.* Pocatello, Idaho: Idaho State University Press, 1967.

Unpublished Articles

Berrien County Day Program for Hearing Impaired Children. *Where normal children with hearing losses learn.* Berrien Springs, Michigan.

Mecham, S.R. Deaf pupils in schools for the normally hearing. Paper presented at the International Conference on Oral Education of the Deaf. Reprinted with permission of Alexander Graham Bell Association for the Deaf, Washington, D.C., 1970.

INDEX

Date Due